ID0343581

A BOXING DYNASTY

Also by Robert Jeffrey

Real Hard Cases (with Les Brown)
Crimes Past – Glasgow's Crimes of the Century
Glasgow Crimefighter (with Les Brown)
Blood on the Streets
Glasgow's Godfather
Gangland Glasgow
Glasgow's Hard Men
The Wee Book of Glasgow
The Wee Book of the Clyde

*   *   *   *   *

Images of Glasgow
Scotland's Sporting Heroes
The Herald Book of the Clyde
Doon the Watter
Clydeside, People and Places
(all with Ian Watson)

A BOXING DYNASTY

The Tommy Gilmour Story

Tommy Gilmour MBE

with Robert Jeffrey

BLACK & WHITE PUBLISHING

First published 2007
by Black & White Publishing Ltd
99 Giles Street, Edinburgh EH6 6BZ

1 3 5 7 9 10 8 6 4 2 07 08 09 10 11

ISBN 13: 978 1 84502 177 1
ISBN 10: 1 84502 177 0

A CIP catalogue record for this book is available from the British Library.

Typeset by Ellipsis Books Ltd, Glasgow
Printed and bound by MPG Books Ltd, Bodmin, Cornwall

ACKNOWLEDGEMENTS

Tommy Gilmour would like to acknowledge with gratitude the assistance of his wife Veronica and his children Christopher and Stephanie in the production of this book and that of Paddy Byrne, noted Scottish boxing historian Brian Donald and Glasgow boxing writer (and fan!) John Quinn, author of *Twenty Five Years On*, the history of the St Andrew's Sporting Club. And Sammy Gilmore. And to also acknowledge the memory-jogging help of a legion of boxing people from cornermen to managers, promoters and trainers, the boxers themselves and the enthusiasts who pay to watch from ringside or from the back of the hall. They all brought the memories back!

DEDICATION

To my mum Lizzie who, I am sure, is always with me in spirit.

CONTENTS

1

THE BATTLE BEFORE THE BATTLE

The roof first went on Glasgow's iconic Kelvin Hall in 1927 after the original building had been destroyed by fire two years before and, on 18 March 1992, it nearly came off again. On a never-to-be-forgotten night of boxing and patriotism Pat Clinton won the flyweight championship of the world in that legendary old place. During the moments after the final bell, the hall fell silent. The crowd sensed it would be close – a split decision was on the cards. The wait was long and agonising as the supervisor Cesar Miranda scrutinised the verdicts of the three judges. Eventually, he handed the result to the MC, Peter Baines. One judge had gone for Isidro Perez, the reigning world champ, and another for wee Pat. The suspense was almost painful. The next few words said it all – 'The *new* world champion . . .' Puerto Rican referee Wiso Fernandez raised Clinton's gloved hand high. The crowd went wild and, for a moment, the old cliché about raising the roof sounded, to me at least, like a genuine possibility. I was part of the wall of noise that echoed round the hall and I was higher than the highest of Pat's thousands of fans. It was the night my dream came true. I was not yet forty years old and I had become the first Scot in almost half a century, forty-six years to be specific, to promote a world-title fight in his home country. And I was also the manager of the man who took the title. My fellow Scot, Pat Clinton, fought out of Croy, a former mining village, with some rough edges, on the eastern outskirts of Glasgow, a city that itself can, on occasion, be an abrasive place to live.

We made a good couple. Pat Clinton knew how to handle himself in a scrap in the ring and I knew how to handle myself in the almost equally tough world outside it. There is no room for 'patsies' in boxing promotion and management. Clinton was, as they say in boxing, a real warrior with the gloves on. To get him into that ring in the Kelvin Hall to face the reigning WBO world champion, Mexican Isidro 'Sid' Perez, involved me in a remarkable battle before a battle.

In November 1991, I lived in Newton Mearns, a fairly plush area of mostly detached houses lying on the south-west of Glasgow and straddling the main road down to the Ayrshire coast. I loved the well-kept three-bedroom place. It was the usual suburban idyll – lounge, dining room and a good bit of garden which was home to a rabbit called aptly, for a boxing family, Thumper. Folk who know me well know I am not totally an animal lover and that, in particular, I dislike the calling cards our furry friends tend to leave lying around. But Thumper had been bought for my daughter Stephanie, twelve at the time, when I was away on fight business in South Africa. It took up residential rights in style and, no matter my thoughts, Stephanie and her brother Christopher were great fans of the lettuce muncher who had the pampered lifestyle of a champion athlete.

Yes, Lismore Place was a nice peaceful spot. Our next-door neighbours both worked for British Airways. Gardens were well kept, the roses and the grass cut at all the right times. It was a long way from my tenement childhood in Oatlands on the edge of Glasgow Green, with the Gorbals and Bridgeton on my doorstep. Oatlands is the correct name for an area squeezed between Rutherglen and Gorbals. Veronica, the kids and I were very happy in 'The Mearns'. And we worked as a team. I can never forget sitting around our dining-room table, in the home of which we were so proud, in the run-up to the Clinton fight. If the neighbours had peeked through the curtains, they would have found me, in shirt sleeves, and Veronica, Christopher and Stephanie all busy collating press passes (getting the wee bits of ribbon through the holes was time consuming), laminating name cards, making up the boards for the ring girls to carry and working on the seating plan. Everything had to be just right – happy days.

I still live in the area but in a house that, I have to admit, is more than a mite bigger! However, it was in Lismore Place in late 1991 that the countdown to my dream began when the peace and quiet of a night in front of the telly with Veronica was broken late on by the ringing of the phone. In my business, the timing was a clue as to who the caller was – because of the time difference, the movers and shakers of boxing in the States tend to start working the phones just at the time normal Scottish folk are thinking of a before-bed cocoa or maybe a wee nightcap of something stronger.

It couldn't have been a bigger call. The man on the other end of the line was indeed on the other side of the Atlantic. He was Ed Levine, chairman of the World Boxing Organisation Championship Committee, a man whose day job was as a razor-sharp attorney in the hard world of Miami legal circles. Although I was, by then, a pretty successful boxing promoter and manager, in a Scottish context, I didn't know him other than by reputation. He talked, I listened. He knew I was now handling Pat Clinton who was, at the time, the number-one contender for the WBO flyweight title. That night, Ed told me Pat was now the mandatory challenger. Perez, the champion, had to fight him. The US east-coast attorney was direct and said I should come to Miami right away to attend the WBO convention to discuss me promoting the title fight. I was to deal with Isidro Perez's connections and, in particular, meet his main spokesman, a character called Pepe Cordero – a 'someone', as they might say in *Goodfellas*, with a serious reputation. Cordero was infamous in the game – he had been involved with the World Boxing Association, a rival of the WBO, with its own world champions. Somewhere along the road, this legendary dealmaker, who took great care to make sure all deals heavily favoured his own interests, had switched sides in the ongoing war to control world boxing. Cordero was the sort of character who tends to turn up in boxing fiction. When I eventually met him, he looked to me a bit like the late Saddam Hussein and I felt that maybe Rod Steiger or Robert De Niro would have been ideal to play him in a film of his life. But in Miami, sitting across the table from him, it was to be real-life drama and Pepe, I found out, was more than a touch fearsome.

Ed Levine had told me to jump and so I jumped. This was a once-in-a-lifetime opportunity and I had no intention of letting it slip past me but I was heading into rough waters and knew I needed a pilot to help me chart my way. However, I did not have any sleepless nights worrying about who to take to the States with me into the trenches in the fight for the rights to the most important fight that had come the way of the Gilmour dynasty in around seventy years in the fight game. There was only one candidate for this role – a man who had worked with my father Tommy Gilmour Sr, known as 'The Starmaker', for years; a man whose help, advice and integrity had played a major role in my dad's career and my own; a man who was a legend in boxing circles, not least for his years as right-hand man to Barney Eastwood, Barry McGuigan's manager. Nicholas 'Paddy' Byrne knew boxing inside out – knew where the bodies were buried, as they say. Name a fighter, name a manager, name an arena and Paddy could deliver the inside story. He was a guy who knew what was what and who was who in the game and he loved to talk about it. Endlessly entertaining in his Irish accent, he is also one of the shrewdest men I have met and, during my years in a boxing family, I had met many. Still active, Paddy made a great impact on the sport as an international agent and as a matchmaker for Terry Lawless, Mickey Duff and Barney Eastwood. This boxing legend had tales to tell and experience of Cordero in his WBA days. There was no question that his help would be invaluable so I knew I had to get him on side for this, the Big One.

It was nearly midnight when I contacted him at his Brighton home, a place packed with memorabilia to the point where you could have created a boxing museum on the spot. Sadly some of Paddy's stuff went missing when he moved to a new home, still in Brighton, but now on the edge of the famous marina and with the smell of the sea on his doorstep – a rather different sort of atmosphere from the smoke-filled halls of boxing. We did not waste time in chitchat or reminiscences on this occasion. Levine had levelled with me – 'Get over quick.' – so I levelled with Paddy – 'I need you to come with me to the States . . . in the morning.' Paddy is a fast mover, always was. Recently I spoke to him and, despite now being nearly eighty, I was told to call back later as he was packing for a trip to Sweden and a world championship fight. It was the same back then in 1991.

He agreed immediately to meet me at London Heathrow the next morning. He would be on the early morning train taking the south-coast commuters to their daily grind in the capital. I took the shuttle down and, just a few hours after that call from Ed Levine, Paddy and I were at the ticket desk.

The first snag was that there were no available seats on direct flights to Miami. However, we got on a flight to JFK in New York at short notice and were soon heading out over the Atlantic. The folk on the big jet were the usual mixture of businessmen and -women and tourists. Most of the other male passengers sipped the G&Ts, eyed the hostesses, ate the tray meals and settled down to watch the movie. Paddy and I were in a different mode and, for the whole seven hours or so of the flight, our conversation revolved around one subject – Pepe Cordero. Right from the start, Paddy told me what a slippery fellow Cordero was and the gist of his advice was that, after I had shaken hands with him, the only sensible course was to count my fingers before we proceeded. Paddy coached me for the meeting in the manner of a cornerman trying to get the best out of his boxer in a tough fight. He knew the ways of the wily Cordero only too well from his own days working in the McGuigan camp. The advice I absorbed on that flight was to be very useful indeed in the smoke-filled Miami hotel back rooms.

The flight passed in a flurry of warnings, suggestions on tactics and other inside info and we were soon back at an airline ticket desk, this time in the buzzing atmosphere of JFK. It was no dice again – no short-notice seats for Miami or even nearby Fort Lauderdale. We had no choice but to take a taxi to the less salubrious surroundings of the city's original airport, La Guardia. If JFK is spaceport USA (or was – it is somewhat tacky these days), then La Guardia is Bridgeton Cross railway station.

But even here, in the tired old terminal, it was the same story
– no short-notice seats to Miami. We booked in to an airport
hotel and, all the way to our rooms, Paddy was still laying it
on heavily about Cordero's character and the way he did business, including a hint or two about some of the people he did
business with. Sunday School teaching, it appeared, was not
on Cordero's CV. It was not a night that I slept dreamlessly
away. My head was buzzing with everything I had been told
and what lay ahead if I was going to make my dream of
promoting a local boy in a world-title fight in my home city
come true.

At least our transport problems seemed behind us and we
had an early breakfast before heading out to the airport for a
flight that we had finally managed to get seats on. The bacon,
hash browns and eggs anyway-you-like-them were probably
great but it was the coffee I remember – strong and black. I
certainly needed it that way to get the brain shifted into top
gear for the day ahead. In Miami, we made it to the taxi rank
and headed for the hotel that was hosting the convention. After
booking in, we set out to find Ed Levine. He was appreciative
of us coming out at such short notice. I told him it was 'no
problem' and it wasn't – when you are chasing a dream, that's
the sort of thing you had to do. A meeting was arranged with
Pepe Cordero and his crowd in an hour's time – time for a
quick shower and not much else. The fact that there was no
time to eat was no problem as my stomach was churning and
my brain buzzing in anticipation of the negotiations ahead. I
was acutely aware that the deal we were going to talk about
was my first world-title fight as manager and promoter. I was
nervous – who wouldn't have been?

We were introduced to Pepe Cordero and his people in a

room that had been set up in boardroom style for negotiations. Before there was a bum on the big leather seats or a bottle of mineral water opened, Pepe was smothering Paddy in a huge bear hug. This, I thought, is in *The Godfather* mould. The expensive suits, the tans, the shades, the thin smiles of the Cordero group all underlined the feeling! But, if Paddy could handle it, so could I. Cordero, it became clear as Paddy had warned, moved in a lot of circles and not all of them were what they might seem – some were potentially dangerous – but, like it or not, this was the man I had to deal with. For fifteen minutes or so, we fluffed around in conversational sparring with no telling punches thrown. At this stage, it was not as hard as I had expected but soon we had to get down to real business. If I wanted the fight on Clinton's home patch and if Sid Perez was to move out from under the safety blanket of fighting in the Americas, Cordero was asking me to put up a crazy sum of money. Thanks to Paddy's advice, I knew what I was dealing with and simply said that this outrageous demand was not on. It was clear that this was the answer they had expected. And, in the time-honoured manner of negotiations of this nature, with the nonsense demands out of the way, we got down to some sensible talk. At this stage, given the nature of the negotiations, things were reasonably cordial and, for a time, I thought we had reached a deal. I laid it on the line and spelled out in detail what I thought I had agreed to but sand was now thrown into the engine. The talks were grinding towards a standoff. No, no, no – they wanted more on top, more perks.

I gave it some thought and, being desperate to get the fight, I agreed to some of the demands. So, once again, I began to detail what I believed we had settled for. No, again they wanted more. This time it was expensive extra hotel rooms in Glasgow for their entourage. I was to pay for Perez's sparring partners, bar bills etc. – it was a long list. I now knew without a doubt what Paddy had been on about – Pepe Cordero was the kind of guy who knew how to take the milk out of your tea and then steal your tea. By this time, I was allowing my heart to rule my head and was having difficulty in seeing much beyond my dream promotion in Glasgow. So, reluctantly, I agreed to the most recent terms but it was still not enough! They went on again, looking for more dollars. It was clear they figured they had a patsy on their hands – a guy so desperate for the fight that they could squeeze more and more out of him.

Suddenly, a touch of Glasgow reality kicked in to my brain as I remembered my dad Tommy Gilmour Sr, a dealer's dealer. He always told me that a deal was a deal and the goalposts were not there just to be moved around to suit some greedy guys – even if they did wear expensive suits and boast darkly of interesting friends. It was then, too, that a touch of gene therapy also kicked in. My grandfather Jim, a champion boxer, a promoter and a gambler, was a man who, at times, had a really short fuse. Old Jim would have approved my next move. I got up from the table, tipped it and everything on it into the Cordero crew's laps, gave them a mouthful of international language and stomped out. This was my *Godfather* moment. I now wish it had been caught on camera. The Cordero mob were given some heartfelt Scottish verbals with directions where to go and where exactly they could stick their demands. They seemed surprised. This was not in the script – the patsy was giving them hell. Paddy had advised against such violent reaction but his advice was too late – I had done it.

I stormed off to the nearest shopping mall, almost taking the hotel doors off the hinges. Away from the heated atmosphere of the convention hotel and the hangers-on and wise guys, I calmed down as I bought gifts for Veronica and the kids. (Now I knew what women meant when they talked about retail therapy.) Deep down, I knew that my show of strength, which had clearly angered not only Cordero but his associates, did not mean I had blown my chance of the fight. But it did mean that, instead of a negotiated promotion which could suit us both, the world-title bout would go to purse offers. This is basically an auction where promoters wanting a fight show how much they are prepared to take out of their wallets in order to get it. I could still win but, if this happened, Pepe and Co. might not get as good a deal and the pursuit of a good deal was what made Cordero such a driven and, I suspect, dangerous individual. The purse offers procedure when all interested parties bid in sealed envelopes and the highest bidders wins might be a bit too democratic for this guy!

Paddy was with me in the shopping mall as we dodged in and out of the stores and past the fast-food joints that pepper such air-conditioned cathedrals of commerce and he told me he thought I'd been way over the top when I'd violently tumbled that table into the laps of the Americans. I told him why I had got so angry. It seemed to me that they were beginning to take the piss out of me and I figured they probably thought that, since Paddy was with me, he was delivering a chicken ready for the plucking. We were still laughing at that when who should appear, trailing us down the mall, but one of Cordero's sidekicks. It was all different now. Would I go back to the hotel to continue negotiations? Paddy was of the opinion that it was a good idea and we agreed. But, of course, I completed my shopping before we went back to the hotel – all that stuff at school about Drake and a game of bowls had not been without relevance to me after all! Back at the table, the Cordero crew were obviously not pleased at all at what was going on but I have to say they were at least courteous. They were throwing small olive branches at me and graciously informed me that we had 'a deal'. It was now my turn to say no. I had had enough of this horse-trading which was clearly designed to milk me. I can still picture with enjoyment their faces when I told them they were not on. Even better was the reaction of Paddy. For once, the old raconteur was literally speechless – the man of a million anecdotes was as stunned as Cordero at this twist in events. This alone made it worth it for me as I never believed till that moment I would see Paddy Byrne stuck for a word.

The ball was now in my court and they listened as I talked. I wanted a deal more than anyone but not at any cost. After some initial shock and argument, they realised they were talking to a Glasgow guy who had grown up in the game and meant what he said. There was no doubt now in their minds that I was not that plump chicken to be easily plucked as they had first thought. I spelled it out – the first deal we had agreed hours ago was the only one I would accept. If they didn't like it, the fight went to purse offers. They were not pleased at all. The faces said it, the body language underlined it. But I had won. Pepe Cordero knew he could make more money out of the fight if it didn't go to purse offers. And money motivated him. The world-title battle was heading for the Kelvin Hall. I was clear in my head about what I wanted in the agreement and headed for the hotel business centre to get someone to get it down on paper for us to sign. It was one of those days – no one at home, the door locked. I went to reception and asked for help, everyone was busy. But I got a loan of a battered old

IBM machine and even that was not what it seemed – no correc-
tion ribbon. I am a talker not a typist but I ploughed on and I
am sure it would have taken the world record for the length
of time taken to put a short agreement together. I stuck at it
and, in the end, everyone signed.

It is hard to say how I felt at the successful completion of
the most gruelling negotiations. The best way of putting it
would be in the words of an old saying I first heard from my
granny, 'I was like a dog with two tails.' But I was knackered
mentally and it was now time for food and drink away from
the fetid atmosphere of that hotel room. Paddy and I went to
a restaurant and it was to be no expense spared for a spot of
what the yanks call 'fine dining'. Apart from fancy food, this
is shorthand for a meal with wine and there was good news
there too. Paddy was pleased to be part of what we had achieved
that day, proud of me and delighted that he had helped the
son of his old pal Tommy Sr to do a good bit of boxing business. He insisted on buying the wine. How could I resist? And
there was the added bonus of an Irishman paying for a
Scotsman's drink. It was the start of a great relationship and
Paddy went on down the years to help me and show great
loyalty to me, in the same manner as he had shown to my
father. One of Paddy's most amusing claims – and he is great
company – is that he shares a birthday with Mickey Mouse.
Maybe, but one thing is for sure – Nicholas 'Paddy' Byrne is
no Mickey Mouse operator.

This crusade of mine to bring the world-title fight to Scotland
cost me a few sleepless nights but that night in a Miami hotel,
after clinching the deal, was not one of them. I was a different
man the next morning as we set off to the airport and home –
I was a man with mission. Although I knew there would be a

few problems ahead, I already had a sense of achievement. Not yet forty, I was making Scottish boxing history. And it would all happen in the Kelvin Hall, such an important place in the history of the great old city of Glasgow. The arena on the banks of the River Kelvin had seen a lot of momentous happenings down the years. During the Second World War, it had even been used as a factory for the manufacture of barrage balloons. And what Glasgow kid can't remember the annual Christmas carnival and the heavy smell of the wild animals in the circus and menagerie, lions, tigers, and elephants, which permeated the whole place for months. Motor shows, the Modern Homes Exhibition, the industrial exhibition for the Festival of Britain in 1951 – the hall had seen a lot of action in its time, including some memorable boxing, such as Jim Watt taking a world title in a classic battle with Alfredo Pitalua. Now another great event was on the way there.

Because of the time difference, I didn't phone home from Miami. I didn't want to wake Veronica and the kids back home in Newton Mearns in the middle of the night so instead I just left a message to let them know what had happened. But, as the jet powered us across the Atlantic, I could not resist doing something I had never done before, something that was a bit unusual in those days – I phoned home from 40,000 feet. It was, I felt, the sort of thing world-title fight promoters would do. Paddy Byrne still talks about the fun of that call to this day. Veronica was as happy about what had happened as I was. But it was when she asked me about the details of the deal that the significance of what I had done suddenly dawned on me. I told her the deal would cost me more than £100,000 – our most expensive event at the time. Veronica has, down the years, always been there for me with good advice and common sense.

She knew this was my dream and her sense of humour soon surfaced. 'Oh, well,' she said, 'you'll not mind going without eggs with your bacon on Sunday!' We had been married since 1973 and she knew how to bring me back down to earth. I knew she would help make it happen and I loved her for it. Still on the phone from the skies, I asked Veronica to get my part-time secretary at the time, Linda Young, who worked from my office on the mezzanine floor of the Forte Crest hotel – better known to Glaswegians as the Albany – to call a press conference and make sure everyone who should be there would be there. I was flying in more ways than one.

2

ON TOP OF THE WORLD

I was still on a high when the shuttle from Heathrow bumped through the usual heavy rain clouds – what else? – hanging above Clydebank and glided in over the remnants of ship-building on the Clyde and across its tributary the River Cart to come to a stop at the Abbotsinch terminal. Time differences were never given a thought. I went home for a shower and a shave and drove straight into my office at the old Albany. The press conference had been arranged and we had to make it a good one. Obviously Perez was training on the other side of the Atlantic and could not be there to help generate the maximum publicity we needed. The red-top tabloids, the broad-sheets and the TV and radio guys needed as much novelty as possible to publicise the fight. We had to come up with some-thing a little bit different to catch attention. The masterstroke came from my daughter Stephanie. (When I look back on my career, I always think of the support I got from Veronica and the kids and I know it has been invaluable.)

At the time of the Clinton fight, Stephanie was just twelve and she had an idea for a bit of fun and publicity for the fight. She remembers it clearly to this day. In those days, we often spent the odd moment wandering around the glitzy shopping precinct in Princes Square, off Buchanan Street. One of the places there was called Chacmool and it specialised in Mexican-style jewellery. But what caught Stephanie's young eye one day was not sparkling earrings or a colourful necklace. She spotted a large papier-mâché model of a Mexican bandit, complete with scarf and huge Zapata moustache. It was, I suppose, the Mexican equivalent of the familiar American cigar-store Red Indian. Stephanie had plans for this little fellow. We approached the shop manager and persuaded him to give us *el bandito* on a short-term loan. Mind you, he took a £1500 deposit just in case the wee guy disappeared when in our company.

A good friend of ours, Bruce Robinson, collected the model and chauffeured him up to my offices in the Albany. The papier-mâché man was destined to play a major role at the press conference – thanks to Stephanie. When we were interviewed, *el bandito* had a place right in front of the cameras. It all added to the build-up for a fight that was capturing the imagination of the Scottish sporting public – even folk who had not paid much attention to the boxing world for years were paying attention.

But I had to juggle more than one problem at a time and something very different from the fun of Mexican bandits began to bother me. Everyone knew that wee Pat from 'Little Ireland', as Croy is often referred to, was a big Celtic man. Apart from his boxing, his sporting life revolved round the adventures of 'the Hoops'. It is sad to have to record that sectarianism in Glasgow was so strong that it had to be taken into account when promoting a boxing match. But it was. The realist in me knew that we did not want one side in the sectarian divide backing the fight and other turning against it. Sixteen years later, as I write these memoirs, the problem is still making headlines. Things are better than they were in 1991 and 1992 but sectarianism in sport is still occupying the newspapers and the Scottish government.

Both the clubs of football's Old Firm, Celtic and Rangers, are fighting it hard at official level but the problem is so deep-rooted that it will take years to completely eradicate the virulent poison that, at times, shames Scottish sport. But, in the way the clubs are fighting it in the twenty-first century, they both helped me to keep the Clinton fight clear of any of the worst excesses of the football's lunatic fringe. The fact that both clubs were willing to sell tickets meant the fight would not be seen as being predominately for supporters of either club. I had good connections with Rangers folk and I was considering the possibility of contacting them to see if they could help. But I hadn't had time to pick up the phone when the Ibrox club contacted me. At the other end of the line was Bob Reilly, commercial director of the Rangers Football Club. Bob and Hugh Adams of Rangers' Pools would arrange for the Rangers shop to sell tickets. This was a great start and a reminder how valuable friends are. There would be no problem at Celtic Park either – they would sell tickets as well. This was no surprise since Pat trained at Parkhead.

The wee guy had been invited to use Parkhead for training by the then Celtic manager Billy McNeill. Amusingly, it took three calls from 'Caesar', as Billy was nicknamed, to get through to Pat who thought the calls were a wind-up. The training at Parkhead was not all one-way traffic. The boxer let the footballers sample his training regime. He introduced them to some of his ten exercise circuits, which included press-ups, squat jumps and bench presses. This was sometimes too tough for the footballers. Incidentally, Pat tells of doing training runs with his Celtic pals and they couldn't keep up with him. Think what a player he could have been! Clinton also recalls that he got the use of the football club's hyperbaric chamber for the treatment of hand injuries (sadly such trouble with his hands eventually contributed to him having to retire). In interviews, Pat talked of the support he got from the Celtic stars. In fact, in Pat's fight before challenging for the world title, he was cheered on at the St Andrew's Sporting Club when defeating Mexican Alberto Cantu by almost a dozen or so of the Hoops – first team regulars, including Paul McStay, Charlie Nicholas and Gary Gillespie.

For a moment or two, I was beginning to think promoting world-title fights was a doddle – what a mistake! I needed sponsorship, TV coverage and an exact date. Bernard Connolly, Director of Parks and Leisure for Glasgow City Council, made Wednesday, 18 March 1992 available at the Kelvin Hall so that was one problem solved. My main sponsor for the St Andrew's Sporting Club at that time was Scottish Brewers who aptly used their brand name Tartan Special. Alistair Wilson, their Director of Sales, was one of the straightest men I have met. The agreement with the sporting club was already going well so I turned to the brewers for help with this venture and a meeting was arranged between me, Alistair and his colleague Roger Crosthwaite. I explained the need for major sponsorship and was asked immediately what I meant by 'major'. With my best air of nonchalance, I mentioned the figure of £40k. The reaction was for Alistair to order pints for Roger and himself and a large glass of cold water for me – a hint that I should cool it! These guys handled the Rangers sponsorship and knew more than a bit about the game. Budgets are tight – when are they not? – and, concerned to avoid the prospect of seeing a grown man cry, they looked at ways to help. I needed to get national TV for the fight to keep Scottish

Brewers happy. The St Andrew's club was sponsored by their Tartan Special brand but, at that time, they were making a major marketing push for McEwan's Lager – the name was on the Rangers' shirts – and that was the national brand chosen to sponsor the fight.

I have always had good relations with BBC Scotland who often televised my club's shows and other shows. They were on side but this was a UK-wide TV call and it was far from easy. The London bigwigs were at first not enthusiastic. The huge interest in the fight and its historic importance to the game in Scotland were not immediately apparent to the movers and shakers down south who thought life revolved round the capital. I had a hard sell on my hands. National TV had shown Jim Watt winning the world title and several of his entertaining defences but this had been done under an agreement with National Promotions, who were based, of course, in London and run by such national names as world-renowned match-maker Mickey Duff, Mike Barrett and Jarvis Astaire. In contrast, the Clinton fight was a first world promotion by a young Scot but, to be fair to the Beeb, I have to say that the then supremo in Scotland, Jim Hunter, along with Director Mike Abbot and Contracts Manager Jim Preacher, pitched in on our side and helped to persuade the Corporation's Head of Sport Brian Barwick to take the fight.

But there was to be a cash slap in the face to me and, indirectly, to Scotland from the myopic Londoners – albeit that Brian himself was a Scouser. I wasn't fighting on a level playing field as I needed national TV to bring local sponsorship. The BBC's offer for the fight was derisory – £15k. In my mind, it should have been far higher but, with the brewers' deal dependent on it, I had to accept what I considered was a seriously low, almost insulting, offer for a live broadcast. Despite my disappointment in our deal, he and I still enjoy a bit of lunch together occasionally although I feel I have to remind him of that miserly £15k, especially over the brandies. Brian went on to be chief executive of the English FA, a position that guarantees its holder getting a lot of flak.

Again, for a moment, I allowed myself to think that all was going well with the promotion – another mistake as a new bombshell had arrived. On the night of the fight, Celtic were due to play Motherwell at home – what a kick in the teeth! I felt sick at the thought of what that would do to ticket sales. I phoned Tom Grant, a Celtic director and life-long friend of the Clintons. I told him of my predicament and, in all innocence, gently suggested that they play the game another night. I was phoning from the Albany in the city centre and he was miles way in the east end at Parkhead but the laughter coming from his end did not need to be amplified by phone. You could have heard it out on the street. Was I mad? Tom pointed out you could have half your team in bed with the flu and the other half injured and the football authorities would still not agree to altering a match date.

Thinking about it, I knew the fight had to go ahead. If the football fixture could not be switched, then maybe I wouldn't even be getting any bacon on Sunday mornings! I summoned up courage and phoned Peter Donald at the Scottish League. As everyone in sport in Scotland knows, Peter is a smashing guy. He took my request with equanimity and I breathed a sigh of relief as he calmly told me that, if both clubs would agree to play on the Tuesday, then the league would switch the fixture. Celtic, of course, were no problem. So then I phoned wee Tommy McLean at Motherwell and he said he was pleased to help the wee man from Croy Miners – Tommy was, of course, from a mining area.

So that was it, we could get on with the press conference. It was memorable. Everyone and their granny, as we say in these parts, was there. Along with me at the top table were Kevin Kelly, from Celtic, Bob Reilly, from Rangers, and Pat Clinton. Sid Perez was thousands of miles away pounding a punch bag and doing a million skips a day but, in his place, our papier-mâché Sid beamed down on the scribblers and made a great target for the legions of snappers who had turned up. It was a fun day and Stephanie's inspired idea to use *el bandito* was proving a masterstroke, especially as we now had the wee guy decked out in lurid red boxing gloves. It was an early example of her marketing skills – she went on to get a degree in business and marketing. The coverage we got was colossal and it seemed like the whole of Scotland was behind us. We also got great support from the city council who agreed to back me for any losses up to £20k in return for 20 per cent of any profits. I liked this as it was a business proposition and not a handout from the public coffers. And, in the event, the promotion was successful and Glasgow got its share of the cash.

On an extraordinary night, the opening scenes were almost as stunning as the finale. The weigh-in even raised my blood pressure. Perez failed to make the weight at the first attempt, threatening the fight. He was given two hours to make the weight and there was talk of a visit to a sauna. At this, the ears of the General Secretary of the Boxing Board of Control, up from London for the fight, pricked up. He pointed out such a visit, with potential danger to the boxer's health, would cause a cancellation. I immediately called on my trusted associate Benny King to take the Perez party to the gym at the Marriott Hotel in Argyle Street, just round the corner from the Albany where the weigh-in was taking place. Benny monitored their efforts to lose the excess weight and it was his opinion that it was all a ruse to give us the feeling that the boxer was weakened by shedding weight. Next time on the scales Perez made the weight.

Back in the Kelvin Hall, we were checking every detail and I was greatly helped in this by my eighteen-year-old son Christopher who kept me on my toes and asked me question after question, reminding me how we, as a family, had planned every detail of the big night. Soon it was time to get into the dinner suits and open the doors to the fans. The undercard was watched in an atmosphere thick with tension and expectation. Clinton v Perez was the only deal in town that mattered that night and the crowd was hungry for it. There is a convention in world championship bouts that the contender enters the ring before the champion appears. I had other ideas on that night of boxing high passion. I smooth-talked the Mexicans into agreeing that their man would go through the ropes first. This he did to the strains of 'The Mexican Hat Dance'. Now, as the seconds to the start of the fight ticked by, everyone waited tensely, watching for Pat to appear and walk in to the spotlight, past the thronged rows of A-list celebrities, towards the ring. He was quite a sight when he finally appeared to a huge roar. He was wrapped in a dressing gown of the special Glasgow tartan courtesy of then Lord Provost, the popular Susan Baird, who also saw to it that the challenger was kitted out in Glasgow tartan shorts. On the back of his gown were emblazoned the words 'Glasgow is Alive'. In the noise and excitement the slogan was something of an understatement.

The challenger strode confidently towards the ring, and his destiny, through an unforgettable wall of noise created by the shouts of encouragement from the crowd and the massive swelling sound of the skirl of the pipes and drums of the

Strathclyde's Police Force's tartan-clad band. In the ring itself, the ritual of playing the national anthems of the fighters took place and the Mexican anthem struggled to rise above the incredible hubbub. Then came an unforgettable moment. Ronnie Browne of The Corries ducked under the ropes and into the ring to lead the thousands of celebrities and boxing fans in the Kelvin Hall in a truly moving rendition of 'Flower of Scotland', the powerful anthem written by his late partner in The Corries, Roy Williamson. I have seldom felt such emotion in the ring and even the English boxing folk who had come up from the south for the world title bout, including John Morris of the Board of Control, were belting it out with passion. These amazing scenes before the start must have helped Pat tremendously – and maybe sent a shiver of fear into Perez who could never have imagined being at the centre of something like this when he had signed for the fight all those weeks ago, thousands of miles from Glasgow and its legions of driven boxing aficionados.

The great and the good showed up for the big night. Politicians, media magnates, businessmen and sports stars were all there and former world champions, like Walter McGowan, Ken Buchanan and Jim Watt, turned out to watch a fellow Scot try to join them on the list of boxing immortals. Sitting beside them were the likes of snooker world champion Stephen Hendry and his manager Ian Doyle and many other celebrities. It must have been the biggest collection of A-list celebs at a boxing night for years. The Kelvin Hall was packed and even long-time boxing fans, who thought they had seen it all before, were caught up in the electric atmosphere. I also felt a tinge of pride in that, when I looked round the arena, I knew almost every face. I had a lot of folk on my side.

Perez began at a blistering pace so it was all the more surprising that, in the closing rounds, he appeared to many observers to be the stronger man. Indeed, at the end of the ninth, Pat looked to be in trouble but, before he came out for the tenth, his brother, who trained him, produced a picture of their late dad Billy and thrust it in his face. The encouragement seemed to work and the next few rounds looked to be going the Croy man's way. During the early rounds, Perez had been aggressive but the Scot expertly blocked his long, lunging punches and delivered telling countering jabs. Many thought it was all going the way Pat wanted but the Mexican moved up a gear in the seventh and the round ended with the challenger on the ropes and under heavy fire. The final rounds see-sawed and there were moments when both boxers looked to be dominant only for them to lose their way.

Most of the ringside sports writers gave the final round to Perez and so the question came down to whether or not Clinton had done enough earlier in the fight to win. At the final bell, few were truly certain who was the winner – it was as close a fight as you will see. The tension as everyone waited for the judges' figures was immense. The MC had announced that the judges were not unanimous. Now we had to find out who had scored it for each fighter. The Danish judge Torben Hansen came first and the hall was stunned when he rated it 116–113 in favour of Perez. The other two judges were American. The first, Bob Watson, announced he'd scored it 115–113 for Pat. Then came the final verdict, that of Frank Brunette, who gave it to Pat by a margin of just one point – 115–114. I had a world champ.

We all pranced around the ring in relief and delight. Wee Pat wore a huge sombrero which made him look even smaller than he was. Then there came a mighty roar of recognition as Ronnie Browne re-appeared in the ring to sing 'Flower of Scotland' again with his arm round Pat. It was as emotional as it gets in boxing. In the aftermath, Pat, an honest guy, acknowledged how close it had been and said he thought he had won six rounds, Perez four and two shared. In the papers next day, there was a lot of argument about the verdict. One Scots reporter was annoyed at the Danish judge scoring it for the holder but that wise old bird, the late Harry Mullen of *Boxing News*, pointed out that many of the rounds were difficult to score and that he would not disagree much with Pat's own assessment.

Anyway, when the lights finally dimmed and dressing rooms emptied, Pat Clinton and his connections left the city and headed out east and back to Croy. Later my friends and family and I followed them out the same road but, before we made it to the village, we were stopped at a police roadblock. The boys in blue were smiling as they said hello and immediately directed us to the party down the road at Croy Miners' Welfare. It was not an early night. Even Rosemary McKenna, Provost of Cumbernauld and Kilsyth Council, who went on to be an MSP, showed up to see the new champion. The newspapers in the days that followed were full of stories about Clinton. It was big national news – so big that the Scottish *Sun* produced an eight-page pullout, something innovative at the time and something rare in boxing coverage. With Clinton finally the champ, I was asked about the possibility of a return match. I said no and pointed out that the Mexicans never granted a rematch at the Alamo.

I have never been as tired in all my life as I was when I finally put the key in the lock of my own front door and hit my own bed. But the aftermath of the fight left work still to be done and I dragged myself into town the next morning to clear up all the niggling little problems that always follow a major promotion – to pay the bills and tie up all the loose ends. For a start, there was a nasty hangover from the negotiations in Miami with the Perez entourage and their ability to pile up perk upon perk in their demands. At considerable expense, I had put them up in the best rooms of what was then the Albany Hotel in Bothwell Street. There were plenty of them and the cost of the rooms and a decent amount of their expenses, for food and drink, would end up on my credit card. I had not, however, allowed for the way the Mexicans would interpret what was decent and reasonable in such circumstances. I didn't expect them to behave like Lifeboys on a trip to town but never, in my wildest dreams, did I imagine what would happen.

Maybe I should have taken the behaviour of one of the Perez hangers-on as an early warning sign. This guy could drink – indeed, his efforts in this field were so impressive that our people, themselves no strangers to the culture of massive daily consumption of hard liquor, immediately nicknamed him Pancho Tequila. Pancho had a notion that life was a dull place if you didn't go for a swim round a bottle of tequila at frequent intervals – say, every hour or so. Now, in those days, you could pop into an off-licence and get a bottle of poison for less than a tenner but I suppose that would not have the style expected of a sharp-suited Mexican mover and fixer in shades (to hide his eyeballs rather than protect them from the watery sunlight of Scotland). So Pancho ordered his medicine from the cocktail bar in the hotel at £40 a pop, leaving T. Gilmour, Glasgow boxing promoter, to pay. Sometimes six bottles a day were going his way.

I was not of a mind to subsidise this sort of lifestyle for anyone and I let the wise guys know it. They ran to the press complaining that I was a 'robber', chickening out of paying up on an agreement. I was raging so I picked up the phone and asked the editor of the *Sun*, a paper that had always had good boxing coverage and knew the score on most things, to get a reporter and a photographer round to the Albany right away. They duly arrived and, before the notebooks were out and cameras focused, I leapt up on to chair and held up a roll of paper from a cash register, detailing the bar bills and extras claimed by this gang of would-be smart asses. It was nine and a half feet long! The point was taken by both the claimants and the press and that fox was shot. There were other arguments over the sort of things reporters and fans never give a thought to – the arcane intricacies of tax and the demands of the revenue's Foreign Employment Unit's complex rules on the earnings of foreigners who have a big pay day in the UK. Sometimes, when I look back on life, I remember a notion that I could have been a chartered accountant rather than a boxing promoter. I love playing around with numbers and I flatter myself that I am pretty good at it. Maybe that, too, is in the genes for my father and grandfather were bookies and gambling men as well as boxing people. Even in these days of glossy bookies' shops on the high street, you get folk on both sides of the counter who would be gold medallists in any mental arithmetic Olympics. And some of them barely went to school.

Whatever, I finally got everything tied up. Wee Pat was at home in Croy with his family and his pals and his championship belt and the Kelvin Hall was quiet again as it waited for its next role in entertaining the citizens, maybe hosting a caravan show or conference, the colossal enthusiasm of that night in March 1992 now just one more chapter in its long history. The papers, which had been full of the fight for weeks, had moved on to new controversies, new sports sensations. I was simply just so tired, worn out and knackered that I took the family off to the Lake District for a break. For six months, the Clinton v Sid Perez battle had dominated my life. Now Pat was champ, the Mexicans and Puerto Ricans were long gone with Pancho Tequila no doubt in hot pursuit of a new drink ticket somewhere thousands of miles away.

That was, incidentally, the last time I crossed swords with Pepe Cordero. For years, he continued to cause problems at the very top of the game. He was certainly a difficult character but I reckon I had won his respect that day in Miami. We became friends and I, for one, had no more hassles with him. I had faced him down and won that day in Miami. In fact, despite his reputation, he was instrumental in helping me on many occasions before his death. He travelled to Glasgow on boxing business from time to time. I remember taking him and a few pals, including out resident raconteur Paddy Byrne, to one of Glasgow's most famous restaurants, the Buttery in Anderston. As I mentioned, Pepe was a bulky guy and, when he pushed his girth into a seat, there was always much stretching and twisting around to try to get comfortable. His weight had contributed to spinal problems and the pain from his back meant that all this twisting and turning was accompanied by some heavy Puerto Rican cursing. The pain was such that he needed regular injections of painkilling potions. This particular evening in the Buttery, he was casually dressed in well-pressed slacks, a polo shirt and a black leather bomber jacket. He looked every inch the big-time international Mr Fixit that he was. We were all sitting around having pre-dinner drinks and chatting about the fight game and enjoying a few laughs when I noticed his face change colour. As the conversation swirled around him he reached into his inside pocket and without pausing he withdrew a syringe out of it and, in one deft move, plunged it into his arm – right through the leather of his jacket. I almost fainted. As my dentist will confirm, I am not good with injections or indeed needles of any kind. It was all done very casually and without any attempt to disguise what he was doing. When the injection took hold I could see that the pain was away and he began to relax again. I don't think any of the other diners noticed a thing. I asked what he had injected to control the pain and he said pethidine which is often used to control the pain of childbirth. To lighten things up, I jokingly said it sounded like the truth drug pentothol to me. Pepe considered the comment and remarked that, if that was the case, in future he would just suffer the pain and take no chances – a truth drug was not anything he planned to experiment with at any time. Pepe had many powerful friends and a share of enemies, too. Although he never had an official title or position with the WBO, the consensus of opinion was that he was The Man.

Not long after he died, I was at a WBO convention in San Juan. This had been his power base and the occasion was a major gathering of the movers and shakers in big-time boxing. We all sat down in a huge and lavishly furnished conference room and high on the wall a large portrait of Pepe gazed down on the gathered boxing luminaries. I was sitting with my partner and co-promoter Barry Hearn and we were all told that this very day would have been Pepe's birthday. As the evening wore on, we were given a signal to stand up at one point and everyone greeted the occasion and the portrait by singing 'Happy Birthday'! It would have made a wonderful final scene for a film about a chequered life.

After all the excitement of the Clinton fight, the break in the Lake District was a welcome one – there's something special in its scenery that makes it the ideal place to relax and rebuild. But initially, for all I cared, it could have been Main Street, Bridgeton on a noisy Glasgow Fair Saturday night. I slept for days so I really could have been anywhere. As I gradually got myself together in the shadows of the beautiful mountains and on the shores of the most famous lakes in the world, a curious thing happened. My dream had come true. I had achieved everything I wanted in boxing. I should, along with Pat, have been on top of the world. But I wasn't. I felt drained and depressed. Years of pressure had taken their toll. It is difficult to explain how you can feel so down and dark at the height of your achievements. But now, years later, I realise I was not alone. What I was going through was nothing unique.

I heard an emotional radio interview with a guy who had served donkey's years in prison for a crime he had not committed. Finally released and with his name cleared, for a few days he felt a high – elation like he had never experienced before – but it was followed by dark day after dark day. He explained to the programme's listeners that the ultimate dream of freedom and of clearing his name had sustained him throughout all the bad years. Now he was free but the focus of his life for so long was nowhere to be found. I suppose I had been in some sort of prison cage myself, albeit at times a gilded one. I'd been driven by that dream of winning a world title in my own city with my own fighter and on my own promotion. Once I'd achieved it, I knew it was going to be a hard act to follow. It took time but gradually I began to feel normal again – maybe I had overdosed on adrenaline in the months before the fight and was suffering withdrawal symptoms. No matter, the mind gradually got back on an even keel, helped by the memories of the fight and the battle to get it to take place in Glasgow.

Sometimes you get so caught up in the nitty-gritty of organising a promotion that you fail to see the whole picture. During the bit of a downer that followed the Clinton fight, I spent some time at home and in the office looking at letters that had come in from fans and dignitaries who had been at the Kelvin

Hall. As I mentioned earlier, one of the most powerful moments of emotion, in a hugely emotional night, came when Ronnie Browne, the man who had sung 'Flower of Scotland' so often before with the other half of The Corries, Roy Williamson, sang it in the ring along with the new world champion. It moved everyone in the hall and, despite the number of times he must have sung it, Ronnie had apparently been moved too. In a gracious letter to Pat, he said:

> To be there in the ring, singing 'Flower of Scotland' with your-self, is a moment in my life I will never forget, and you must forgive me if, in my mind, as a Scotsman who has worn his patriotism on his sleeve all his life, I bask in your glory of that occasion for the rest of it.

Ronnie went on to note how lavish Pat had been in praise of his family's support and the effect it had on him. He added a poignant personal note:

> I know full well how much that [family support] has meant to me throughout my career and especially after Roy [his partner in the legendary folk group The Corries] died and so I feel I know something of their pride, and no doubt relief at this momen-tous outcome, so please convey our sincere best wishes to them.

He signed off on a happy note, saying, 'Cheers, champ'.

I was particularly pleased to get another letter from wee Jack Irvine a former editor of the Scottish *Sun*, spin doctor extraordinaire and all-round media guru. No wonder Jack liked a night at the boxing – anyone in the media and many beyond it will testify to his combative nature (something of an understatement). Jack likes a scrap but you know where you are with this talented guy. When he says it, he means it so I was touched when he wrote to me to say:

> I had a lump in my throat watching you and Pat last night. You put on one of the finest spectaculars Scotland has seen in many a long year. I can't think of anyone who deserves the success and acclaim more than you. You are a nice man and I'm proud to know you.

That put a lump in *my* throat, I can tell you, and it gave me a wee mental lift just at the time I needed it.

I was also delighted to receive a note from John Morris, the General Secretary of the British Boxing Board of Control. John of course congratulated Pat but I took some satisfaction myself when he spoke in his letter of the way the night was organised. He wrote, 'It was, to say the least, highly professional and to see such a wildly enthusiastic crowd controlled perfectly and behaving impeccably was a great credit to boxing.'

Back in the buzz of the city after the tranquillity of the Lake District, I was able to reflect on this and lots more. I thought quite a bit about wee Pat Clinton who had just made history. The Croy flyweight came from a boxing family. The village itself had an interesting history. It was a mining village and most of the folk who lived in the vicinity were Roman Catholics of Irish stock. These days when people think of the potato famine and the bad times that drove many of the Irish from their homelands, the assumption is that they all took off to America as indeed the forefathers of a famous namesake of Pat, ex-president Bill Clinton, did. In fact, the rush to get away from Ireland was such that those without even the few quid needed for a voyage to the land of the free had to settle for a new life nearer home. The pits and steelworks of Scotland offered alternatives.

The immigrants, mostly poor farm folk, got to Glasgow and followed the rail lines out of the city on the assumption that there would be a village down the line with work available. Many of them found themselves in Croy, a stop on the main line to Edinburgh, and, as I've already mentioned, over the years, it became a 'Little Ireland'. The tag was well merited. It was once said that the only Protestant in the village was the copper and he could be a busy man at times. Croy may have been a god-fearing sort of place but it had its share of hard men. So much so that one former denizen says to this day that, forty or so years ago, it was the sort of place where 'they ate their first-born'. A bit over the top perhaps but the guys who earned their meagre wages in the pit had it hard. The Scottish coalfields had long, hard seams of black gold. Mining here involved the use of pick and sledgehammer to break up the tough layers of coal to be loaded on to the underground trolleys. Rather different from work in a mine in, say, the Nottingham coalfields down south, where it could be like 'picking popcorn off the roof', so soft were the seams. At least that is what they said in Croy. But the Croy miners and labourers did not just pay lip service to their religion for the chapel house was never short of free coal. And, when the mines eventually began to close and the miners turned to working the local quarry, they negotiated a deal that part of their wages went to maintain the chapel house.

Pat's father, Billy, from a Croy hamlet called Auchenstarrie, met and married Sadie, a lassie from the nearby area of Smithston, and, over the years, they had ten children, six boys and four girls. Billy's brother Jim had been an amateur boxing champion in the forties and he himself won the Scottish pro flyweight crown in 1940 (a title his son was to take forty-seven years later). Billy might have dreamed of great things for he did once beat a little-known Dundonian called Freddie Tennant, who had out-pointed Benny Lynch. But another famous flyweight, Jackie Paterson, took only two rounds to beat Billy and hopes of world fame such as Benny enjoyed, before his downfall in a bout with the bottle, were over. Billy had six boxing sons – Michael, William (known as Billy Jr), Peter, Danny, Bernard and Pat – and, of them all, he thought young Pat had the most potential. At one stage, Pat had an idea to be a jockey but, when a heart attack killed Billy, Pat made up his mind to realise his father's dream of being world champion for himself. However, I still sometimes wonder what might have happened if he had taken to football like other 'pocket demons' such as Wee Willie Henderson and Jimmy 'Jinky' Johnstone.

Pat began the long road to boxing superstardom by turning to the professional ranks under the highly rated London-based Burt McCarthy. Burt knew his stuff but so did Billy's father. Ring historian Brian Donald quotes Pat acknowledging what he owed in boxing to his dad: 'He taught me everything – how to move, how to counter-punch, not to mix matters in the ring unless desperate, how to box for all my openings.' The time after his amateur career spent south of the border produced some big wins, culminating in the European crown taken from Salvatore Fanni in a bruising battle in Caligiari, the Italian's hometown in 1990. The Italian connection was apt as Croy had fighting connections going back to Roman times when it was a key point in the Antonine Wall defences.

I also reflected on how Pat had come to be handled by me. The opportunity came out of the blue. With Pat still in London, the late Jim Reynolds gave me some interesting news. Pressmen and promoters like regular natters on the phone comparing notes, speculating on what might happen next in the fight game. Often the pressmen can point you on the right track. Jim Reynolds was a remarkable man and the boxing world paid him a lot of attention. From time to time, he enjoyed a wee dram or two with my dad, Tommy Sr. He had our respect. Not flash, his one-liners could raise a laugh but they were delivered quietly. He had something about him of the dignity and authority of *The Herald*, the paper he ended his career with. Jim covered football and boxing but I suspect boxing was his secret first love. The English like to sneer that Scottish sportswriters are 'fans with typewriters'. In my book, that is no criticism – these guys – and, nowadays, sometimes girls – have passion for their work. The fan in them makes them great sportswriters. Jim was, I suppose, that sort of old-fashioned sportswriter but none the worse for that. He took care, he knew the games and he was a statistics freak, always a good sign in a sportswriter.

These days, if you want to know who has scored most goals in a season or defended a title for the longest run, you simply look up a website. Computerisation has made the compilation of stats a piece of cake but, at the time when Jim was working, he would put in a hard day at the office, go to a game or a fight and then give his all in a report that would always be perceptive, accurate and never nasty. Afterwards, he would go home, get out some school jotters, his scissors and the old Gloy paste and fill them with team lists, times of the goals, round-by-round reports on the boxing etc. And, whenever he needed stats for a story, he just got out his own notebooks. It is a long way from hitting a few keys on a laptop.

Anyway, one fateful night, Jim brought me news that he understood Pat was in the mood to return home to do his boxing out of Glasgow. Pat was leaving Burt McCarthy on good terms – so much so that we invited Burt north as our guest for the Perez fight – and, if he wanted a new man at the helm of his career, I planned to be that person. Pat's elder brother Michael was looking after his boxing affairs after he had split from McCarthy and he came to see me. I promised the Clintons a shot at the world title after two fights under my flag and I delivered. My faith in the Croy warrior's ability was justified – he won his first contest with me as manager when he defeated Armando Tapia, fighting him at my St Andrew's Sporting Club in the old Albany. It was a win but the fight had nothing of the stature of that wonderful night in the Kelvin Hall.

Sadly, after the world-title win, Pat Clinton's career fairly quickly lost its shine. Thereafter, like many a Scottish flyweight before him, from Lynch to Jackie Paterson to Walter McGowan, he was dogged by weight problems. He managed an unimpressive defence of his title a few short months after winning it, this time in the SECC arena in Glasgow, and lost it in 1993 when a little South African, Baby Jake Matlala, stopped him in eight rounds. A foray into the bantamweight ranks was also a failure due to the combination of weight worries and hand injury problems. But the likeable little man from Croy had repaid his father's faith in him and won a world title for him. The bond between the two Clintons was underlined, as I said, when Pat had that photograph of his dad shown to him at a crucial point in the fight. I could well understand how the boxer felt for I too was part of a boxing dynasty and, in my case, it spanned four generations. I am told that in itself is a world record. The Gilmour boxing dynasty began at the Olympics in Belgium in 1920 although, in those days, the name was Gilmore – something that emerges in the remarkable story of my grandfather.

3

OLD JIM'S STORY

Although the story of the Gilmours revolves round Glasgow and hard-working folk in such down-to-earth places as Bridgeton, Rutherglen and the east end, generally, in bookies' shops, boxing gyms, pubs and packed arenas, it really started in, of all places, Belgium in 1920. The First World War was barely over and, throughout Europe, people were struggling to get over bereavements, make sense of national triumphs and disasters and get out of uniform and back to some semblance of normal life. Then, as now, sport had a role to play in turbulent times. The idyllic dream of Baron Pierre de Coubertin, the force behind the modern Olympics, survived the war, the death of millions and years of the great powers at each other's throats but it wasn't quite business as usual in the stadiums of Belgium in 1920. Nation continued to take on nation at sport but with some important qualifications. Germany, Austria, Hungary and Turkey were not welcome at the party in Antwerp. The war left a long legacy even in the Olympics.

A modern Games can involve almost 20,000 athletes but, back in 1920, only 2668 athletes took part in the first Olympiad since the First World War ended and only seventy-one of them were women – changed days indeed. The worldwide audience for the Sydney Games was more than a billion viewers. The heroes of Antwerp toiled before much smaller audiences – there was to be no hour after hour of wall-to-wall TV and radio for them. The exploits of those who didn't make the medal tables were severely under-reported although, even then, winning a gold or two made headlines round the world. Who has not heard of the Flying Finn, runner Paavo Nurmi, who won the first three of his nine gold medals at Antwerp? A legend, he ran with a stopwatch in hand to keep control of his pace.

My grandfather Jim, who boxed for the Great Britain Olympic team that year, had, however, to be content with the glory of simply being able to compete – to enjoy the taking part above all. This spirit was something that de Coubertin considered to be so important although, nowadays, the cynic might remark that having a good Olympics is the prelude to making a fortune. Many of the modern boxing greats first became world figures when they represented their countries at the Olympics – Muhammad Ali being a prime example of this trend – and, in a strange way, the Olympics were also to prove a turning point for old Jim.

Jim's career as a boxer, promoter, bookie and all-round sporting man took off after Antwerp although, as an Olympian, he didn't have the success of an Ali. Critics of boxing often overlook its long history and it is astonishing to think that boxing very similar to the form we have now was featured in the original Games way back hundreds of years BC when the contestants fought with hands bound in leather. In Belgium in 1920, Jim fought in the lightweight division and lost on points in the preliminary stages of the boxing to a Norwegian called Johan Sæterhaug who, as far as I can find out, did not go on to a glorious career despite his success against Jim.

Jim was, however, a remarkable boxer – at one time, he was champion of Great Britain and Denmark. The Danish title came his way because, in those days, if the champion of one country fought another, then the winner assumed both titles. Again this system is rather different from and much more simple than the current mess of several world boxing bodies all holding world championships – though it has to be said that the so-called unification title fights can sell television rights and provide some good boxing. Jim also gained fame in Glasgow and beyond for defeating a legendary figure in the old game, Alex Ireland, in the first round. Alex, who boxed for Leith Victoria, was the real deal, as they say – the first Scot to win silver in the boxing Olympics, a feat he achieved in Antwerp. The Leith man went on as a pro to win the British middleweight title.

Jim had not been in the services for the First World War. Why I don't know and neither, it seems, do the family historians I have consulted. However, he did lose a brother, Felix, a teenager in uniform, to enemy action. No doubt this had something to do with the fact that, in later life, men who knew Jim remarked on his ongoing hatred for Earl Haig, the general many blamed for much of the colossal loss of life by the British army in the horrors of trench warfare and the pitched man-to-man battles of those black days.

Back home after Antwerp, 'The Auld Yin', as we call him, began to carve out a remarkable career as boxer, promoter and bookie, laying the foundations for a dynasty that now sees my son Christopher as a fourth-generation boxing promoter. Incidentally I believe this family connection with the sport over so many years is unique – there's nothing else like it in the world I'm told!

But, of course, it all began with Jim. The family had come over from Antrim to Bridgeton where many Irish families, on both sides of the religious divide, had settled, staying in the solid tenements of Main Street, which ran like a spine from Richmond Park and Shawfield stadium, straight as a die, up to the 'Umbrella' bandstand, at Bridgeton Cross, and the many smaller streets that branched off it. It was a lively area especially around the twelfth of July each year when the Orange order marched behind flute bands, with their big drums beating menacingly. A favourite ploy was for the march to divert down streets known to be largely Catholic. There, the inflammatory music was greeted with a hail of objects from the open tenement windows of the residents who felt under attack by the marching bands and sectarian music. Glasgow's famous chief constable of the day, Sir Percy Sillitoe, said that sometimes in Brigton, as the locals called it, it was almost like a medieval siege – though some of the stuff that was thrown on to the marchers was not boiling oil. What rained down was indeed partly liquid but nastier even than oil or tar.

Bridgeton, in those days, was a hard place to live in. Everyone knew each other's religion. Even the way your name was spelled was a giveaway. Back in Ireland, the Gilmours were the Gilmores. The boxing side of the family decided to adopt the 'Gilmour' spelling and I grew up with the understanding that the change was made by my grandfather in the early days of boxing promoting as the antagonisms between Protestants and Catholics in Glasgow were so strong that the name 'Gilmore' on a bill could have hindered ticket sales. It is hard to believe this in the twenty-first century but, back then, there were countless examples of how a spelling identified the religion of the holder of a name.

It seemed everyone was obsessed with everyone else's religion and even the school you went to was a pointer to 'what foot you kicked with' as the bigots would say. Sometimes even the pronunciation was important, as in Devine which could be *De*vine or De*vine*. And it was also wise to make a difference between your McGinl<a>ys and McGinl<e>ys. I'm sure we did change the name for purely commercial reasons but some of the family who stuck to the spelling Gilmore didn't like it. However, having two spellings of a name was not all that unusual and sometimes there was an innocent explanation. One old guy from the boxing world told me that it often happened accidentally, say, when an Irishman, straight off the Burns-Laird line's Belfast boat at the Broomielaw, first registered for work. Many were illiterate and form filling was done pretty carelessly, with the applicant often just talking to the clerk rather than writing down the correct spelling and, hence, many Irish Carrs, for example, became Kerrs in Scotland.

The Auld Yin was one of six brothers – Frank, Jim, Charlie, Harry, Felix and Maurice. Big Catholic families were common in Brigton and the girl Jim married, Mary Cairns, my granny, had four other sisters though I only knew two, Kate and Lucy. Kate was a widow and stayed in Bains Square near the famous 'Barras' street market and Lucy, a spinster, stayed with my granny. After their wedding, Jim and Mary lived for almost all their married life in a tenement up a close at 10 Tullis Street, not far from Main Street and near to what were to become famous boxing venues, like Premierland, 136 Main Street, the Scottish National Sporting Club at 36 Charles Street and the Olympia gym.

I remember Tullis Street well and was never far away from it, as I grew up. I lived with my mum and dad in Rutherglen Road, a mile or so away on the other side of the Clyde, across Glasgow Green. I suppose everyone remembers visits to their gran or grandpa and the extra little indulgences that are part of the relationship and that special freewheeling friendliness that comes from the fact that, at the end of the day, the kid goes home to his mum and dad. Grandparents can dish out love without the baggage that goes with being a parent. Certainly I loved my trips across the Green. Granny was a dab hand at homemade soup and I had more than my share. Mind you, it's Mary's pancakes that first come to mind when my cousin Sammy Gilmore remembers his visits to Tullis Street.

Their flat had two bedrooms, an inside bathroom (not necessarily the norm in the east end in those days), a living room, with another bed set into a recess in the wall, and a scullery. It was a comfortable place. I remember that, when you entered the lobby, as we called the hall, the first room on the left was Aunt Lucy's. Lucy was a real character. A life-long spinster, she lived with her sister Mary and Jim for around thirty years. Spectacular home-made tablet – rather than soup – was her speciality. Again I had more than my share. Lucy worked in a local licensed grocer, handy no doubt when a 'carry-oot' was required to celebrate a win in the ring or a good day at the races. Although my grandad smoked, Lucy would never smoke in front of Granny Gilmour as she felt it wasn't ladylike. I think she thought that Granny didn't know she had a secret puff or two in the bathroom. Old Jim knew but never divulged the secret. This behaviour continued till their dying days.

That job of Lucy's was responsible for a curious episode in my young life. I really wanted to learn to swim and, thanks indirectly to Lucy, I almost did but my ambition was thwarted by an odd turn of events. Lucy's job was in Jimmy Whitelaw's licensed grocer's in Rutherglen Road, less than 100 yards from our house, and, during the school holidays and busy periods in the shop, I was encouraged to help by stacking shelves and doing deliveries. In those days, it was normal for the beat 'polis' to drop in on such shops to check that everything was OK and to get a quick cup of tea and a biscuit. I liked to talk to these guys in uniform and, in conversation, I mentioned to one of them that I could not swim but wanted to learn. No problems, said one copper. The police at the time had the use of a pool at Adelphi Street School and, the next weekend, I was picked up by the copper I had spoken to and taken to the baths with his wife and family. Over the next few weeks we went regularly and I was beginning to gain confidence when my friend in blue told me that he was leaving the force to start up a business and that our jaunts to the baths would have to end. It was a blow to me as I enjoyed the baths and had visions of becoming a good swimmer. My friend told me he was starting a greengrocer's shop and that was that.

In 1969, I got a shock from the papers that littered our house in Rutherglen Road and, for once, the big news that caught my attention was not on the sports pages. The papers were full of a shooting in Alison Street, Govanhill, just off the famous Victoria or 'Vicky' Road. A cornered would-be bank robber had shot two cops. Turned out it was my swimming instructor Howard Wilson and he ended up serving thirty-two years in jail. As a kid, I found the whole business unbelievable as Howard and his family had treated me so well.

And, many years later, there was another odd link with Howard Wilson. One of my dad's boxers was Willie Armstrong, a good-quality middleweight who had beaten the famous

Nigerian Dick Tiger. Tiger also beat Terry Downes and eventually became world champion. Willie became a prison officer when he left the ring and ended up working in Peterhead during the infamous riots there, when one of the inmates involved was none other than Howard Wilson!

The Cairns (Granny's maiden name) were strong and attractive women and I remember that Aunt Lucy had a long-term boyfriend called Willie Gray although they never married. Lucy was careful with money and Willie was told he had to save a pound when Lucy saved a pound if he wanted to cement the relationship. Willie was not exactly an eager beaver in the work stakes and that seems to be the reason they didn't marry. However, there is an alternative suspicion was that they didn't get hitched because Willie 'kicked with the wrong foot' and this made matrimony an outside bet in those days. Whatever the reason, till the end of their days, Willie was a weekly visitor to the home shared by Jim, Mary and Lucy for a bowl of soup, a plate of chicken and a wee hauf. Interestingly, Jim himself was not at all religious. Indeed, Sammy Gilmore remembers him as being far from pious!

Granny, though, was different and, according to Sammy, she was a 'saint' who went to 10 a.m. mass in Bridgeton's Sacred Heart every morning. She was also pretty saintly in the way she looked after The Auld Yin. Again, according to Sammy, she happily lifted and laid for him all day long – she was the sort of wife who stirred your tea for you. Life was pretty different then and, when Lucy had visitors, maybe even the long-term boyfriend, the front door was left open as a signal that no hanky-panky was underway.

Along the hall in the flat was a big bedroom which my dad and his brother Harry had shared. It had a good view over John Street School, one of Glasgow's most famous, and there was always something going on in the playgrounds and in and around the buildings to attract attention. One rather sad side to this was that I suspect that room had a damaging effect on my father's own career as a boxer. All his life, from his schooldays, he had to wear strong spectacles to correct a vision problem. The 'pebble' specs became something of a trademark and contributed to Dad having an often-remarked on likeness to TV's Sergeant Bilko as played by that great comedian Phil Silvers. At one stage as a kid, Dad took chickenpox and the doc's advice was to keep out of sunshine and direct light as much as possible as the illness ran its course. It was not advice that a lively boy found easy to keep and Dad spent too much time gazing out of that window in the sunshine, keeping an eye on the goings on in John Street. As a result, he developed cataracts and his career as a fledgling boxer suffered – what a great pity! I'm told that Grandad's brother, Maurice, regarded Dad as potentially the best fighter in the family.

Inside this room, there was plenty of evidence of the fruits of success that boxing can bring. There was a dressing table, another table and a big Welsh dresser laden with silverware, cups, medals and shields won by Jim Gilmour as an amateur and professional fighter. It was impressive to a youngster. It emphasised to me, even as a primary school kid, that life as a Gilmour was something a bit special and different from that of my schoolmates whose fathers worked in the yards or steel-works and who had never seen a silver trophy at first hand.

The living room, with its bed recess, was the heart of the home. Apart from the bed, it had a sideboard and a gleaming well-blackened fireplace with comfortable chairs either side of it. The fireplace had a built-in bunker for the coal and the windows of this room looked out on the backcourt. The scullery had a sink for washing, a cooker and storage cupboards. It was all warm and welcoming – the sort of little palace that you found often in Brigton or the Gorbals where, despite the hardness of life, neighbours mostly had a cosy and cheery relationship.

When old Jim was away bookmaking at the races, my cousins and I spent hours listening to Granny's tales. She, like many an Irishwoman, was a talented storyteller and her mind ranged far beyond Bridgeton and a life spent looking after a boxer and bookmaker, to produce imaginary adventures that held her grandchildren spellbound. It was better entertainment than the daytime TV garbage that is often used to occupy kids these days. Maybe I should have written the stories down and done a J. K. Rowling and made millions.

Granny and Grandad were great friends with a couple known to me only at the time as Mr and Mrs Lyall – later in life I learned they were Archie and Daisy – and they shared holidays at each other's homes and got on famously. Incidentally, looking back, I realise it is not at all unusual that I never knew the Lyall's Christian names. Meet someone for a minute or two these days and you are instantly on first-name terms. Back then, people were much more reticent and, indeed, there was an inherent respect, especially from youngsters, in the use of the titles 'Mr' or 'Mrs' rather than saying Jack or Josie or whatever.

I remember my grandparents as a loving couple although, in their era, tough guys did not wear their hearts on their sleeves. But, in his heyday, my grandfather was a great provider. My dad, too, when in funds, knew how to spend. I remember my granddad and granny's golden wedding and my dad and mum bought them a stylish Sobell TV – and this was in the days when it was something special to have a set at all. And, when Granny was not in the best of health, Mum and Dad sent her on a Mediterranean cruise with Kate who still lived near the Barras.

4

BETTING AND BASEBALL BATS

The main source of the family's money apart from boxing was bookmaking and The Auld Yin had learned his bookie skills in the shipyards. He worked in Fairfield's in Govan for a time as what is called a 'hudder oan'. This required holding a red-hot rivet in tongs at just the right angle and in just the right place while your mate hammered it into the hole in a shower of sparks and a wall of sound. Watching hundreds of riveters and 'hudders oan' at work was spectacular and incredibly noisy. When welding later took the place of riveting, the Clyde was a quieter place and there was a lot fewer half-deaf folk in the riverside pubs.

The yards were highly disciplined places in those days and the workers put in a hard shift. You had to be fit. Surprisingly Jim was, according to Sammy Gilmore, a bit too fit to be the best 'hudder oan'. Hour after hour in the gym training for the ring had left him a bit 'muscle bound' for the job which required litheness as well as brute strength, turning from the cold steel of the giant hulls to pick up the glowing rivet and in a swift rhythmic swivelling movement hold it, before it could cool, to the spot where it was banged home. Incidentally, one of Jim's pals in Fairfield's was Sammy Wilson who was

47

to play a key role in the career of Scotland's greatest flyweight, Benny Lynch.

The yards had huge notices all round the place warning that no football was to be played so, at lunchtime, there were often two or three pitch-and-toss schools in action at one time. Jim was more suited to this work than 'hudding oan'. His boxing skills and reputation made him a good protector of the cash that was bouncing around between the gambling workers. No one took liberties and his nimble brain made him a good book-maker. It was here he honed his real skills as a bookie. He was not well educated but was an ace with numbers. When he went to the racecourse and his prime pitch on the rails, he took a clerk with him because it looked good and the punters expected to see one at the bookie's side. But Jim's brain was working harder and faster than the clerk's pencil, recording the bets and altering the odds to suit a shifting market. I have been told that, in his day, he was the most skilful of the bookies around.

When he left Mary at home to go about his work at the race-tracks, he looked the business in sharp suits – waistcoats, gold watch and key fobs adding a touch of what we would call bling to the well-cut dark serge. A soft hat was a must and, in winter weather, so was a long coat. He was a smoker, as most folk were back then, and he enjoyed his fame and success. I suppose these days he would be regarded as something of a celebrity with top pitches at the rails at Lanark, Hamilton Park and Ayr. He was a founder member of the Scottish Bookmakers Protection Association and a major player in the bookmaking game in the city and the surrounding tracks.

Jim was a natural. He could go to a racecourse with only the money to pay for the pitch in his wallet and roll up really big takings from the way he ran his book. I have to say though that sometimes on good days, with the cash rolling in, he would turn punter himself. Unfortunately, he was not quite as good a gambler as he was at running a book and could turn financial triumph into financial disaster without too much bother.

In his later years, The Auld Yin's own bookmaking enter-prises had scaled down a bit and he had a wee office in my father's betting club in Olympia Street, Bridgeton. The place had telephones and even a gigantic switchboard allowing our various betting shops to be linked – something that was vital as the information that was coming in was used to lay off bets. No doubt The Auld Yin played a role in that. It was a business arrangement and, at this stage, old Jim got a wage for his efforts. A man's man, Jim spent some of it, sometimes too much, with his cronies in the Station Bar or the old Waverley Bar. But Dad made sure Granny never went short.

A curious fact about the betting shops is that each one had its own type of customer. The punters had what today we would call a 'profile'. A good day for favourites winning would hit the Bridgeton shop hard – especially on Fridays when the punters would flood in with their wage packets and try to increase their value by backing favourites. Most of these gamblers worked for the old east-end engineering firm, Davy United. Across the city in Hollybrook Street, Govanhill, Dad had another shop with a different clientele. These were guys on the hunt for high-price winners. Juggling the cash coming into the various shops and making sense of them and laying off risks was an art. And you needed a lot of telephones and telephone time to run the operation and not get financially burnt.

In his days at the top no one, but no one, mucked The Auld Yin about. In the thirties in Brigton, the gangs like the Catholic

Norman Conks and the Proddie Billy Boys played a major role in day-to-day life. They would battle each other in Glasgow Green, often on Sunday afternoons, and on the streets, attacking each other's patch. And, like the gangs of New York or Chicago or Marseilles, they were into protection rackets. My cousin Sammy Gilmore can tell a tale or two about this. Sammy himself is a West of Scotland celebrity and a folk hero to trade unionists, particularly those who toiled in the yards. Along with the late James Airlie and Jimmy Reid, he led the Upper Clyde Shipbuilders' sit-in in 1971. This was another example of the fighting Gilmores (if not Gilmours!). But it wasn't boxing and the opponents were Ted Heath's Tories. UCS was made up of five yards – John Brown, Connell, Yarrow, Alexander Stephen and Fairfield's – and they were getting into some financial difficulties. Heath ruled that lame-duck yards would have to go but, led by Reid, Airlie and Sammy, the workers decided to control the yards themselves. They won success, with a sit-in rather than a strike, when the government keeled over and injected millions into the struggling consortium. The U-turn produced a short-term victory – take a look at shipbuilding in the Clyde now – but Sammy and Co. had written themselves into trade union history. It was said that James Airlie was the brains of the struggle and Jimmy Reid was the legendary orator who stirred the crowds and managed the media. Sammy was the man of the people – the ordinary guy who led the ordinary workers. This makes a nice sidebar in the story of a battling dynasty.

Sammy Gilmore, a fighter for trade unionism, was not much of a boxer but of course he moved around the family and, like me, he listened to my granny's stories and popped in and out of old Jim's betting shops and gyms. He remembers a particular incident with the Billy Boys. As I mentioned, bookies were a target for the gangsters. Dog racing was big in those days and there was one story of a Carntyne dog track bookie called Green who was shy of paying his protection money and ended up running up a close in Main Street to hide from a gangster with a loaded revolver. These guys meant business. But, when the Billy Boys came calling on old Jim, according to Sammy, he had the answer. He had a few Brigton boys of his own in his team and he opened a cupboard in the betting shop and handed round a few baseball bats and they went to pay the would-be extortionists a visit. After that, there was never any more protection money trouble. Maybe this was where another family trait came into play. Sammy Gilmore says old Jim was too daft to feel fear but he certainly he had the guts to take on the Billy Boys.

Interestingly, Billy Fullerton, the legendary leader of the Billy Boys, having finally eschewed gangsterism after the Second World War, ended up working at times for the Gilmours as a ring whip, a term that survived from the bare-knuckle days though it latterly simply meant a sort of cross between a steward and a kit man. Fullerton even helped in a promotion we ran at Celtic Park of all places. And the notorious hard man showed a changed side to his character in his later years by organising special events for the kids from Brigton and around. Old Jim paid for buses to take the kids from the Olympia on picnics to places like the David Livingstone Museum in Blantyre which had nice grounds suitable for sack races and all the fun of a day out.

But this hard-man stuff, taking on the gangs who threatened him, was only one side of old Jim. He had a softer side. The family often talks of the old Olympia betting club. There was a cat on the premises to help control mice and Jim loved animals. One day he came in the door to find a losing punter pausing on his way out to give the cat a vicious kicking. In return, an enraged Jim gave the punter himself a real doing.

Sadly the cat died, but she left some kittens. One of the feline survivors ended up in my granny's and Buster became a family legend. When Jim went to work, Buster would keep his seat beside the fire warm for him, waiting for him to come home. The Bridgeton folk also remember that Jim was a generous figure on his walks from Tullis Street to his work – half crowns galore were handed out to the needy he met on the street. And, although he did not accompany my granny on her regular visits to Sacred Heart, he had a soft spot for the Salvation Army. He was generous in support of them because of their mission to help anyone and everyone. I think the character of the man was neatly summed up in a piece he wrote himself for a promotion in the late forties at Central Park, Airdrie. On a warm August evening, Jim Kenny of Polmont, managed by my dad, was featured against a prominent ex-amateur champion called Ernie Ormrod. On the back of the 'offishul' programme, price thruppence, Jim gazed out in full dinner dress, black bow and white shirt, with the piercing gaze I remember well. And he has some advice for the less well-dressed folk who had flocked to the arena for the boxing:

It is with intense pleasure that I bring another boxing show to this spacious arena. In so doing I know that those gathered around the ring, in which I am confident we will witness many thrilling bouts, will see to it that the boxers are shown the true sportsmanship of which Airdrie is noted.

It is essential that the spectators, who have come to applaud, will have a hand clap for the loser as much as the victor. Scottish boxing audiences need only to keep in tune with tradition to see that every boy feels he is getting the square deal outside the ropes he's assured of receiving inside.

That, I feel, says a lot about The Auld Yin. And I hope that his sentiments with regard to the welfare of his boxers, inside and outside the ring, have been carried on by my dad Tommy Gilmour Sr 'The Starmaker' and by me too.

Incidentally, the choice of Airdrie, miles away out in Lanarkshire, was not a foolish one for the town was at the end of the line for the Glasgow trams and therefore easily accessible for fans. The tram system in its heyday stretched from Airdrie in the east as far as Paisley in the west and you could take a 'caur' to almost every nook and cranny in the city for a few pence. These days, fans arrive by Roller, Jag or Beemer to watch the fights but, in old Jim's day, the mode of travel was mostly tramcar. The routes were identified by colour as in the 'blue caur' or the 'yellow caur' which meant that even those who could not read the destination board knew where they were going. Airdrie was a popular spot for evening or Saturday afternoon promotions and the fact that most of the fans did not have their own transport did not matter. Bob Jeffrey, my co-author, remembers being taken to a show in Airdrie, when in short pants, by his father, a fight fan.

Not all Bob's tram escapades were as successful as that. In the early forties, his dad also took him by tram to see the model of Cock Robin, a stuffed bird that was then being exhibited in the wee museum in Tollcross Park in the east end of Glasgow. Every kid knew the Glasgow rhyme 'Who killed Cock Robin?'

and the park was something of a place of pilgrimage. The rhyme, by the way, was, I believe, English in origin and the Robin not a bird but Robin Hood. It goes on and on but most Glasgow kids knew the first few lines at least:

'Who killed Cock Robin?'
'I,' said the Sparrow,
'With my bow and arrow, I killed Cock Robin.'
'Who saw him die?'
'I,' said the Fly,
'With my little eye, I saw him die.'
'Who caught his blood?'
'I,' said the Fish,
'With my little dish, I caught his blood.'
'Who'll make the shroud?'
'I,' said the Beetle,
'With my thread and needle, I'll make the shroud.'
'Who'll dig his grave?'
'I,' said the Owl,
'With my pick and shovel, I'll dig his grave.'

But Bob and his dad never made it to their destination thanks to the attentions of a certain Adolf Hitler. The air-raid sirens shrieked and the caurs stopped and the passengers made their way home on foot, glancing a little fearfully at the sky from time to time. The tram system, though, was, for years, the pride of the city. Bob also remembers as a young cub on the *Daily Record* accompanying the famous flyweight Elky Clark, by then the *Record*'s boxing reporter, to a show in the old St Andrew's Hall. Elky had had a remarkable career including fighting the legendary Fidel la Barba in New York in 1927, a battle he lost on points. Coincidently the American, like Elky, became a sports-writer after his ring career was over.

Bob expected at least the glamour of a taxi to take them to their place of work but wee Elky would have none of it – the tram was good enough for him. And that is how they travelled from the *Record*'s old Hope Street premises, opposite the Central Station, to the hall. Then, as now, sports stars often picked up the typewriter after their career was over. A famous successor to Elky, as a *Record* boxing writer, was dapper Dick Currie who covered the fight scene in the post-war years, after a great flyweight career in the ring which included winning an Empire Games gold medal in 1954.

The noise of the trams rattling up and down Main Street, either heading out to Rutherglen or Burnside via Farme Cross or taking the denizens of Brigton into town, is fresh in my memory. Before they were foolishly swept away, the trams added much to what would now be called the quality of life in the city. Sitting in motorway traffic jams I and, I'm sure, thousands of other motorists think of them fondly.

5

FITBA' AND FLYWEIGHTS

Jim Gilmour was much more than a successful pioneer bookie. He had a major role to play in boxing in the twenties, thirties and for years after the Second World War. He promoted not just at Premierland, he also put on shows at Firhill, home of Partick Thistle, and at Cathkin Park on the south side which was the ground of the long-gone-but-not-forgotten football team Third Lanark. Jim was also a founding licence holder of the British Boxing Board of Control and his career stretched over five decades. When Jim began to make his name, boxing was not as tightly regulated as it is now although the bare-knuckle era was long over by the time he was climbing into the ring to start his career as an amateur. In fact, the last bare-knuckle championship was as long ago as 1889 when John L. Sullivan beat the American Jake Kilrain in Rinchburg, Mississippi. From then on, gloves gradually took over.

Pre-1929, the regulatory body was the National Sporting Club but, after that, the British Boxing Board of Control took over and, down the years, the safety of the boxers became much more closely monitored. But, in old Jim's early days, booth boxing was still around in the touring fairgrounds. My granddad used the famous promoter Mickey Duff – a high roller in Vegas as well as a British boxing legend – as a matchmaker. Years later, I also worked for Mickey as a matchmaker.

In his youth, Mickey toured as a booth fighter. Mind you, his own career as a pro was successful but undistinguished. Thankfully he never met old Jim in the ring. The booth system gave a fiver or a tenner to anyone from the crowd who could go three rounds with the professional. I was told Jim had a habit of knocking out the so-called star in round one. I hope he still got his cash even if the punters did not get three rounds of fighting. But his real trade was in the ring fighting as a professional and amateur. On one occasion, he fought three ten-round fights in one night, winning them all on points. And five or six fights a week was not unusual. The purse on these occasions would be around a week's wages or even more. So, for those days, large sums could be earned quickly.

Just as the Clinton fight was a highlight for me, I suppose Jim would say the same of a fight he promoted in 1931, eleven years after his Olympic exploits. The Scottish flyweight title, the same crown held by men like Benny Lynch, Jackie Paterson and Lanarkshire's Walter McGowan, was at stake. And there was a purse of around a thousand pounds to be had – a massive sum then. The fighters both came from the west of Scotland – Jim Campbell and Jim McHarg. The venue was Firhill Park, home of Partick Thistle to this day. And the promotion was an early example of using football grounds for big fights and attracting huge crowds. Latterly, this was to become common-place with such as Mike Tyson fighting at Hampden, which was also where Paterson fought against the colourful Hawaiian Dado Marino. And then Jim Watt made a great world-title defence at Ibrox. Looking at it now, the most astonishing thing about this fight was that it pulled in a crowd of 12,000 to the stadium in Maryhill (an area with a great number of boxing fans and the latterly the boxing fiefdom of the great John 'Cowboy' McCormick.) It is a tribute to the Auld Yin and his promotion skills that he could have such a crowd attend a fight in the middle of the Depression with more than three million unemployed.

Firhill is a place close to the heart of Glaswegians. Peter Keenan was later to fight there on one of my granddad's promotions and many are the tales of Partick Thistle and its players who showed their skills and eccentricities there (some might say they still do). Old-timers still talk of 'Ma Ba' McKenna' who thrilled post-war crowds. He claimed any high ball or cross as his own, elbowing anyone in the way aside as he jumped to head clear or maybe make an attempt at goal. It was joked that his shout of 'Ma ba'!' could be heard outside the stadium at Maryhill Cross. The Maryhill folk themselves liked to get into the action. McKenna and Co. performed in the days long before smokeless fuels and the stadium was surrounded by tenements, with every house in the close boasting a coal fire. The thick clouds of choking black smoke pumping out of the hundreds of chimneys could turn a clear winter day into a foggy one. It was even said that, if Thistle were in the lead and the wind was blowing the right way, the Maryhill folk would heap dross on the fires during the final moments of a game to give the Thistle any advantage going – well, that's what I've been told! A long way from gas central heating.

The size of the crowds in the twenties and thirties is astonishing. Jim for instance fought in Edinburgh's old Waverley Market Arena (now an upmarket shopping mall) in front of 12,000 in an amateur match between Britain and Denmark. This is an all-time record for amateur boxing in Scotland. The

Edinburgh connection, according to boxing historian Brian Donald, reveals another key quality of Jim's. He never studied management or read any of those manuals that promise to teach you instant managerial skills, which you can now pick up in any bookshop. Jim had it naturally and was an expert at what the blackboard and flip-chart management gurus like to call networking. According to Brian, it showed up in the shrewd way he linked his amateur and pro boxing career to that of Scotland's leading promoter in the twenties, the Leith-based pawnbroker Nat Dresner.

Dresner was a terrific operator. He promoted the first British and European title bouts in Scotland and, in November 1924, established a Scottish indoor attendance record of 24,000 for a British title fight. The Auld Yin fought on many of Dresner's Edinburgh promotions but the relationship was deeper than that of fighter and promoter. Dresner and Gilmour were 'shrewd men cut from the same enterprising cloth,' says Brian Donald. They say that some of Jim's gene pool of business acumen has filtered down to me and I don't argue with that but there is another strange link, the touch of another dynasty involved. The aristocratic master of ceremonies at many of Dresner's Edinburgh shows was Sir Ian Colquhoun of Luss. Jim struck up a friendship with him. Sir Ian was a glorious name to have in the contacts book – personal friend of King George VI, a First World War Guards hero and a champion amateur boxer himself.

Sir Ian's role as MC at many of old Jim's fights made him a useful ally later in his career as a promoter when the Luss aristocrat became the first chairman of the newly formed Scottish Area Council of the British Boxing Board of Control in 1929. Maybe I inherited my grandfather's business acumen and maybe

I inherited his contacts book too for, when the St Andrew's Sporting Club began in Glasgow in 1973, a major patron for years was Sir Ivor Colquhoun of Luss – Sir Ian's grandson.

Not all of Jim's fights were in the east of Scotland of course. He even appeared at the famous Hengler's circus in Sauchiehall Street, Glasgow. Hengler had circuses in many British cities but his Glasgow venue became an institution in the city before it closed in 1924. It featured a lot more than boxing and was on the site of what eventually became the ABC1 cinema. Known as the Hippodrome it had a famous manager, William Powell, who let children from charity schools in to see the events free. It often featured Wild West shows and had an amazing motor-powered circus ring that could sink into the floor, converting the arena into a ten-foot-deep lake into which horses would plunge from a great height. I suppose a night at the boxing was a quiet affair after that.

But not too long into his professional career, Jim Gilmour realised that, skilled as he was, he was not going to win world titles and maybe the promoting and the bookmaking were better bets. He succeeded in both. In his early days, Brigton was a world apart from what we know today. Jim promoted fights in Premierland (attended by his friend Sir Harry Lauder) and regular fight nights were also held in the National Sporting Club in Charles Street. Bridgeton may have been a little working-class place in the east of Glasgow, almost a village – a place where people were fiercely proud of their roots and their ability to carve out a life for their families in tough times – but it had connections with more glamorous areas far from Main Street and its gyms, pubs and betting places. No less a celebrity than the famous Georges Carpentier – 'the hero boxer of France', according to the billboards – gave an exhibition there.

Another legend from boxing's past, Battling Siki, was advertised to appear in Glasgow in November 1922 and he got the full PR treatment: 'The man that beat the French idol Carpentier in six rounds. His last appearance in Public prior to his meeting Joe Beckett, for the European Heavyweight Championship, at the Royal Albert Hall, London, on December 7.' But, in this case, it did not happen. Leith promoter Nat Dresner had announced that the Senegalese world light-heavyweight champion was coming to the old Waverley Market in Princes Street and the Glasgow promoters planned to have him appear in their city as well. But the then Home Secretary refused to let Siki into Britain for racial reasons, a decision provoked by the behaviour of the black American heavyweight champion Jack Johnson who had reneged on a promise to defend his title in London. It sounds odd today but the thinking at the time was that, because one black boxer had reneged, they feared all black boxers would be unreliable. On St Patrick's Day 1925, Siki did finally make it to the British Isles when he lost his title in Dublin to an Irishman, Mike McTigue. Siki, incidentally, shared some of his temperament with some of today's boxing heroes. Away from the ring, he loved to have fun. He partied a lot and, occasionally, his violent temper got him into trouble. A flamboyant character, he loved to walk around Paris parading lions on a lead and was once nabbed for firing a revolver in the air. No wonder his nickname was 'Battling'!

Exhibition bouts featuring the likes of Carpentier have largely fallen out of favour in the TV age although Muhammad Ali did make a similar appearance in Paisley, an event involving myself as a boy and something I'll cover later on. But, at one time, exhibition bouts were a rare chance to see world stars in the flesh.

There is a curious connection between old Jim and one of Glasgow's more memorable boxing exhibitions. Earlier, I mentioned the end of the bare-knuckle era and the fight between John L. Sullivan and Jake Kilrain in 1889. Years after this battle, John L. was still cashing in on it. He came to a Glasgow theatre in 1910 and the *Evening Times* carried an advert for the exhibition, which was billed as 'Sullivan v Kilrain Mark Two'. It seems the trend for snappy titles like 'The Rumble in the Jungle' is no new gimmick. And the desire to milk a triumph for all it is worth is, likewise, still around. The visit to Scotland was part of a honeymoon tour for Sullivan and his second wife and, remarkably, his opponent, Jake Kilrain, accompanied the couple on something of a working holiday. No doubt the re-creations of the famous match paid for the honeymoon. The link with old Jim comes from the fact that a Bellshill boxer called Harry Owens, British welterweight champion in 1936, was such a big fan of the American that he took the name Jake Kilrain for his own use in his professional career. After his retirement in the mid 1940s he continued to use the name Kilrain when he became a referee who officiated on many of The Auld Yin's promotions. Incidentally, Jake was managed by my dad at one point.

Old-timers, especially those with east-end roots, still remember the National Sporting Club. The 'National' was a Bridgeton institution. It had been founded in 1905 and, in the twenties, on the membership card, the secretary John A. McConnachie proudly announced, 'members now being enrolled'. The annual sub was twenty-one shillings (one pound five pence). The back of the card carried an 'important special notice', informing those interested in joining that the committee had decided that 'The

Boxing Member's Subscription shall be 10/6, which entitles them to TUITION IN BOXING, WRESTLING AND PHYSICAL CULTURE, HOT AND COLD WATER BATHS and all the latest and most scientific methods of training by proficient instruction. Signed J.A.McC.' The reverse of the card carried the fight programme for the next pro night. One features The Auld Yin himself and tells the members that he is prepared to box any lightweight in Scotland for £100 a side. The 'National' was clearly the forerunner of all today's glossy hi-tech gyms in five-star hotels – though you would not get service like that for 50p a year nowadays, I suspect. It was all part of a magic era for boxing fans.

Maybe it all looks better in retrospect but there is no doubt that, in those tough times, life in Brigton was much brightened by the sporting clubs. At least for the men – some of the women folk might not have enjoyed their earner blowing what scarce money there was on backing nags that just could not run or boxers who could not punch their way out of paper bag, as they say. But it is all colourful stuff – life in Scotland lived with a touch of the Damon Runyon, with old Jim's big hats, flash suits and long overcoats adding to the effect.

My cousin Sammy Gilmore, now retired, likes to have a drink or two in his favourite bar in Cambuslang, not far from where he worked in the old Hoover factory, before he went to work in the yards. He remembers the Brigton Main Street of old as a vibrant cheery place, as well as sometimes being a violent one. Sammy's pub is well frequented by Celtic fans – a fact demonstrated in spades on the day of an Old Firm match when you would have had to have dropped in from Mars not to realise which side the punters were pulling for.

A regular in the place is an interesting old fellow called

James Sweeney. Glasgow folk have a penchant for bestowing nicknames that don't exactly take a lot of effort and James Sweeney was known sometimes as Todd for short. Old James grew up in Brigton and, during his rough and tumble youth, he was, for a time, a member of the area's infamous Pen gang. (This is the outfit that had a junior section which often toured the more affluent nearby neighbourhoods of King's Park and Croftfoot terrorising the locals and was wittily known as the Biro Minors.) James Sweeney remembers the boxing 'academies' of Brigton where men like Jim Gilmour passed on their boxing skills. To this day, he can give you some good boxing advice – weave, don't bob, is his mantra. Trainers still tell their charges just that. Old Sweeney knew Jim in his heyday. His verdict as he looks into his pint? 'The Perfect Gentleman.'

There are no sure things in boxing, horse racing or, indeed, life generally and, in later life, Jim took some knocks with promotions that didn't always make money. He was, however, very proud of his son Tommy, my dad. Tommy rose to the top in the fight game. With connections round the world, he operated in a much wider arena than Jim had. There was a certain rivalry between them at times but Dad looked after The Auld Yin even if, at times, they might have words about the fight game. Towards the end, when Jim was still living his life as the big-earning local celebrity but not earning in the way he had in the past, they had a good arrangement. If a Jim Gilmour promotion lost money, Dad took the hit. If it made money, Jim was in funds. Maybe my son Christopher, a fourth generation promoter, will takes this to heart though I hope he never needs to – only joking, Christopher! Incidentally Christopher and I don't promote jointly as we both know and accept there is only one boss when you are running a boxing show.

Jim died in 1963 and his funeral was memorable, with the great and the good in attendance in large numbers. The papers were full of stories of the old era in Bridgeton. And, if the head-liners were there all right, so were the boxers who never quite made it, the guys who old Jim had urged the crowds at Airdrie to applaud. The verdict was the same as that of old James Sweeney – a perfect gentleman had passed on.

6

AT HOME WITH THE STARMAKER

It is undeniable that boxing has produced more quality writing than any other sport. In *The Guardian* recently, the perceptive columnist Marcel Berlins mused that the reason for this is the nature of the elemental, one-on-one battles of the ring offer a rich seam to be mined by writers. The game has attracted the best – among them Norman Mailer, A. J. Liebling, Budd Schulberg, Ring Lardner, Nelson Algren and our own incomparable Hugh McIlvanney. The list is lengthy and you could spend a lifetime reading fact and fiction about a sport that can be both repellent and fascinating and, yes, sometimes noble, in the space of one three-minute round. Berlins acquired his Christian name as a result of a family affection for the famous French boxer Marcel Cerdan. A lover of Edith Piaf, at the height of his fame, Cerdan died in a plane crash on his way to see her.

I was reminded of all this in a chance meeting one night when out for a meal at the old Deerstalker in Bath Street, in the city centre, with my mum and dad. A tall, extremely handsome guy approached us, apologised for disturbing us and asked Dad, in a sexy Sacha Distel French accent, if he was Tommy Gilmour. Dad confirmed that was the case and the guy introduced himself as Marcel Cerdan Jr. They then chatted about Marcel and his career and it turned out that Marcel Jr had, as I had, followed in his father's footsteps. Cerdan Jr had a successful career as a pro and I am sure his father would have been as proud of him as my dad was of me.

Incidentally, Bert Gilroy, who was managed by Dad, boxed Cerdan in the Regent Crest Hotel in London in 1947 but was beaten in the fourth round. A fight follower, Marcel Berlins interestingly points out that boxing is not a sport you 'play' unlike cricket or football. Anyone who has been in ring knows that. One anecdote underlines the point perfectly. The light-heavyweight Willie Pastrano was down on one knee and the referee solicitously leaned over him to ask if he knew where he was, in case he had to step in and prevent further punishment. The boxer replied, 'You are damn right I know where I am. I am in Madison Square Gardens getting beaten up.' That was reality.

Yes, there is a lot of great boxing writing about, including in the fiction of Damon Runyon, Jack London and Conan Doyle. Schulberg, who is still writing perceptively about the game today – one of his outlets is the *Sunday Herald* – is most famous for *The Harder They Fall*, a story about an innocent boxer betrayed by the sharks in the US fight game who live off his back. It's a plot that can still resonate today and, of course, his screenplay for *On the Waterfront* produced that unforgettable one-liner 'I coulda been a contender'.

Yet it is also true that the fight fans of today are in danger of dying from being smothered in a blanket of clichés woven by the writers in the lurid red tops. The ring is always square, always the loneliest place in the world and there is never a hiding place. All in all, the 'leather trade' is a tough one.

Referring to A. J. Liebling's collection of boxing writing, the wannabe intellectuals like to call it 'the sweet science'. But it has to be said clichés become clichés because they sometimes brilliantly express a truthful concept in the minimum number of words and so it can be with boxing. If it is indeed a 'trade', I served my apprenticeship in it under the tutelage of a master – Tommy Gilmour Sr, who is often identified by the cliché 'The Starmaker'. He, in turn, had learned from Jim Gilmour and I hope I have something to teach my son Christopher now that he is in the early days of his own career as a promoter.

But anyone who thinks that I was pushed into the fight trade and moulded by the dynasty is wrong. To succeed in anything, you have to want to be in it – you have to want it desperately – and my dad let me decide for myself whether or not I wanted to follow in his footsteps. Sometimes he was the hardest of taskmasters and, while making my way in the game, I often had to justify my moves to him. It was no soft option walking in the footsteps of a great. Like me, Christopher is in boxing because that is what he wanted to do.

I can remember my dad coming home at night after a hard day at the 'office' which, in his case, was his gym or his betting shop. Like any other dad, he just wanted to enjoy his evening meal – or tea, as we called it in those days – in peace but I was always full of energy and bursting with questions: who had he met that day?; what fights were coming up?; what was it like out there in the world of big-time boxing? The questions tumbled out and, over the bit, I got all the answers I wanted but a bite to eat in peace was the priority for The Starmaker. Now that I'm running the St Andrew's Sporting Club, managing a string of fighters and promoting shows, I know how the old man must have felt! But, thinking back on my childhood, I see now that maybe I was always destined to be a promoter even if I did resist it for a spell.

In the heyday of The Starmaker, we lived up a close in Rutherglen Road, an area squeezed between the old Gorbals and Shawfield, the famous dog track and home of Clyde FC before they succumbed to the pressures of changing housing patterns and followed the folk who moved out of the east end to the new town of Cumbernauld. Home in Rutherglen Road was a comfortable corner flat above Logan's Bar – two rooms, a kitchen and lobby (hallway), in a traditional tenement flat. We had the luxury of an inside toilet and my mother never wanted to move. And she was not alone in that as some families lived in Oatlands for generations. Once, when he was flush, Dad bought a bungalow in High Burnside, a posh area indeed. But it was bought one day and sold the next. It seemed that Mum just wanted to stay where she was comfortable and happy. I have often wondered if there was a deeper reason for the sudden sale of what seemed a lovely house and the decision to stay put and perhaps it had its roots in something that happened on our family visits to America.

Mum was christened Elizabeth Burns Bryson and she was known as Lizzie. In the fifties, she would have been pretty well off with Dad at the peak of his career in boxing and the bookies' shops doing well. Some of that financial comfort cushion was reflected in the travelling the family did. Most of our friends and neighbours would regard a trip to Blackpool or the Isle of Man as serious travel. In contrast, visits to New York and Detroit were taken by us in our collective family stride.

I particularly remember hearing of the trip my mum, my sister Rena and my brother Jim made to America in 1950. They travelled in real style on the *Queen Elizabeth* at a time when

Britain was just beginning to recover from the austerity of war. Sailing under the Verrazzano Bridge and up the Hudson into the berths used by the great Atlantic liners, in the shadow of the great skyscrapers, must have been a wonderful experience after day-to-day life in Oatlands.

The Gilmours were met by my aunt Kathy Logie, my mother's eldest sister, and Peter Burns, my mother's cousin, and, before travelling to Detroit, there was a round of sightseeing including Niagara Falls. Detroit, motor city as it was known, had a large ex-pat Scots community made up mostly of folk who had fled the Depression at home to find work in the many factories there. Mum's brother Matt met them in Detroit. He was a maintenance man at the Sacred Heart Seminary for trainee priests. Uncle Peter worked, naturally in Detroit, in a car factory and Kathy was a cook. This last is no surprise as a love of cooking and a talent for it have run through the family from Granny Bryson's day. Mum herself was what we in Glasgow would call a 'dab hand' at it. Mum stayed with Kathy and her husband John Logie who I remember as always smiling and somebody who loved playing with the kids. They had a son Jackie and a daughter Trina. Aged seven at the time of this visit, Trina was the same age as my brother Jim. A couple of years later Mum and Dad went back to Detroit to show off yours truly. The Scots were all happily settled and doing well in the New World.

But fate can often have a shock or two in store. We were not long back in Glasgow when terrible news arrived – Trina had a brain tumour. It was most unusual for a youngster to have such an illness and she needed urgent and skilled surgery if she was to survive. The unusual nature of the illness was such that the local papers ran features on Trina. The snag was that such treatment as she needed was expensive and the family soon discovered that, even if America was still the land of the free, there was no free medical treatment. This was no NHS country. The surgeon who operated donated his skills but the hospital bills were hefty, as was the continuing treatment needed. This was where our then affluence helped. Mum had a hugely generous nature. She had a genuine desire to help folk who were less lucky than she was. She always remembered that she had escaped the hard times of life in the infamous The Dwellings in Brigton, where people struggled in poor housing and grinding poverty. Here was a chance to do something special and Mum and, for a long period, Dad gave financial help to the Logies.

The operation was a success in that, against the odds, it saved Trina's life but it left her paralysed down one side and forced her to wear a calliper. However, Trina was a fighter. She never gave in to her illness and led as normal a life as possible, graduating from college, marrying and having kids. Today she lives in Florida, enjoying the Sunshine State to the full. We went back to America again in 1959 when the medical bills were still coming in and we were glad we could be of help. I wonder if her passion for helping people had been in the back of my mum's mind when she rejected that move to genteel Burnside. Staying in Oatlands would leave a lot more of the readies splashing around to help others.

In any case, I was happy we stayed put and that a move to High Burnside was not on. In Oatlands, across Rutherglen Road, lay Glasgow Green and the attractions of its neighbour Richmond Park. There was plenty of greenery and open space for fitba', with the traditional jumpers for goalposts, and a pond with swans where you could sail a model yacht and dream of one day owning the real thing – or at least one of the floating gin palaces of yachts that now litter the Clyde coast marinas.

Mind you, in my young days, I thought Marina was a girl's name.

Despite the struggles of life in Oatlands in the days when money, for most folk, was not too easy to come by, it was often great fun. The neighbours in any close kept a watchful eye out for each other. In our close, the Morgans, the Scanlons, the Andersons and the Dynans all pulled together. Most doors were never locked during the day and were kept on the latch. Visitors just knocked and opened the door and shouted who they were. There was truly remarkable openness and trust. There were kids galore around. I had my own pals but, if they were not about, my older brother Jim's mates let me play with them.

We got up to all sorts of high jinks but football we took seriously. We had challenge matches in the street with lampposts as goals. At other times, we would climb the iron railings to get into Wolsely Street School or, when the parkie was not about, we would play on the grass of Richmond Park. These games featuring the Gilmours, the Blyths, the Cowans, the Motherwells, the Dochertys, the Murrays and the Mooneys were competitive. And we could play for three hours at a time – at least until it got dark or the parkies or the polis chased us back into our houses.

At the entrance to the close was parked the ultimate status symbol – a big Ford Zephyr saloon car – as like all the ubiquitous sandstone Glasgow tenements, ours did not run to a garage. We were the only family in the area with a car and it added to the glamour of it all that Dad had purchased it from Kenneth McKellar. The singer, who knew something about cars and liked to spend some of his huge fees from his great career making best-selling albums and filling concert halls, on high-power motorbikes. And this, of course, was long before the phenomenon of stars with a mid-life crisis spending thousands on big toys for big boys. Kenneth was a pacesetter. And that big glossy Ford he sold us was great for giving my pals and me a wee run around the area – most of my pals had never been in a car up till then. We also used it for visits to relatives in Penilee where it was spotted by the locals, young and old, who enjoyed a bit of celebrity popping in to the area. And occasionally it was used for jaunts to friends in Dundee or Aberdeen – long, exciting journeys in those pre-motorway days. And when, as a treat, Dad would take my pals for a wee run in it round the neighbourhood, they all looked up to him and called him 'Mr Gilmour'. But it didn't stop them giving a wee bit cheek from time to time. In areas like Oatlands, the kids were, as they say, 'wee men cut down'. Some of the kids, even as young as nine or ten, smoked and they would run after Dad, obviously a man with a bob or two, shouting, 'Hey, Mr Gilmour, can we get your douts?' They got a surprise when Dad gave them the end of his King Edward cigars – something of a change from the Woodbine singles on sale in corner shops at the time.

Looking back now, I realise how different my childhood was from those of some of my neighbours and pals. World travelling started early for me as, at the age of three months, I was crossing the Atlantic in a Boeing 377 Stratocruiser, stopping in Iceland to refuel. We were on our way to visit my mother's sister Kathy, brother Matt and other relatives, including a cousin from the Dundee area whose daughter Marie was married to a guy called Tony Nowaczewski. Tony and Marie were keen to have a family and they were excited to see me, a wee Scottish baby. After we went home to Glasgow, Marie fell pregnant and told everyone who would listen that I had brought her luck. Now in her eighties, Marie and I still correspond.

Even my own birth was a wee bit special for a baby going home to live in Rutherglen Road, Oatlands. I first saw the light of day in a private nursing home, called Park Grove, in the august Park Circus in the west end – a fair indication of Dad's earning power. Most of my schoolmates were born in state maternity hospitals or even at home up a tenement stair with midwives scurrying about and calls for hot water from the kitchen bouncing round the walls.

Incidentally, there was a further show-business connection to my days in Rutherglen Road as our near neighbours were Glen Daly and his wife Ella. Their daughter Mary went to school with my sister Rena and their son Terry was my best man when I married Veronica. In those days, big-time stage performers such as Glen often liked to live close to the folk who flocked to see them – no Beckingham Palaces for them. Glen made his name as a feed to the great Pavilion comic Lex McLean though he went on to be a star on his own, adding a bit of singing, most probably the 'Celtic Song', to the comedy. It has to be said the singing was an acquired taste though the guy was a great comedian in the days when it seemed as if Glasgow was home to hundreds of them. Glen, Chic Murray, Tommy Morgan, Billy Rusk, Jack Anthony, Hector Nicol, Jack Milroy, the Logans and more – everyone, it appeared, was a comic back then and the old Metropole at the bottom of Stockwell Street, the Empress in Queen's Cross and the Pavilion in Renfield Street were packed from Monday to Saturday with fans desperate for a laugh.

My dad, moving as he did in sporting and newspaper circles, got plenty of 'comps' for the theatres and on Monday nights, he regularly took a jaunt into town for the first house – and, on occasion, we got a wee treat and went with him. The Mondays were always a bit special for the cast were giving a first try-out to a new series of sketches and material for the week ahead. At the end of a week's run, the performers would be spot on, their gags would be word perfect, the punchlines would be delivered right on cue and the scenery and the curtains would do what they were intended to do. Not so on Monday nights! After a few minimal rehearsals of the new material the previous day when some of the cast would still be hung over after the Saturday night party, much could go wrong – lines would be forgotten, scenery would totter, singers would miss their cues – but Lex McLean could ad-lib to great effect and often the Monday performance was funnier than the more polished ones later in the week.

I remember Lex had a regular routine for the first night. He wandered on in a baggy suit and took a slow, languid, some-what contemptuous, look at the first few rows of seats which were normally 'papered', as they say, with the newspaper critics and the jack-the-lads about town like my dad. Lex would then announce to the ordinary paying punters in the circle and gallery that he was delighted that 'the cream of the Arabs are in tonight'.

Being a Gilmour had its moments for a youngster. Dad was a real Mr Fixit – the sort of guy with a network of friends and associates who could arrange almost anything. My brother Jim, for instance, wanted to meet the famous film cowboy Roy Rogers who was in town appearing at the old Empire, at the bottom of Sauchiehall Street, with his famous horse Trigger. This was the hottest ticket in town but Dad fixed it and Jim met his hero backstage at the Empire. As a kid, I liked to listen to Tommy Steele's songs and, when he was in town playing variety, I asked if I could get to meet him and, again, Dad did his Mr Fixit bit – great times, great memories! Mind you, I don't really know why I was so keen to meet a musician since I am tone deaf. My sister Rena could play the piano we had in our flat and Jim played the accordion – he was taught by a well-known character on the music scene, Tony Vericho. There was family pressure for me to learn an instrument but I fell out with Mr Vericho. Much later in my career, I would be entertained, after a few drinks, by my friend Barry Hearn doing his Larry Adler routine on the 'mouthie' and I couldn't even join in on the spoons.

7

THE HIGH LIFE OF A SOMEBODY

It was in Rutherglen Road that I spent my days from primary to secondary school with Mum, Dad, older sister Rena and big brother Jim. I was the baby of the family – Jim was seven years older and Rena twelve – but, even from an early age, I liked to get my own way and surprisingly the family often deferred to me – most of the time, it happened the way Thomas wanted it to. However, if I stepped out of line, I would be grounded and I particularly remember one case in point in the sixties. It was the early days of big-screen cinema and, on the Green and around Richmond Park's 'swanny' pond, the kids playing football and climbing the trees could talk of little else apart from the film *How the West Was Won*. You had to see it – you just had to! This was the biggie in more senses than one – a Cinemascope epic with John Wayne, James Stewart, Henry Fonda and Gregory Peck. It came to the old Coliseum in Eglinton Street, a few miles from Ru'glen Road. I don't remember my crime, other than I suppose I was being cheekier than usual, but, while my pals made the short trip to the cinema (we usually got a tanner, three pence to get in and three pence on sweets), I was kept at home. It hurt but I didn't change my ways!

Overall, it was a lot of fun and a bit of a privilege to grow up with The Starmaker as a dad. Most of the time, he was away at the betting shop and gym in Olympia Street earning the cash to keep us in a bit more style than our neighbours enjoyed. A phone in the house was a bit of a luxury in Rutherglen Road. Most of the folk around us didn't have one and the alternative was a trek to the old-fashioned red box at the end of the street with a handful of coins in the pocket to drop into the chrome-fronted box at the appropriate time. The Gilmours, however, had no fewer than six telephone points installed in their flat and you could just plug a handset in and off you went. Despite the inside toilet being so small that both elbows almost touched the walls, Dad would sit in there and do deals on the phone as if he was in a suite in a Vegas hotel. Just as well that this was before video conferencing! The phone, though, was freely given to the immediate neighbours so that they didn't have to go out in the rain to call an old aunt, the doctor, their work or whatever.

The phone was vital to keep up to date with the latest from the racetracks and the boxing world. Dad had a routine that saw him have a leisurely breakfast and then 'work' the phones with boxing writers like Davie Stewart of the *Citizen* or Matt Irwin of the *Evening Times*. Then, as now, you need a good contacts book in the boxing promotions business. After this, Dad went off to work at the betting shop and gym, where he'd deal with the punters, supervise the training of his fighters and discuss possible bouts with matchmakers. For me, if I wasn't at school, it was usually out to the park for some mischief or a game of football with my mates. Mum and Dad's best friends were the Sutherlands, neighbours in the next close. I called them my 'uncle' Bob and 'aunt' Margaret – though I called Margaret 'Aunt Matt' because I could not get my tongue round the word

Margaret when I was young. They were, of course, not real relatives but what we call Glasgow aunts and uncles. This was a common term for your parents' friends in the close-knit world of the tenement. It was, I suppose, a kind of extended family.

Mum and Dad and Bob and Margaret would have nights in playing cards at the weekend and maybe a wee drink or two. We would all holiday together so we were closer than most real relatives were. Indeed, after Mum died in 1968, I lived with Bob and Margaret for a few years to allow Dad to run his businesses without having to worry about me. Dad and I, however, had a spell when we fended for ourselves and it nearly ended in tragedy. Dad was no cook and, at this time, we often took our evening meal at Granny's. But I remember one night, after I had gone to bed, when Dad had come home feeling peckish – maybe he'd had a couple of drinks with a contact, who knows. In any case, he got a tin from the cupboard, put it in a pot of water to boil on the gas and fell asleep. The explosion as the pot boiled dry and the tin burst open woke me, wrecked the cooker and gave us both a bit of a shock. The cooker's replacement was electric and so a bit safer but Tommy Gilmour Sr was never going to be a Gordon Ramsay.

It was a cosy relationship and I could work it to my advantage, especially since we had a phone connection between the two houses. If I figured something healthy but not too appetising – say, fish – was coming up for our tea, I would find an excuse to pop round to Uncle Bob's where there was a good chance of some nice mince and tatties. Bob worked the night shift as a carpet weaver in Templeton's factory and he could walk to work across the Green in just a couple of minutes or so. And the factory was one of Glasgow's landmark buildings – an ornate place styled along the lines of the Doge's Palace in Venice.

Its striking architecture was a memorial to workers who had lost their lives in a fire on the same site years earlier. On Saturdays, Bob would help my dad in the betting shop but Sundays were the real treat for me. This was the big day in the gym and Bob would take me over to the Olympia with him most Sunday mornings. Dad would be there already, supervising training.

It was an exciting world. Thursday was the big fight night in those days and Sundays were devoted to final preparations for the fights. People like Chic Calderwood would often be there or other famous fighters like Charlie Hill or Jackie Brown. Calderwood was my idol and there is more about him later on. Those Sunday mornings were unforgettable. The place was mobbed. In the big ring, fighters would be doing some final sparring and figuring out how to deal with an upcoming opponent. The sparring partners tried their best to mimic the style of the opponent on the forthcoming Thursday night. Around the rest of the hall, guys worked out on the punch bags and there would be the constant whack, whack, whack of leather on leather. Others were on the benches, stretching and doing lifts, while some worked with the medicine ball or the Indian clubs.

Talk about second-hand smoking! The air was thick with cigarette smoke and this smog was intermingled with the heavy smells of embrocation and sweat. Bandages were unravelled by the mile as the ring men strengthened the hands of the fighters before lacing on the gloves of the would-be champs. Sundays were the only days the boxing guys could really all get together for, back then, few were full-timers. Even the big names had Monday to Saturday jobs. Chic Calderwood slogged away as a brickie on building sites between spells of making headlines in the papers. Those few hours on a Sunday were precious to the fighters and their 'connections'. And it was also a good time to sell tickets for the Thursday fights. It was a bit like a punter looking at the horses in the show ring before a race. Fans could watch some sparring and decide to open their wallet and make sure they caught the action on the Thursday.

And there was a constant chatter as the has-beens, the never-wases, the wannabes and the dedicated fans mixed with boxers and trainers – all the time, they would be talking up the next fight or making excuses for the last or remembering the old-time greats or maybe just reading the yellowing bills, advertising the fights of the past, that were pinned to the walls. It was an addictive experience for a wee lad lucky enough to be in the midst of all this manly action and male fellowship – another world. It was all part of a world that has gone.

In the Olympia's great days and for some years afterwards, there were around 100 gyms and boxing clubs in the city. Many flourished into the thirties and it was only by around the seventies that the decline in private gyms and boxing clubs began. The grip the sport had on the city has by now largely been forgotten but, like dancing, boxing was one of Glasgow's great passions. One of old Jim Gilmour's rival establishments in the early days was run by a character called Judah Solomon in Florence Street, where Benny Lynch stayed. Some of the clubs had evocative names like the Parkhead Physical Culture Club and there was even a club in Weaver's Pend near Anderston Cross, an area that was traditionally home to weavers. There was the LMS Rovers for rail workers and even the Meat Trades Club in the meat market – at least these guys were well used to the sight of blood. There was the Adelphi Club in Adelphi Street, the Dalmarnock Club and dozens of others. The east end and the south side in particular were dotted with gyms.

And when finally the Sunday session in the Olympia was over there was another treat to come for me. The Starmaker had an unlikely passion for ice cream – something that I shared. We would walk up the short distance to the famous Glasgow 'Barras' street market off London Road. The Barras on a Sunday were mobbed by bargain hunters and there would be hoarse-voiced salesmen loudly hawking the latest kitchen gadget or pushing the 'must-have' doll for Christmas. Mixing with the crowds, there would be street acts like a violinist or a piper or strongmen, escapologists or cardsharps. And then, as now, the local cops kept an eye on the crowds.

But we headed not for the Barras themselves for, when it came to buying furniture or household goods, we could shop up town for the best. We were there for the ice cream. And not just any ice cream. The big treat was ice cream from Rossi's café. This was a wonderful very sweet ice cream unlike any other available. All ice cream in cafés then was handmade, of course. The Rossi family had other cafes in the city and in each there was a subtle variation in the taste of the product. For us, it had to be the café opposite the Barras. Other Rutherglen Road folk favoured a rival family of Italian descent, the Crollas, who had a place on Main Street, Bridgeton, but the Gilmours, in their wisdom, judged this product to be too milky and overly smooth. We were big Rossi fans.

This pernickety, nothing-but-the-best part of Dad's make-up showed itself in other ways too. Coopers, the famous old-fashioned grocers, had, around this time, decided to modernise their shop off St Enoch Square in Howard Street. It was turned into what you could say was among the first of the supermarkets.

Instead of white-aproned assistants slicing bacon or butter, you could walk the aisles admiring exotic produce not too often seen in the city. In the days before delicatessens, this was as good as you could get for fancy food, tins of paté, delicate sauces, salami, anchovies and the like. Often Dad used to phone home and tell Mum and me to meet him in Coopers and off we went on a trek round the well-stocked aisles. I once worked out just how many miles you could cover in such a place. It was a lot. This search for exotica on a plate is a trait that my son Christopher has inherited. He likes nothing better than jaunt round the aisles, filling a trolley. Delicatessens in the genes of a dynasty? It's a strange idea but who knows?

Dad was always keen to turn a pound or two and in the difficult post-war years that could include selling eggs, a rare commodity at the time, or even a bit of cloth for a suit. I remember hearing about one guy who turned up at the gym and asked him if he would like a fresh egg or two from the countryside. Dad nodded a yes and, not much later, a van appeared and the egg or two turned out to be box after box of the much-in-demand product. Dad simply unpacked the boxes and, along with his pals, set about handing out a wee treat of half a dozen fresh eggs to many of the neighbours who had not tasted anything like it since before the war. To someone used to powdered eggs, the straight from the hen variety was something else.

My old pal John Quinn also tells the tale of getting a call in his office at the *Evening Times* from Dad. Pop in to the gym on your way home, he was told. The gym, at that time, was in Ingram Street not far from the *Herald/Times* offices. John wandered round to the gym expecting a titbit of boxing news but, instead, Dad produced a suit length of top quality cloth and said, 'How do you like that?' John was impressed and rated what was on offer as top Austin Reed style stuff at a bargain price. He took the suit length home and told his wife Kathleen that it could come in handy for a function. It was not long before an opportunity arose. John and Kathleen were invited to the wedding of wee John McCluskey, the British flyweight champion, in Wishaw. The suit length was duly taken to a tailor and made up. Resplendent in his new gear, John rolled up to the function in a taxi. There were three other guests arriving at the same time and, as they leapt from their taxis, they all suddenly realised they were wearing suits made from the same material!

That old gym in Ingram Street was the backdrop for a 'fight' that showed how Glasgow's religious bigotry can affect even folk from lands far away. The gym was always busy with boxers working out and often full of old-timers reliving past glories, while watching the current crop prepare for action. Dad had a wee office in the back where he could work away from the hubbub or have a private chat with a contact. One day, he heard a lot of shouting and came out of the office to find two of his ex-boxers shouting and screaming obscenities at each other. One was apparently a Fenian B****** and the other an Orange B******. It was serious stuff and the old man had his work cut out to separate them. He administered a serious telling-off then, laughing, he took them to the gym's full-length mirror and stood them in front of it, inviting them to note the colour of their skin and remember that they both came from the Gold Coast. Dad pointed that we have enough problems of our own with home-grown Rangers and Celtic supporters and that they should take life a little easier!

I suppose all this was very different from the life my pals

led but we didn't really think much of it at the time. We could afford good holidays at least twice a year and, like almost everyone else in Glasgow at the time, we went to Douglas, Isle of Man, for the 'Fair'. Everyone and his granny did the same but we did it in style. Glasgow Fair fortnight in July saw the city almost shut down. All the factories and yards and steelworks closed and the workers and their families headed off for a well-earned couple of weeks at the seaside. The Friday before the Fair was chaotic. Workers collected their holiday money and headed for the pub at lunchtime and, for some, that was it till closing time. Others did manage to make it home at least, if the worse for wear, and collected their families and headed for the traditional Isle of Man Steam Packet Company midnight sailing from Ardrossan to Douglas. We were more fortunate and could travel by plane.

The sailings at the start of the Fair were the busiest and most drunken of the year. If we ever had to sail to the island – perhaps because we were unable to get a seat on a plane – we had the wherewithal to hire a private cabin. This was luxury and set us aside from our less well-heeled neighbours and friends. But, as I was growing up, I was not conscious of our lifestyle being all that different in any real way. My best pal at school, Mick Blyth, would come with us on holiday (My other great friend from my school days was Frankie Docherty and we all kept up our friendship as adults although now we're at the stage where we only exchange Christmas cards). Mum paid Mick's fare and Aunt Margaret his digs and his own parents chipped in with his pocket money. Mick was a great mimic and kept us entertained day and night with impersonations. His speciality was parodying TV commercials. The community spirit of the old tenements has been much written about and, on occasion, exaggerated but it did exist. Away from the tenements of the city, we'd live it up on the holiday island. We played together like one family – the kids on the beach and on the prom, the parents dancing at the famous Villa Marina and everyone taking the occasional tram trip along the seaside to the White City amusement park at Onchan.

One year, the planes were full and Dad had left it too late to get a cabin on the steamer. A racing acquaintance helpfully pointed out that he knew a man who worked at Ayr racecourse and who had a private plane. It would be ideal to pop us over to the island by air. He also said that the aviator was fond of a dram and it was wise not to pay him till we landed . . . just in case. So we headed down to Prestwick and this character from the racing world turned up dressed like a First World War flying ace, complete with leather helmet, silk scarf and goggles, and ushered us aboard. We made it to the IOM but we had our moments high above the Irish Sea on the way there. At one point, a door vibrated open and this Scottish Biggles calmly urged us just to shut it – no panic – so Uncle Bob reached out into space to do just that. And, as Douglas neared and the fuel load dissipated, he moved us around like chess pieces to balance the plane.

Looking back, I see more clearly that private planes and cabins on steamers were only part of it. The Starmaker was a big figure in the city, recognised all over the place by punters and boxing fans. He liked long coats, big cigars and jaunty hats and looked the part of a boxing manager. Central casting would be proud of him. His picture was on the sports pages on an almost daily basis. He was a somebody in a city where respect was hard won. As well as the swanky car, expensive clothes, holidays and the many phones, he and Mum would have special nights out in exclusive restaurants like the old 101 in Hope Street.

Dad, like old Jim, was good with figures and, on my forays

Two faces of the man who founded a dynasty. Jim Gilmour in the thirties as a boxer, a fearsome opponent, and later in life in the suave dinner suit favoured by the successful promoter.

This is the entire British Olympic team for the Antwerp Games in 1920! Then fewer than three thousand athletes from around the world took part – now around 20,000 is the norm.

'The auld yin', as the family called Jim, at the wheel of a gleaming limo – testimony of the good life he built from his career in boxing. Not many of his neighbours in Bridgeton had his style.

Scotland's most famous comedian of all time and friend of Jim, Sir Harry Lauder, was a boxing fan and a regular at the Premierland nights in Bridgeton.

A treasured item in my scrapbook – old Jim's licence as a promoter and proof of how the hoi polloi loved the sport in the old days. Included in the list of stewards are three lieutenant colonels, a colonel, a major, two judges, an MP and three QCs.

BRITISH BOXING BOARD OF CONTROL (1929)

President:
J. ONSLOW FANE, ESQ.

Vice Presidents:
COL. THE HON. HENRY C. GUEST
RT. HON. EARL OF DROGHEDA, P.C., K.C.M.G.

A. VAN GELDER, ESQ.
COL. VISCOUNT SCARSDALE, T.D.
LORD BURGHLEY, K.C.M.G.
ALEXANDER H. ELLIOT, ESQ.
DR. R MELVILLE HILEY
KENNETH EWART, ESQ.
LT.-COL. R. G. GROSVENOR

Stewards:
LT.-COL. J. W. GRAHAM
J. BASIL HERBERT, ESQ., Q.C., M.C.
M. R. NICHOLAS, ESQ.
W. H. BARRINGTON DALBY, ESQ
J. WENDELL, ESQ.
N. L. C. MACASKIE, ESQ., Q.C.
DAVID KARMEL, ESQ., Q.C.

COL. J. C. B. STEPHENS, T.D.
E. MARNAN, ESQ., M.B.E., Q.C.
DEREK CURTIS-BENNETT, Q.C.
HON. RICHARD STANLEY, M.P.
LT.-COL. W. H. BROMLEY DAVENPORT,
R. C. VAUGHAN, ESQ., O.B.E., D.L., T.D., M.P.
JOHN R. WILLIS, ESQ.

LICENCE No. 72670

This is to Certify that

MR. JAMES GILMOUR,
36 OLYMPIA STREET,
GLASGOW, S.E.

REGISTRATION No. P 36

as been granted a Licence by The British Box...
ontrol (1929) to promote

American Henry Hank takes it on the chin from a kiltie in the Olympia Gym in Bridgeton. Henry was training for the fight against John 'Cowboy' McCormack.

The Tommys and the Johnnys, the Gilmours and the Smiths ... Dad managed the Smiths, father and son, and young Johnny was the first champion I trained when he won the Scottish light middleweight title at the St Andrew's Sporting Club.

Me with Tommy Steele, the man of the day. Dad, Glasgow man about town, had arranged the meeting.

With the late great Chic Calderwood in Blackpool in 1963. Legendary corner man Dunky Jowett on the left and wee Tommy Smythe, designated as Chic's minder amid the many temptations of the resort, on the right.

Mum, right, with Jim and Rena, second left, on top of the Rockefeller Center on a visit to New York in 1950. Mum is surrounded by her own family, the Burns and the Brysons, who lived in the states.

Dad looked after his boys well. When Roy Rogers and Trigger came to town, Jim wanted to show off his cowboy suit, again, Dad arranged it.

Sugar Ray Robinson with me and Peter Keenan Jnr in the Keenan gym in Grant Street.

With my childhood pal Mick Blyth in the Villa Marina Gardens, Isle of Man.

Tommy Gilmour Snr, the Starmaker, was a name known and respected worldwide. Here in New York he chats with the legendary Nat Fleischer, who founded 'Boxing's Bible', Ring magazine, in the early twenties.

Talking again ... Tommy Snr and wee Peter Keenan feuded for years but, later in their careers, they were at least back on speaking terms. Here they are in 'costume' to plug a play on the tragic life of Benny Lynch.

The Gilmours dickied up for Mum and Dad's silver wedding in the Trocadero in West Regent Street, Glasgow. I am between Mum and Dad, old Jim is on Mum's right and Granny is beside Dad. At the back are my brother Jim and sister Rena.

The wonderful couple I called Uncle Bob and Aunty Margaret were close friends of my parents who shared the fun of life up a close in Rutherglen Road and helped to shape my life and values.

Alan Oag, Henry Hoey, Dunky Jowett and me in the Ingram Street gym.

Hughie Smith being presented with the Tennant Caledonian trophy for the best boxer of the year by Alan Buchanan, brother of Ken.

The irrepressible Paddy Byrne, dispenser of good advice and laughter.

At the height of his fame Peter Keenan was one of the most popular sportsmen in Scotland. Here Glasgow's finest protect PK from his enthusiastic fans.

Referee Tommy Mulhinch, Frank Blaney, MC, Tommy Snr and Jim McHarg, retired boxer, get together in the Ingram Street gym.

to his bookie's at the Olympia at a really early age, I found I shared that trait. I found the old pre-decimal coinage easy to calculate mentally and working out payouts for odds like 7/4 and 15/8 presented me with no problems even when I was around ten or so.

Bookmaking was, of course, illegal in those days but, for us and other back-street operators, the police raids were few and far between and mostly we got tip-offs that the cops were on their way. It was the same for all such establishments from Govan, the Garscube Road or wherever. The famous city ex-detective Les Brown, now a crime writer rather than a crime fighter, remembers raiding a place near Gorbals Cross and the bookie concerned started investigations as 'it was not his turn to be raided'. If, occasionally, the punters in our shop were nabbed, Dad paid their fines and added in a ten bob note as compensation. It would have been more accurate to describe the compensation money as a loan because it quickly came back over the counter in losing bets. Sometimes we did lose out to the boys in blue, though, and, during one unexpected raid by the police, Uncle Bob jumped out of the window carrying the cash bag in order to avoid, he hoped, the cops confiscating it. For his trouble, he broke both his legs. And we still lost the cash.

The exposure to money and calculations must have helped me at primary school for I was always near the top of the pile in most subjects. I did not play hookey much but was posted missing on one occasion when Peter Keenan took me with him to the Ulster Hall, Belfast, to hold up the cards showing the numbers of the rounds during a Sonny Liston exhibition match.

The Gilmours and Keenan had an odd relationship. Dad and wee Peter, one of Glasgow's best-loved boxers, fell out big time in 1952 and, later on, I'll tell the story of their feud but Peter was always kind to me even after the bust-up. Maybe the fact that his own son Peter was born next to me in the old Park Circus nursing home helped. I came home as a newborn baby with a black eye and my older brother Jim often joked that he blamed young Keenan.

8

HOLYROOD'S GOOD DAYS AND BAD DAYS

The primary school days were fun for me and I remember my mum having her happiest days at that time, chumming around with some of the teachers and other mums from the Union of Catholic Mothers. There always seemed to be a fête on the go and home baking galore. And there would be cigarettes in the staff room and occasionally a wee nip of whisky after red-letter days like a first communion. One of the teachers, Sally Smith, was married into the family of John Smith a famous bookie with a place in West Nile Street. So there was something of a shared world to life in Rutherglen Road.

Primary school was OK by me and my teachers – happy memories all round – but secondary was a tad different. My parents would have liked me to go to St Aloysius, as would Jimmy Darcy, a superb teacher but there was a snag – I was mad keen on football and played in trials for such as the Glasgow Schools XI – and at St Aloysius the game was rugby. So I ended up going to a famous south-side school where the round ball was the game of choice. In fact Holyrood Senior Secondary had good connections with senior football in Glasgow. That remarkable polymath Bob Crampsey, headmaster, novelist, TV and radio commentator and county cricket buff, taught there but had left for a post in Lanarkshire just before I arrived although he continued to live round the corner from the school. I'm sure I would have enjoyed being taught by him. And the gym teacher I had, John Murphy, did the announcements at Celtic Park on Saturday afternoons after supervising the school team in the morning.

Holyrood, just down the road from Hampden, was an amazing breeding ground for young footballers. Pat Crerand, Mike Jackson and Charlie Gallagher went on to play for Celtic. Boys like Mick McDonald, our goalkeeper, and Fred Pethard, our centre-half (central defender these days!), became professionals. But one of the most talented players of my age group was Tony McBride who went to St Margaret Mary's in Castlemilk. We had a good team at Holyrood, winning the league and getting into the semi-final of the cup one year. Tony was a great rival who kept me out of playing for Glasgow and Scotland as a schoolboy. He went on to play for Celtic though eventually his senior career sadly went downhill – despite the late Jock Stein saying he had the potential to become another Jimmy Johnstone.

Tony was some character. He used to turn up in battered sand-shoes, ragged shirt, unkempt hair and generally looking like Alf Tupper, the Tough of the Track, whose adventures featured in the comic books we awaited eagerly each week. This was not American Captain Marvel strip-cartoon stuff. The stories in such as the *Wizard*, *Adventure*, *Champion* and the *Rover* ran to thousands of words a week, with minimal illustrations – a great way to get young boys reading. In the Alf Tupper tales, the Tough of the Track always ran rings round the well-turned-out opposition. No doubt about it – Tony was the Alf Tupper of St Margaret Mary's. He could put on a dazzling show in any football game.

So all was well on the football field for me then but, at secondary, my schoolwork did not go just as smoothly. I remember taking one maths test and providing all the right answers but getting a poor mark. The teacher, a Miss Maley, who I was told was the daughter of Willie Maley, the famous Celtic manager, had marked me down for not showing the workings of my calculations. And yet that is something I have trouble with to this day. I can do massive calculations in my head and at times arrive at the right answer by something akin to intuition. How I get there is another story. But even the right answer wasn't enough for Miss Maley.

Teachers can have a remarkable effect on pupils – for bad as well as for good – and it is interesting that my mother who came from a poor background, growing up in much written-about The Dwellings in Bridgeton, had come across Miss Maley at one point in her schooling. Mum, too, was not impressed.

It was during my early years in secondary that I began to lose what today we call 'focus'. My head was full of football. My relationships with some of the teachers were not what they had been in primary. And my mother was gradually beginning to suffer from ill health. The old family albums show a strong, good-looking woman and you get a sense from them of her smiling, vibrant personality. She got a lot of fun out of life and her pals. I felt very close to her and it was desperately sad to see her go downhill, eventually dying in her early fifties from stomach cancer. My dad was naturally badly affected, especially as the final illness had been preceded by stays in hospital with a broken leg and pneumonia. It was a difficult time all round. My sister Rena had gone to live with relatives in America, where she prospered, and my brother Jim had just got married. My dream at that time of being a chartered accountant was in tatters and I left Holyrood at fifteen with no real qualifications. However, a new chapter was beginning.

9

LESSONS IN LIFE IN THE DAY JOB

January in Scotland is always a depressing month. The Christmas and New Year festivities are over and the weather is at its worst. In the city, the wind and rain, sleet and snow, or sometimes all four at once, whistle down the canyons between the bleak tenements, gathering power and malevolence as they go. It seems to be dark twenty-four hours a day. And, before central heating and two-car families arrived, even keeping dry and warm was a problem. Thousands of coal fires belched out choking black smoke, adding to the gloom of midwinter. The first month of 1968 was perhaps the low point of my life. Being out of school and into the world with no qualifications was bad enough but I spent a bit of time developing an uncharacteristic touch of bitterness that a school career that had promised so much in the early days had withered. Because of my own lack of focus during my final school years, my hopes of success in a profession like accountancy had been swept away. And amid all the gloom was a young man's certainty that, no matter how much she said she was 'all right', I knew deep down that my mum was in trouble with her health.

I needed a job. My dad, as I mentioned earlier, did not push me into bookmaking or the boxing game. I feel now that he wisely waited for me to make that decision for myself. At fifteen, I was too young to get involved in such a business but he did help me find work and, in a way, his life as a bookmaker was an asset. He had a pal called John Dick who had a small business dealing with bookmakers and specialising in printing betting cards, race cards and programmes and the like. I liked the idea of being a compositor and had developed an interest in the printing trade.

This was in the days before IT and computer typesetting. Compositors were well paid, well unionised and often, by the very nature of their work, well-read, rounded individuals. They say that, when one door closes, another slams in your face and I soon found out how true that is. Breaking into the printing trade was not easy. Jobs were passed down from father to son and it really helped to have a relative in the trade. I just could not get into that game. None of the Gilmours were in printing. Engineering apprenticeships were almost as hard to get and we didn't have any relatives in that trade either. But I did get lucky with the offer of a start in John Laird's in Carstairs Street, Bridgeton. Laird's were an old family-run printing works with a reputation for high-quality work. I thought that, if I could not be printer, then working as a printing engineer was the next best thing. So I became an engineer.

When you step through the door for your first job at fifteen or sixteen you have no thought that you might be there for nineteen years but that is how long I worked in Laird's. These were really happy years with lots of laughs mixed up with the work and I forged friendships that have lasted forty years. I was fifteen when I started and I had to wait till April that year, for my sixteenth birthday, before I could begin serving my time.

So, for the first three months, I worked in the engineering office helping Bob Farquhar. A lot of the Laird's folk lived locally and Bob had a house down the road in Rutherglen. With his meticulous style of working, he taught me a lot. He was the sort of person who, like me, liked to dot every 'i' and cross every 't'. The printing game has a terminology all of its own and Bob introduced me to it. And he also gave me a baptism in the grimy side of the business. He was in charge of collating information on the plant and the machinery and he had me crawling around dark and dusky corners of the factory to get the information he wanted for his records but it was all a valuable introduction to the world of work.

However, a cloud hung over my early weeks in engineering. In February, I got the worst news of my life. Mum had cancer and the medical people gave her only months to live. Six weeks later she was dead. I was away from Carstairs Street for a short time and everyone there, from the bosses to the guys on the floor, could not have been more understanding and supportive. I returned to work in early May. I then had a short time off in June to go to the States to give my sister Rena away at her wedding. This was a poignant trip. It had been intended that Mum would go as, at the time, Dad just hadn't the funds for the two of them to make the trip – bookies, like punters, do have their ups and downs! In any case, he felt that it was more important that Mum was at the wedding. But it was not to be. Our manager Mr Simpson was, again, sympathetic to my request and I got a friendly nod that it was OK to go.

When all this was happening, I was assigned to work with a character called George Marshall. He was one of the longest serving employees at Laird's. A friendly guy who could remember his own days as an apprentice, he knew how to handle a young fella. He had wispy hair and an unkempt moustache and was known to everyone on the floor as the Duke. It took a little while before I summoned up the courage to make inquiries as to how he had acquired the nickname. The reason for his aristocratic moniker was it seems that he lived in Duke Street so he was known as the Duke of Dennistoun. When the Duke became a foreman, I was sent to work with George Dallas, known to his mates and everyone in the factory as Dal. He became my friend as well as my mentor and he was a genuinely good bloke – he would even pick me up and drive me to work. We had some great times and I was saddened that he died a relatively young man.

Apprentices were moved around to pick up all the techniques of the trade and, when I was sent to 'turning', my teacher was Jimmy Timney. His family were famous coal merchants in the east end and Jimmy could keep us entertained for hours over endless cups of tea with tales of the scams and dodges of the old-time coalmen, an imaginative bunch when it came to squeezing an extra pound or two out of a lorry load of coal. We became pals. Jimmy liked to go to the football and Dad got us tickets for the North Stand at Hampden for the famous and still-remembered Celtic v Leeds battle. We finished work at a quarter to five and went to Jimmy's house in Springfield Road for a legendary helping of my favourite meal – mince and tatties. Jimmy and his wife Jean had no family and I became a sort of adopted son to them. Jean, in that way Glasgow wives often have, always called her husband James. And James was a man who did not much like change. Every working day he turned up in the factory with the same 'piece' – bread and cheese.

Factories are a fertile feeding ground for jokers and the lads in Carstairs Street could not resist the opportunity for a little fun. One such joker was an engineer called Willie McDonald. Fed up with seeing Jimmy eat his cheese sandwiches day after day he composed a letter to Jean, which we all signed. It was a demand that she gave Jimmy a change. Off it went and we waited to find out the result. Sure enough a couple of days later Jimmy opened his piece to find the filling was gammon. Normally mild-mannered he, as they say in Glasgow, 'did his nut'. He ranted and raved about the change and, for a time, it looked like we would all be witnesses in a divorce case. But Jean saved the day and it was soon back to cheese sandwiches for her James.

As the days in Laird's went on, I began, in a small way, to drift into the boxing business, training a few fighters and putting on shows. I suppose that, all the time, that is what my dad and grandfather thought might happen – it's that dynasty thing! During this time, I got great support from my workmates – they bought tickets and generally assisted me. Many a time they covered up for me when I was away doing a little wheeling and dealing in the public phone boxes, dropping the coins in as the conversations went on and on. For this, I want to publicly thank them! The bosses at Laird's helped me too but in a slightly different way – they sent me to college. There I recovered my early interest in learning and I was named 'top boy' and eventually got my City & Guilds certificate, passing with distinction.

In my time at Laird's, I also encountered a culture that you don't see much of in boxing promotion – the unions. I had to help Willie McDonald collect the union dues and, since I went for my lunch – we called it dinner – at my Granny Gilmour's in Tullis Street, I was given the job of going to the branch office in Landressy Street to pay the dues in. There was always a bob or two extra for me for delivering the monies and the books. All my life I have been ready, some say too ready, to speak up if I feel I see any unfairness or injustice. It is a trait that has brought me into more than one or two serious conflicts, particularly with the Boxing Board of Control. At the print works, I was the same and found myself, at twenty-one, a deputy shop steward and, before too long, I was the shop steward. As a kid, I liked to get things done my way and nothing had changed. I suspect that my election to the elevated position of shop steward was a result of the fact that no one else really wanted to do it. I didn't see my union career as political – just as a natural extension of my interest in fair play and equality. And I think my brief excursion into the world of votes, strikes and committee meetings did me no harm in my future career as a businessman. It was all a bit of an eye-opener. I was even sent by the union on a course in Ayrshire where shop stewards were coached in the skills of representing the guys on the shop floor and squeezing the maximum cash out of employers.

The other students were natural militants, guys who had grown up in union families, the sort of folk who read the left-wing press and paid more attention to politics than they did to the sports pages. Frankly, I was a fish out of water. The folk on the course talked a different language and, if their concern, which you had to respect, was bettering the life of the work-ingman, it seemed the only solution was one word – strike. I was, at this time, beginning to build up my career as a boxing promoter while still working in the factory and I felt like a fraud, even an infiltrator. I was driven to tell everyone my position in the Great War between employee and employer. But they asked me to stay and I did. Honesty never goes out of fashion.

I have to say life was good during my time in Laird's, though the firm changed its name a few times, and, as I was now married to Veronica and had two kids, Christopher and Stephanie, it provided security when I needed it most. When I meet up with guys from the old days, we still have a few moans about our time in Laird's but, by and large, it was fun. I remember the laughs best. Veronica has always been a pal as well as a wife and she understood me at times better than I understood myself. She knew that, despite all those years in the factory, deep down I wanted to follow my grandfather and dad into the fight game. More than once, she voiced her opinion that I should quit the day job and go full-time into boxing promotion.

For a long while, I resisted. I didn't have the confidence to give up a pleasant lifestyle to chase a dream that could go wrong. Maybe, at that time, I just did not want it enough – being in the world of promoting took a lot of guts and hard work – but Veronica always seemed to know it would happen. Her faith in me is enormous and her encouragement invaluable. She would always take the risk.

It has to be said that Veronica's attitude in this was a bit different from that of my mother. She had married Dad and escaped from a difficult life in the infamous The Dwellings in Bridgeton. She had a great lifestyle with The Starmaker – big holidays, fancy restaurants and cash in her handbag – and sometimes she was just a little cautious as she didn't want to risk losing what she had. Looking back, I wonder now if that attitude might just have rubbed off a bit on Dad, making him more cautious in his career than he might have been. Veronica, though, was different, always encouraging me to take a risk.

But, as the politicians say, 'events, dear boy,' sometimes make the difference. In a sense, my decision to leave engineering and take the plunge to stand on my own feet was made for me. The factory in Bridgeton was too old and out of date and the firm planned a move to a purpose-built place in the new town of East Kilbride out in the countryside south of Glasgow, a few miles up the road from Rutherglen and Burnside. The new place with new equipment needed fewer workers and a cut in the work force was one of the attractions of the move for the company. Voluntary redundancy was on offer. I discussed it with Veronica, we agreed I should apply and I got it. The pay-off was good but, nonetheless, Veronica knew I would worry about supporting her and the kids in a new career in boxing, a world where your money didn't pop into the bank in nice round sums month after month, a world of no paid holidays, no sickness benefit and no guaranteed pensions. In reality, there was not a problem with cash – the redundancy money gave me a bit of a cushion – but Veronica took a job to ease the early years of my career change. She didn't have to but she did to make it all a bit sweeter for me. Once again, she was in the frontline, supporting me and my ambitions.

I was lucky to have her. We had both gone to Holyrood Secondary in Crosshill but, at school, we never seemed to meet and I have no memory of her as a schoolgirl. Holyrood was the place for those who had passed the eleven-plus or the dreaded 'qually', as it was known. In the area I grew up in, if you failed this make-or-break examination at a ludicrously early age, you went to St Bonaventure's Junior Secondary. It was a system that drew a lot of criticism from folk who thought that eleven was too early to split kids into successes or failures. Your birthday even had an effect on your education. Veronica was what they called 'winter intake' and her early part of secondary education took place in an all-girl annexe where the pupils did 'prep' for a few months. I, on the other hand, went straight into first year since I was 'summer intake'. We did not meet till our school days were over and one of the reasons we did, I like to think, was an early demonstration of my ability as an organiser.

Our local priest, Father Gerry Fitzsimmons, decided that a disco would help keep the local youth out of trouble and generally add a little fun to life in the area. It was to happen on a weekly basis and a committee was formed. My pals and I were on it and one of the main tasks was to deck out the local primary school dinner hall appropriately for the disco. This we did and I enjoyed helping to organise the nights. I like planning for events. A bonus was that I met Veronica at the disco. It took a bit of courage to ask this good-looker out but eventually I did it. A night at the pictures was the usual first date then. We went to see Sinatra in *Tony Rome*. I often think back to that night when I am in the States – Tony Roma, the Place for Steaks, is a major restaurant chain and its ads always prompt memories of that first date. It was the start of our courtship and many Saturdays were spent at the cinemas in town or in the Electric Garden disco in Sauchiehall Street. Such venues change their name frequently and the place is now the Garage and is occasionally visited by the now grown-up Christopher and Stephanie.

Our trips to the Garden (not Madison Square!) took place

about the time there was a huge revolution in the habits of Glaswegians. Up until then, eating out in restaurants was the preserve of businessmen with plenty of cash. Working folk would save for weeks to splash out at birthdays, wedding anniversaries or whatever in such places as the 101, Ferraris, the Malmaison, the Royal or maybe a few miles out of town in such as the Buchanan Arms in Drymen. The thought of routinely popping out for a meal, as is normal now, just didn't happen.

The man who changed all that, in Glasgow at least, was an energetic Cypriot called Reo Stakis. He arrived to walk the streets selling lace out of a suitcase but saw a great opportunity in the restaurant business. The steakhouse was on its way. Reo, like all good entrepreneurs, knew what the punters wanted. The huge fancy menus of the classy places, often in French, were off-putting to the working guy and his girl – as were the fancy prices. Reo realised that, when a youngster took out a girl and a toffee-nosed waiter gave her a huge à la carte menu to choose from, the guy would be a worried man. It would be a case of the girl choosing whatever dish she wanted, regardless of the price, and not her picking something her escort could afford. The answer was the famous Stakis set meal – most often, it was prawn cocktail, steak and chips and Black Forest gateau. You knew where you were then and there was no big unpleasant surprise when the bill arrived. What's more, for the time, the food was good and the places were stylish.

For Veronica and me, a night at a steakhouse alternated with a night at the pictures – although, sometimes, when we were flush, we did both in the same night. The Blenheim in Sauchiehall Street and the old Berni Inn at the top of Hope Street were

101

favourites. As time went on, I was spending more and more time in Veronica's home, particularly on Saturdays and Sundays for a meal. My own mum was a cracking cook and so was Veronica's mum, Jeanie. I still regret that Mum died before I met Veronica and they never knew each other. Veronica's dad, Larry, liked me but was a wee bit sceptical about his daughter taking up with a guy he used to see on occasional visits to the bookie.

Mr Curran had a good job with the Corporation – always important in the old Glasgow. As a chief inspector with the cleansing department, he had that badge of honour, the sober green Corporation uniform. My dad, on the other hand, looked at times like he could have stepped out of a Damon Runyon short story.

But we gradually all became close friends and, appropriately on Boxing Day 1970, Veronica and I became engaged. We waited for three years, till June 1973, for the wedding. A traditional reception was held in the Co-op Halls, Main Street, Rutherglen, and it was such a great day. A planeload of my relatives came over from America, sporting more sunglasses than you would see in an airport chemist's, and Veronica's mum and dad, Jeanie and Larry, laid on a top-class 'do' – a strong hint as to how they expected their daughter to be treated.

There was an amusing, ironic touch to the Catholic wedding. June was part of the marching season in Glasgow and, as the guests arrived for the reception, an Orange Parade rolled noisily past. The Deputy Grand Master, in the lead of the marching ranks, was none other than Archie (the Craw) Crawford – my uncle! He made sure that the guy beating the big drum in the flute band gave it a few extra whacks for us. This was maybe a little bit embarrassing for some guests but at least everyone was pulling for us. It is rumoured that Archie later went to reception and asked for carrots rather than green peas with his main course – very Glasgow! I thought back to that day years later when both sides of the Old Firm got behind the Clinton fight. The honeymoon night was spent in a place that, for years, was part of my life. The Albany was then nearly new and *the* hotel in town. In later years, of course, it was to be the head-quarters of the St Andrew's Sporting Club and would play a major role in my life and that of Veronica and the kids.

It is always valuable to look back at the cost of things as it can bring you back down to earth. Our stay at the then new Albany cost £12.50 which was more than a quarter of a week's wages for me. The honeymoon itself – ten days in Lloret de Mar on the Costa Brava – cost £55 per person but that was not my worry as Veronica paid. Lloret was one of the most popular of Spanish resorts at the time but I only met one fellow Glaswegian there, John Quinn. John was a famous name with the *Daily Mail* and the *Evening Times* in the days when jour-nalists regularly double-tasked. He was a hard-nosed diary reporter and news editor and a respected boxing writer with one of the best contacts books in the business. John and his wife Kathleen became great friends over the years, even if I might have heard John's party piece 'Stand Up and Fight' from *Carmen Jones* once or twice too often.

John was in touch daily with my dad about the goings-on in the boxing world and, when I got my first licence in 1970, he was the first to write about me. He is retired now but we are still mates and speak at least once a week. He has seen more boxing shows than even I have and has a great memory for fights and fighters. He is a writer who comments on the game with huge authority. Mind you, we still had fun and high jinks in Lloret with boxing, for once, in the background.

The first home Veronica and I shared was a four-in-a-block house in Castlemilk Road, Croftfoot, in the south side. When advertised in the papers these days they call such places 'cottage flats'. It is not a bad description – you had your own front door, a bit of a back green and a nice wee garden at the front. To us it was just beautiful – a dream. Veronica's dad and her brothers Lawrence and Thomas decorated it for us and Aunty Margaret and Uncle Bob, the carpet weaver from Rutherglen Road, carpeted the lounge and hall. Friends and relatives helped with the furnishing. We were a lucky couple. They were great wee houses – even if the soundproofing left a lot to be desired. Not so far away, one of Glasgow's top journalists, Russell Kyle, had a place and, with his show business connections, he even managed a party or two with such as Rod Stewart and Billy Connolly as guests – not bad for wee Croftfoot. And some of the neighbours must have got top entertainment free, thanks to those thin walls.

Our mortgage was around five grand to be paid up at £40 a month. We could handle it as I had my good job in Laird's and Veronica worked in the office in the giant Weir's factory down the road in Cathcart. We were doing OK.

At this time, I was also training boxers for my dad and that pulled in a little extra. Sometimes, though, the extra was not quite enough. I remember training Johnny Smith to box for a Scottish title against Derek Simpson. If Johnny did the business, my commission would be £40 and I promised Veronica that the cash would pay for new venetian blinds in the lounge. Johnny duly claimed victory and became my first champion. Veronica had heard the result on Radio Clyde and was sitting up in bed waiting for me when I eventually got home. Right away, she wanted to know when to order the blinds. There was just one problem – I had paid for the champagne to celebrate Johnny's win. The blinds were eventually bought but I had to work two Sundays on overtime to pay for them. That's boxing. But Veronica, as always, understood. No wonder she is still my best pal as well as my wife.

10

BIG CHIC, COWBOY AND WEE PK

Flicking through the photograph album of my career, you'd be struck by the number of shots taken at ringside or in the ring itself which feature me with a wide, wide smile – provided the decision has gone our way, that is. At times like those, I have a trademark grin that shows just how I feel and it attracts the newspaper snappers who fill the back pages. But that show of emotion in public is not the full story. Sometimes, in the boxing game, a poker face is an advantage. When you're deal-making across the table facing some of the sharpest guys in the game – and with a lot of money at stake – you have to put your facial emotions on hold. I can do it. I like to think I can make decisions without emotion, rationally, weighing pros and cons.

Maybe I could have made some money at the tables in Vegas like my dad's old friend and rival Mickey Duff. Mickey was in the Nevada charmed circle, a high roller as well known at the tables in the casinos on the strip as he was ringside at the biggest fights in the world. If he took the notion to hit the tables, no matter where he was at the time, a quick call to Vegas resulted in air tickets deposited at the nearest airport and a reserved suite in Caesar's Palace, Circus Circus or whatever gambling joint he fancied – a bit different from a wee game or two of pontoon in a Bridgeton printing plant. Mind you, Mickey was pretty good at the tables and pretty good at making money out of boxing. Now retired, he likes to remind folk that he left the game a millionaire. Mickey was one of the most knowledgeable men in boxing. He was someone from whom I learned a great deal as he sat in our home sipping a cuppa and regaling everyone there with his stories of the great and the good and the not so good, in the fight game. A wonderful raconteur.

My ability to control my emotions never served me better than during the week my dad died in October 1979. By then I was building a career for myself as a promoter. I was in partnership with Henry Hoey who was, like me, a shop steward in the engineering game. He also trained fighters for Dad. We knew that Willie Booth, in Dad's stable, was what we call in the business a ticket-seller. But there was no one to promote him. In the seventies, boxing was in one of its cyclical downturns, apart from at the St Andrew's Sporting Club, and there were not enough venues for the boxers. Henry and I put Willie into action in the canteen of Henry's employers Terex, with their help of course, out on the Edinburgh Road but more of that later. It was the start of something of a comeback in the game.

One of the other venues we used, at this time, was the famous Plaza Dance Hall at Eglinton Toll at the end of Victoria Road. This was a place rooted in the folk memories of Glaswegians. The city was a place that was, in the days before wall-to-wall TV, twenty-four hours a day, 'dancing daft'. The halls like the Locarno, The Majestic (aka the Magic Stick), the Dennistoun Palais and the Albert in town and dozens more attracted dancers by the thousand. The girls went there after work, dolled up to the nines as they say. The guys changed out of factory or office gear, maybe splashed on a little of the aftershave they had received at Christmas and went on the hunt for a 'lumber', as they called a pick-up. Sometimes the more middle-aged simply went on their own or as husband and wife for the pleasure of a neatly executed quickstep or samba to the rhythm of a swing band belting it out under sparkling lights. There was even the chance to take a dance lesson or two if you were not up with the latest natty steps.

Spangles on dresses were a must for the girls and men wore polished pumps as they greased round the slippery dance floor. It was a touch of glamour in grey lives. But a night at the jiggin' was mainly a weekend attraction. Getting the punters into the halls on Mondays and Tuesdays was not so easy. So the legendary manager of the Plaza – a famous, immaculate, dark-suited gentleman called Adam Sharp – saw the financial advantage of a boxing show early in the week. A ring was assembled on the dance floor, suppers like scampi or chicken in a basket were laid on and, after the boxing, the floor was cleared for cabaret and a wee spot of dancing. Incidentally, I still get a bit of a lump in my throat when I pass Eglinton Toll and look at the site – the old Plaza has been swept away by the wreckers' ball and, surprise, surprise, flats erected in its place. However, there's a nod in the direction of nostalgia as a wee bit of the old entrance remains. These were normally really happy, carefree nights – a nice mixture of the boxing and the show business – and the fans loved them.

But that week back in October 1979, we put on a Plaza show in sad circumstances. The Starmaker, Tommy Gilmour Sr, a man recognised as one of the leading managers, not just in Britain, but also in the world, in the forties, fifties, sixties and seventies, was in the Royal Infirmary fighting for his life after a stroke. He was taken in just twenty-four hours before the promotion. The immediate reaction in such a situation is to cancel but then you think what it means, folk with tickets in their pockets, boxers looking forward to a bit of much-needed prize money – money they had trained hard to earn. We all talked it through. It was never going to be a happy night but the consensus was that the old cliché 'the show must go on' said what had to be done. And all the time we hoped and prayed for a recovery while putting the worst-case scenario to the back of our minds.

I was very mixed up indeed. In the run-up to the show, my brother Jim and I were in and out of the Royal at Dad's bedside. It was a tough time – snatched cups of tea, talks with doctors and nurses and those upsetting journeys across town in traffic to the hospital, with a million things going through your mind. Whenever the phone rang you jumped never knowing whether it was the hospital with news or a well-wisher asking after Dad or some problem that had turned up at the venue. It was really difficult to concentrate on the minutiae of detail required in advance of putting on a show.

One of the boxers on the bill that week, Hugh Smith, was particularly affected. A good pal of my dad, he was initially for cancellation but changed his mind and fought with a heavy heart. Hugh is still much talked about in the fight game, even today. Incidentally, his sister is the novelist Anna Smith who made a good career for herself as a *Daily Record* reporter. The promotion went on. Sadly Dad died later in the week and in the next few weeks and months I had plenty of time for memories and to reflect on my happy days growing up in Rutherglen Road. The news of his illness had come out of the blue.

The illness struck in the old Ingram Street gym and he was taken to hospital by one of the trainers, Chic Brady, and I was phoned at my then home in Cambuslang. Jim and I rushed to hospital. We were told that there was some hope that he might survive though he might have been disabled and that the next forty-eight hours would be critical. The nurse in charge asked us to take away his effects. It was a sad reminder of some of his eccentricities. He always kept a record of his business affairs in a tattered collection of old jotters and notebooks. But, before he filled the jotters in, he packed the pockets of his expensive suits and coats with little notes – scribbled pieces of paper were everywhere. I remember Mum giving him hell for the way this habit misshaped expensive suits but he never took a telling. Nothing changed and, on that sad day when Jim and I took away his stuff, he had more than £25 in coins in his possession, ready for the payphone in the gym. His pockets were stuffed with cigars, sweets, notes on people who owed him money and little scraps of paper with info for his journals. He even had a set of pocket tools, with a screwdriver etc., though it had been years since he used such thing.

In the good times in the old Olympia gym and around the big fight nights, I suppose the two fighters most associated with my dad were Chic Calderwood and Peter Keenan although there is a legion of other big names. PK, as everyone in Glasgow called him, ended up feuding with my dad but Peter and I always got on well and he was involved in one of my greatest boxing memories. It was August 1965. Keenan was promoting at the time and had some great shows at the old Paisley Ice Rink, which had a capacity of around 5,000. Londoner Mickey Duff was also involved with PK at this time. Home of the Pirates ice hockey team, the Paisley venue was a remarkable place and, at various times, indoor tennis there had featured such famous names as Ken Rosewall, Pancho Segura and Rod Laver but the biggest star to appear in the Renfrewshire arena was undoubtedly Muhammad Ali. This was during the time when he was in the process of changing his name from Cassius Clay. When Ali flew into Glasgow for his exhibition show in Paisley in a small plane, the Coatbridge Ladies Pipe Band was on hand to greet him. From there, he travelled to the old MacDonald Hotel at Eastwood Toll (now bulldozed to be replaced by, surprise, surprise, luxury flats).

I had my own moment of glory at Paisley. Ali was due to defend his title against Floyd Patterson a month or two after his appearance at Paisley so there was no way he would put that at any real risk in a hard-hitting exhibition but, nonetheless, the place was sold out and pictures and stories about Ali filled the papers. I found him far from the bumptious figure he cut on TV. My co-author Robert Jeffrey also remembers the big man visiting the old *Daily Express* offices in Albion Street and that although famous executives and writers almost fought for his time and to have their pictures taken with him, the champ took time to chat to the young copy boys who were in a high old state of excitement about meeting one of the most famous men in the world face to face.

Ali, who later always travelled with a cast of thousand (many of whom would bleed him dry financially), was restrained on his visit to Scotland. His regular sparring partners Jimmy Ellis and Cody Jones came to town as did his trainer Angelo Dundee and Angelo's brother Chris. Based in Miami, Chris was a big, big figure in the fight game in the States. A man with 'connections', he was not the type you would want to get into an argument with. He also came to the house in Rutherglen Road – two world figures dropping in on a flat up a close across the road from Glasgow Green. Memorable!

At one of his many press conferences, Ali told the fans in Paisley that they would see him against Jones and Ellis and that 'you people in Paisley would see more action than all those who paid millions to see me destroy that ugly big bear Liston'. This had to be somewhat of an exaggeration considering he was taking care to keep in shape for the Patterson bout.

I held up the number cards indicating what round it was for PK promotions. I was the best card boy in the world or so I thought. I was the number one kiddie. I was to be paid a couple of guineas or so for doing the business and I had my own mini feud with PK when he tried to pay me in straight pounds. Demonstrating my belief that a deal is a deal and that attention to detail is vital, I held out for the fee to be paid in guineas! Peter, of course, coughed up with a smile. I had held the number cards up for Liston (when Peter took me out of school to Belfast), Sugar Ray Robinson and now Muhammad Ali. I used to be rigged up for fight nights in my best shirt and trousers and I had a huge eye-catching bow tie. I leapt into the ring like spring-heeled Jack and stood to attention for a second or two showing the number of the round to one side of the audience. Then I turned left, marched eight steps and stood for a second or two facing another side of the ring. Then it was a few steps to the right before going back to where I had started. Veteran boxing observer Bert Watt, cousin of the world champion Jim, says it was as if I was doing a carefully rehearsed dance routine.

Holding up the round cards has always been a bit of a Gilmour family tradition. My dad did it as a kid, before he managed his first boxer at fourteen, my brother Jim did it and, of course, I did it. So did Jim's son Ricky (now a timekeeper) and his brother Anthony. My son Christopher was the last number boy. The job is now done by glamour girls of the sort *The Sun* calls 'stunnahs'. Two beauties who carried the cards at the St Andrew's club were June Lake, much featured on Tennants lager cans, and Michelle Mone who became a millionaire bra tycoon.

All I remember of that night in Paisley was getting my picture taken with a smiling Ali. It was a bit odd because, in the dressing room, he was not his usual self but Dad had a word with Chris Dundee and the happy snap was taken. For some reason, there was a rumour going about Glasgow that Ali had been booed at the end of the exhibition. Frankly, I don't remember that though all I was interested in was my picture and I got it. Mickey Duff, who co-promoted with PK at the time, is on record as saying the rumour was a damned lie. Another rumour around the pubs at the time was that wee Peter had slapped Ali on the head, alleging that the big man had not put his heart into selling tickets for the event. Now PK was brave enough to have done it but I don't believe a word of this one either. The show was an easy sell-out and there would be no conflict of the kind suggested by the rumour. Duff is interesting on PK and his comments throw some light on the feud with Dad. According to Duff, Peter was a decent man, capable of great kindness – a 'nice fella' – but he could be difficult.

Chic Calderwood was a dour fellow – the opposite of perky Peter who had an opinion on everything and everyone – but he was one hard, hard fighter who could have become a huge name in the game. He always had time for me when I was a youngster and he simply became my idol. After workouts in the Bridgeton gym, I was the kid who cut the bandages from his famous fists and wiped the sweat off his brow.

Chic, from Craigneuk, died in a car crash in the Clyde Valley in November 1966. He had been driving a new Mini, which is not exactly the size of limo needed to comfortably accommodate a heavily muscled light-heavyweight, but the wee car was the talk of the day and Chic was one of the first to have one. The crash, at a place called Fidler's Bridge, was front-page news, a major sporting tragedy. I learned of it at home in Rutherglen Road. The phone rang fairly late at night and that first call was from James 'Solly' Sanderson, looking for my dad who was out. Jimmy just said to say he had called. Dick Currie of the *Record* also called and there were other calls from the boxing writers wanting to speak to Dad so I knew something was wrong. These guys called at ten in the morning for sporting titbits, not at ten at night. I soon learned the sad truth. Big Chic was dead.

The accident happened just weeks after he had fought for the world title against José Torres in San Juan, Puerto Rico. The heat and humidity there gave the big Scot problems as did Torres, an accomplished champion. Calderwood only lasted two rounds. In a different sort of climate, he still may not have won but it would have been a much closer fight. I met Torres, an erudite and intelligent guy, many years later at a WBO convention in San Juan, Puerto Rico. At the time of Chic's death there were rumours going around that, as they say in these parts, especially in the city's always busy courts, 'drink was a factor'. You've got to expect such things – boxers are often spied on by the public. A modest half pint or even a soft drink in your local and someone is on to your trainer or manager with lurid stories of overindulgence. I know, as a manager, I have taken many a similar call and, more often than not, it is fantasy although, of course, some legendary Scots fighters did enjoy a refreshment or six away from the ring. However, such tales are far from the truth where Chic Calderwood was concerned – it was a road accident pure and simple.

Down the years, some of the most successful boxers, really big earners, have had more trouble with bank managers, bookies and bottles than they ever had with opponents in the ring. The stories of boxers bled dry by connections or simply dissipating their money in fast living are legend. Unfortunately, many of these anecdotes are true and there is nothing sadder than seeing a sporting legend who has had thousands pass through his hands living near the poverty line in later life. Truly fame does not pay the rent.

Dad used to tell a story about big Chic that made the point. Good managers try to point their fighters in the right direction when it comes to looking after the cash when it comes in. Dad gave Calderwood one of his lectures, told him to see the bank manager, get some solid advice and look after his earnings. The bank manager sorted out things with Chic and, with the aim of looking after him, issued him with a chequebook. Dad also arranged for the fighter's money to be paid by cheque into his bank account to help control any spendthrift urges.

It didn't work. After a few weeks with the chequebook, Chic turned up at the gym with a long face. He was worried as he had had a call from the bank manager who told him that he had no funds left. At this point, Chic pulled out a still fairly thick chequebook and pointed at it inquiring at the same time how he could be skint with all these cheques left. That was fifty years ago and things have moved on. There are exceptions still, of course, but, nowadays, a boxer is more likely to ask a manager about pensions, stock exchange tips and financial advisers. However, Dad got a few good laughs with the Chic and the chequebook story.

Another Calderwood escapade that makes us smile when we reminisce is the story of his time in Blackpool when he went south to fight Ron Redrup. Chic went down early to promote the fight and train in the south and Dad despatched one of the team, wee Tommy Smythe, to act as his minder amid all the temptations of drink, gambling and women in the Lancashire holiday resort which was at the height of its popularity in 1963. I don't know if Chic liked a punt – I suspect he did – though he was generally well behaved in training. But he was a big good-looking guy in a glamorous sport and Blackpool in the summer was a place packed with showgirls. And Chic caught the eye of many of them – even a couple of headliners who had their names in lights outside the many theatres in the place. He was staying in that huge place on the sea front, the Imperial. The old hotel – a great favourite of the politicians during Labour Party conferences in the town – was packed with show people.

Chic had a reputation for enjoying himself so Dad charged wee Tommy to make sure he did not get out to play. Chic was a powerful six-footer and wee Tommy could not even make the five-foot mark. But there was only one boss in this duo – wee Tommy. One night, they went for a stroll on the prom with the intention of doing little else than breathe in the bracing sea air. When they got back to the hotel, Chic was locked in his room and Tommy trousered the key. This was not in the big fellow's game plan. He was determined to get out. There was a fanlight connecting to the next room. Calderwood moved the furniture around, climbed on it and attempted to get through the fanlight. His broad shoulders got stuck halfway through. If it was embarrassing for the boxer, it was worse for the couple in the room next door who were enjoying the delights of a honeymoon to the full. It must have cost Dad a bottle or two of champagne to smooth that one over. We managed to keep the incident out of the papers so all was well – especially when Chic won the fight.

Wee Tommy Smythe was one of the great stalwarts of Scottish boxing at both pro and amateur levels. When I started promoting, Tommy, as well as building the rings, acted as what is called the 'ringmaster whip'. In that job, you are an important figure who keeps a finger on all parts of the promotion and sees that things go as smoothly as possible – even down to ensuring that the boxers wear the correct colour of shorts. I remember one night at the Plaza when I heard a row coming from the dressing room and decided to investigate. I found Tommy arguing with the managers of two of the boxers and demanding that one changed the colour of his shorts. I pointed out that, since one of the guys' was coloured and the other's white, did it really matter? Tommy insisted the rulebook was adhered to and so I left him to it. It was a tragedy when wee Tommy, then in his seventies, was killed in a street car accident outside a boxing event. He deserves that over-used adjective 'legendary'. My whip these days is my niece Joan's husband Jeff who, like Tommy, also builds my rings for the St Andrew's club events. Talk about a family business.

Many years after Chic's sad death, I got the chance to put my idolisation of him on a more permanent basis. After the accident, the Calderwood family put his Lonsdale belt up for auction in McTear's just off Glasgow's George Square. Dad was out of town and left a reserved bid but the belt went to agents of a Russian sports museum. I never heard anything more about it till a couple of years ago. Someone in Lanarkshire got in touch with me to say he had Chic's belt. We met, I had a look and, sure enough, the gold belt was in its red leather box, resting on ivory silk – the real deal. I had a few contacts at police HQ in Pitt Street and thought it prudent to check out what the score was. I even contacted the famous Nipper Reid in London, the man who will forever be known as the cop who nicked the Krays and who was a top man in the Metropolitan police. Nipper was Chairman of the Boxing Board of Control after his police days. He knew what was going on even in Interpol and he contacted them for me but they knew nothing that would cause a problem. Nipper is a real gentleman and we are still in touch to this day. He was one of the first to congratulate me when I was awarded the MBE in the summer of 2007.

Once I had established that there was clearly no problem regarding the sale of Chic's belt, I decided to make an offer for it. The guy selling the belt had found it in a relative's attic when he was clearing out after his relative's death. It seems the Russians had failed to take the belt abroad – maybe the museum never materialised or maybe they just did not pay up. I bought it for a sum not too far from £10,000 – not small potatoes but I had my permanent reminder of my idol and my youth.

A game that boxing folk like to play is to imagine fights that never happened and come up with a result. Now sadly Chic had died when he was not quite at his peak but I have often wished he could have fought that truly great world light-heavyweight, Archie Moore. Archie was good enough to fight up a weight, as a heavy, against the best. It never happened but it nearly did. The Old Mongoose, as the boxing press called Moore, came to Scotland to see Chic fight and this wise old warrior didn't like what he saw in the fearless youngster from Lanarkshire. The gist of his off-the-record comments were that Chic was too young (and maybe too good!) and that he, Archie, was too old. The American did everything he could to avoid the fight, including asking for a purse of $100,000, a huge sum in the sixties. Archie, incidentally, followed a well-worn path for ex-boxers in appearing on stage and in film. He starred in the film of *The Adventures of Huckleberry Finn* as a black slave. Moore was a genuinely nice man; it was a pleasure to have met one of the true greats of the game.

From his attempts to avoid Chic, you could surmise that Archie was a cautious guy who took care to have opponents he could handle – no first-round surprises for the old champion. In contrast, Chic himself was the sort of bold fighter who, like Ali, would travel anywhere to take on a local hero and risk the dreaded 'hometown decision', convinced his fists would see him OK. Fans love that and, for the huge numbers of supporters who followed Calderwood, this was part of the attraction. He travelled to Detroit to face a fearsome battler called Henry Hank and was on the canvas in the third round but proved his toughness by getting up to finish. The Yanks loved his courage despite the loss on points. I went to the States with Dad and Chic for the fight in the city's Convention Arena. Aged nine and wearing a kilt, I was Chic's official mascot and even found myself pictured in the local papers as a mini celebrity.

Dad mixed business and pleasure in Detroit by visiting my mum's sister Kathy and her brother Matt Bryson who had settled in Motor City. Harry Baxter, a guy described in the papers as a 'part Scot', was president of the local Sports Guild and had Dad as guest of honour at a fancy dinner at the British-American club. For me, at the age of nine, it was all a bit above my head but Dad was lauded as a 'genuine sportsman' in the papers. One of the most frequently asked questions from the local scribblers was about why the UK crowds love to see wee men fight in the ring. Dad said, 'The British people just love the little guy. When you get above the middleweight class, people lose interest. Maybe with the little guys they see themselves in the ring.'

Calderwood and Cowboy McCormack are obvious exceptions though the theory has something going for it when you think of Lynch, Jackie Paterson, Walter McGowan and Pat Clinton etc. Calderwood was a huge draw in the States and the Detroit 'Scots' really looked after him well. He had a big limo for his personal use and a wealthy businessman, Jack McPhee, who had been born in Scotland, arranged for him to do his running at the plush Western Golf Country Club. Four or five hundred folk would turn up just to watch his training sessions – more, he joked, than the crowds at some of his fights back home. Big Chic also fought a draw with Henry Cooper's brother Jim and defeated one of the all-time greats, Willie Pastrano. Chic won a British title and had a shot for the world title against Torres. Who knows what would have happened if that little Mini had not crashed in the Clyde Valley.

Calderwood was a rising star in the Gilmour stable in the late fifties. Indeed, I have an advert for Dad's boxers that lists Charlie Hill, the British featherweight champion, above Chic. Curiously the advert claims to be for the Tom Gilmour stable rather than the 'Tommy' used by the reporters. The full list was: Charlie Hill, Chic Calderwood, Jimmy Croll, John Smillie, Arthur Donnachie, Dave Croll, George McDade, Pat Glancy, John O'Brien, Len Mullen, Jackie Brown and Hugh Riley. And there were no security worries in these days as the ad gives our home address, 682 Rutherglen Road, and helpfully supplies the telephone number, SOUth 1708, and adds that the gym number is BRIdgeton 4512. Another ad published around the same time included the invitation, 'We extend a cordial invitation to boxers, managers and all connected with the fight game – when in Glasgow visit our well equipped gym, where all training facilities will be provided free of charge.'

I can't say often enough how much I owe to my dad. We often chatted for hours about the training of fighters. He told me and I now know for myself how important it is to instil confidence in a fighter. Folk who have never been in the business of dealing with celebrities, big names in show business or sport, have no idea about how many of them lack self-belief. I remember reading that Robert Taylor, the Hollywood actor, thought he wasn't good enough to be a 'star'. He used to say there were dozens of actors more deserving of that accolade than he was. He simply did not know how good he was. It is the same with boxers.

Amazingly Chic Calderwood came into that category. Dad would tell me and any newspaperman with a notebook handy that the first lesson he learned in management is that a boxer must have supreme self-confidence and, said The Starmaker, if he hasn't got it, you give it to him. He is on record as saying that it is surprising how many men with a reputation as a hard man in the ring believe that they are not in the top drawer. Dad was quoted as saying:

> My present British cruiserweight [nowadays that would be light-heavyweight] champion Chic Calderwood is a case in point. I expect Calderwood to go further than any boy I have ever handled – and I have handled a few – but it is an almost constant job telling the 'big yin' that he is better than any fighter at his weight in the world today. He just doesn't believe me . . . When he came to me some of the wise guys around the game claimed Chic wasn't game. He is just a few steps off the world crown and these same characters cling to their belief though by now they are saying it out of habit. Calderwood is game enough – and good enough – to win the world title. But I have to keep telling him he can do it.

Dad told me that the turning point in Chic's career was when he fought Yolande Pompey at the Paisley Ice Rink. I was at this fight in March 1959 and, this time, it was my brother Jim who held up the cards. Seemingly, up to this stage, Chic had been making steady progress up the ratings but just how good he could become was not apparent. Chic was a bit shocked to hear he was to tangle with Pompey who had fought for the world title against Archie Moore. When Dad told him, he replied along the lines of, 'You must be joking!' He had to be given what was called a massive dose of Doc Gilmour's confidence pills. 'Son,' Dad said to him:

> I told you I would never rush you . . . that I would pick opponents that you would start level with. You haven't lost a fight

so far. Now it is Pompey's turn – you can go for him and you can take him.

On the big night, Chic was pretty nervous about taking on the man they called 'The Trinidad Terrier' – especially when he saw Pompey calmly sitting on his stool across the ring, looking as if he had not a care in the world. It all started pretty evenly but, at the end of the fifth, Calderwood needed no verbal confidence pills – rather the reverse. There is lot of psychology in the fight game and Dad was not too pleased to see Chic now straining like a racehorse waiting for the off and cockily saying, 'I think I will have a go now. I can trim this one.' 'Aye, aye,' thought Dad, 'I have given him an overdose of confidence – dangerous against an old fox like Pompey.' But, as the last round approached, Chic demanded to be allowed to cut loose. Dad gave the OK and said, 'He's yours.' Calderwood proceeded to knock the Trinidadian out and Pompey never fought again.

The way Chic was dismissed in his early days for lack of courage in the ring reminded me of Ingemar Johannson who was labelled a 'choker' after failing to win the heavyweight final in the Helsinki Olympics. Ingo the Bingo went on to be professional world champ. And down the years I have noted that many of those quick to criticise some boxers and say they have no 'bottle' often get their courage out of a bottle. It is easy to criticise ringside, especially if you are never likely to be inside the ropes yourself.

Sometimes it is reality rather than psychology that a boxer needs. I still laugh to this day when I remember Dad telling me of how nerves affected his boxer Jackie Brown who won the British and Empire flyweight title in the early sixties. Jackie, an Edinburgh man, fought his nerves with a toothbrush. He would clean his teeth a dozen or so times between arriving at the stadium and getting into the ring. Eventually Dad had to inform him, 'You're no going to kiss them, son – just fight them.'

Dad used psychology with Calderwood and other boxers and he could also use his verbal dexterity to his favour in his dealings with other promoters and matchmakers. I remember him telling of the time he was asked by an English matchmaker to provide an opponent for European and Empire welterweight champion Wally Thom. Dad put forward the name of one of his boxers, an African called Vincent Okine, and he told the Englishman that Vincent was 'not much of a boxer'. But, when they met in the ring, the contest was stopped in favour of Okine. Thom's corner were not exactly what you could call happy and challenged Dad about his remark about his man not being much of a boxer. 'That's right,' said The Starmaker, 'but he is a hell of a fighter!' It was honesty without showing all of your cards, you might say.

Another great favourite from around the same era as Calderwood was a remarkable boxer called John 'Cowboy' McCormack from Maryhill. And this is as good a chance as I will get to give the reader the answer to what is a great pub quiz or trivia game question: Who is the only boxer in the history of the sport to be beaten by a fighter with an identical name? Step forward Cowboy! He didn't do much losing in a great career but, in his last fight, he suffered a points' defeat at the hands of an Irish boxer called Young John McCormack. If this little piece of intelligence wins you some cash in a pub bet, I will expect a cheque in the post. The nickname Cowboy came from the shape of his legs – one that was well suited to horse riding. After his retirement, John turned to doing a bit of public speaking and he would remark that, if his legs had been a might straighter, he would have been several inches taller.

Calderwood and McCormack had something of a bitter-sweet rivalry. Both generated immense loyalty in their fans. And despite their weight difference – Cowboy often fought as a middleweight – they did meet in the ring. In 1965 the Maryhill man opened a cut in Calderwood's eye that ended the shoot-out in round two. There was a lot of hype about this bout with some scribes calling it a grudge match but it was all just paper talk.

Mind you, papers can sell tickets for shows and this fight offered a classic example of that. Due to an airport strike – what's new? – Cowboy's training in the Kelvin Arena was disrupted because his two sparring partners from the south failed to appear. Tommy Gilmour Sr pulled a masterstroke. He turned up at the arena in a long coat and a big hat, with a large cigar. He had two fighters, Willie Hart and Willie Fisher, in tow. The boxers stripped and McCormack's training session was saved thanks to the manager of his opponent. Wee Peter Keenan saw an opportunity. He announced to the press guys, 'Methinks that it is something out of order that Mr Gilmour should be present when John McCormack is training. I will call some of my serfs (sic) and have him ejected.' Dad swelled up with dignity and said, 'I grant the point but I will not be ejected. I will quietly walk to the portals and wait there until the training is finished.' 'No, no,' said PK, 'I will have you thrown out – it will make a better story.' Who says there is no fun in boxing?

Cowboy was a one-off, a real Glasgow character. Becoming

the dux of his primary school – St Marie's – was just the start of a career at the top for this smart man. And, according to many ring experts, he could have gone further if he had been a little more of a hard trainer and a little less of a playboy intent on getting the most out of life. But he was fun to be with and, if he smiled a lot, maybe he had a lot to smile about. What a character! He once boxed Len Mullen, known as 'Lenny the Clutch', who my dad managed. He spent a lot of time in the ring holding opponents. He was also a tiptop tailor as a day job. And the tale is told that, when in a clutch with Cowboy, the Maryhill man asked Len if he could run up a suit for him.

Cowboy McCormack boxed out of the famous NB Loco as an amateur. He fought in the Melbourne Olympics and won a bronze. He was defeated by José Torres, mentioned earlier, who went on to win a world title and make a name for himself as an author. Torres said that Cowboy was his toughest-ever opponent. The depth of John's potential as a pro can be gauged by the fact that Sugar Ray Robinson's manager George Gainford wanted him to join his stable in the States. But America was a step too far from his beloved Maryhill. Men who knew boxing saw what he had to offer. He had a couple of memorable fights with Englishman Terry Downes and they ended up mates but their first fight had a sensational ending with Cowboy down on one knee while Downes was disqualified by referee Ike Powell for a low blow. The return was a bloody battle, won by Downes, but the *Daily Mirror*'s famous boxing writer Peter Wilson praised Cowboy for 'some of the rawest courage I have ever seen in a boxing ring'. No wonder he had such a huge fan base in his home area.

And some of his fans were in the press – like that great

character Charlie McGinley who, amongst his other journal-istic skills, was a fixed odds pundit in the days when betting on the result of individual football games was big time. Charlie had grown up in Maryhill and would yield to no one in his admiration for Cowboy. They were both 'Butney Boys' – a proud reference to their home turf. The Butney was a hard tenement area and the name is interesting. It seems that it is derived from Botany as in Botany Bay in Australia. Assorted toerags from around Britain were billeted in this area before heading out across the world in convict ships sailing from Port Glasgow or Greenock. I doubt if the penal settlements they went to in Australia were any tougher than Maryhill in the nineteenth century. Gamblers in Glasgow followed Charlie McGinley's tips in the *Evening Times* with fervour – though he was seldom allowed to forget one bad call. One season Celtic, then in good form, were drawn away to Airdrie in an early round of the Scottish Cup. The bold Mr McGinley advised all his legions of readers to 'put the mortgage on Celtic'. Sadly the hoops had an off day and, for the rest of his career, Charlie had to endure pub talk about lost mortgages.

The folk in Maryhill to this day still love the characterful Cowboy. And no less a connoisseur of the game than former world champion Jim Watt MBE, who these days travels the world commenting and who is respected for his knowledge of the game, says that his favourite Scottish boxer is John 'Cowboy' McCormack, not to be confused, of course, with Young John McCormack who ended his career! Jim Watt and I are great pals and maybe our choice of idols, Calderwood and McCormack, says something about a great era in Scottish boxing.

But the relationship between that other ring giant from

Glasgow, Peter Keenan, and The Starmaker is something else. The word feud is justified in this context though there is no doubt in my mind that, in this dispute, Dad was the legal and moral winner.

The background is complicated. Peter had risen to the top of the heap under the management of The Starmaker. Towards the end of 1951, he was British and European bantamweight champion. The European title had been claimed at Firhill football stadium in a battle with Spaniard Luis Romero. I still have some of the financial records for this fight. The numbers put today's earnings for boxers and managers in a different light. Dad kept meticulous notes, sometimes handwritten in school jotters, of what came in and what went out in the way of money. It is a trait I've inherited. I keep my own records of dealings in a cashbook. If there's a penny out in a total, I will spend hours looking for it despite the fact that the accountants assure me that the figures are rounded up or down to the nearest pound. I want my books to balance. And to be honest I like the challenge of tracking down the source of a discrepancy. I can spend enjoyable hours doing just that. The same trait applies to seating plans for shows – I have got to know exactly where everyone is. Placing the press and celebrities in the right spots is a pleasant duty.

It is interesting today to pore over Dad's records. The terms of a fight with Luis Romero on 5 September 1951, plucked at random from the notebooks, made interesting reading fifty-six years after the event. The terms (what Gilmour let Keenan fight for) were £2,242 12s 6d. At the end of the day, the boxer got £1,567 15s and the manager £489 5s. The expenses for the Romero fight came to a grand total of £467 12s 9d. Of that, £33 9s went in things like taxis and photographs of the fighters.

Another £32 11s was paid out for complimentary tickets as follows:

Father McBride	3
Chic Brogan	4
Jimmy Doyle	4
Butcher	6
Grocer	6
Sparring partners	6
NB Loco hall keeper	2

No wonder we ate well in Rutherglen Road. And our spiritual welfare was in good hands! Other expenses were:

Trainer	£120
Sparring partners	£140
Specialist	£40
Board tax	£96 19s 9d
C.A.	£3 3s
Training camp	£33 9s
Tickets	£34*

*These were probably for sparring partners and helpers.

Keenan is a classic example how a boxer's income fluctuates with the drawing power of the opposition. The terms for a fight in the Kelvin Hall in the spring of '53 against a journeyman called Stan Rowan, two years after the success against Romero, was a mere £400 and the boxer's share just £271 10s. And, in November of that year, PK fought in the Albert Hall, London, for terms of just £350. In between these fights, Keenan

129

took on a much better known man, Maurice Sanderyon, at Firhill Park and the terms were £3,000.

Dad and Peter were not getting along. The problem was money. It is the same these days. When a boxer is fighting for small purses, the manager's 25 per cent does not seem as much. When the boxer, with the manager's help, moves up in class and the purses get bigger, so does the cut and the boxer does not always take that as good news. I make no apology for the manager's commission – anyone who has read this book through will have a pretty good idea what the manager does for his money. In any case, this seems basically the cause of the bad blood between The Starmaker and his biggest star – though I can't resist pointing out the real significance of the nickname always attached to Tommy Gilmour Sr. Stars are made as well as born. Dad told journalist Malcolm Munro of the old *Evening Citizen* that in the early fifties:

> I was Keenan's manager – the guy who arranged his fights, saw that he was making a lot of the folding stuff and that he was in the right place at the right time – but that was all. We didn't speak and the atmosphere that surrounded us both must have affected anyone who came in contact with us. To Keenan I was an extra weight on his finances – an expensive luxury.

At this stage, Keenan was unbeaten in thirty-two fights and some say looking good for another thirty-two. One day, Dad got a call from Glasgow promoter Sammy Docherty who introduced him to a South African businessman who was a member of the Transvaal Boxing Board. This guy came to the point without any delay. Fifteen hundred pounds was on offer for

PK to fight Vic Toweel for the world-title fight in Johannesburg. Malky Munro said it was like a scene from a Hollywood film with the reporters present all the time and buzzing about the offer made to Keenan. At this time, no one was thinking much of the fact that Toweel seldom left his redoubt in South Africa – 6,000ft above sea level – to fight.

On the offer, Dad indicated that he thought the money was not enough but he wanted time to think about it. He meant two or three days for Keenan was on holiday in Dublin and no one knew exactly where. As a manager myself, I know how Dad felt. If he turned the fight down, Keenan, especially the way he felt about his management at the time, would be bitter that a chance for the world title had been missed. The £1,500 was not great since PK had already fought for twice as much. But what would his purses be like if he won the title? While all this was going on in Dad's head, the South African took out a travelling clock and put it on the table in front of him and indicated Dad had an hour to decide.

To stall for time, the South African was asked to send contracts on. Dad only wanted time to contact Peter and see what was what but the reporters jumped the gun and left the meeting to announce the fight was on. At the time, no one knew the trouble all this would cause. A few days later, Jack Solomons, the London promoter, contacted Dad and said, 'How about a world-title fight with Toweel for me. I will give you £2,000.' Solomons was a canny man with money and it did no good to his health when Dad asked for another £500. Remember all this was almost sixty years ago. Solomons was reminded of the verbal offer from South Africa but Dad said, 'I have not heard a cheep from them since. They must have scrubbed the idea. But, just in case, give me a few more days.' No further word came. Keenan was, by now, home from Ireland and didn't like the idea of a title fight with Toweel in the rarefied air of Jo'burg. He wanted to play a waiting game. But Jack Solomons had, by now, set a date for a fight in South Africa. And the British Board of Control ordered PK to fight there in January 1952.

Keenan and Dad were barely talking but the boxer asked the manager if he was going to South Africa with him. Daft question: what manager would not go out for the fight? But Dad was only going for the last few days so Keenan set off with his trainer to prepare and, shortly after he left, all hell broke loose. Word was coming out of Africa that they thought the title fight was theirs, not Jack Solomons'. They told Keenan this. They claimed that The Starmaker had agreed to the fight though no contract or word other than the ones spoken at that first meeting ever materialised. Dad was in trouble. Apparently word-of-mouth agreements were legally binding in South Africa. He was told that, if he kept his word, given to Keenan, to travel to South Africa he would be slapped in jail. He went to the Boxing Board in London who confirmed that was what was likely to happen. All this was happening at a bad time for the family. Mum was worried about what Dad was going to do and they talked it out into the night – they must have been long, anxious hours – but, in the end, Dad said that he always stuck by his fighters and that his place was with Keenan. It was not a pleasant flight to Jo'burg. Keenan and Dad weren't talking. Two different promoters were claiming the fight. And there could be cops at the airport waiting for the plane to land.

Representatives of the two groups, South African and Solomons', connections, waited for him. 'Which lot are you with?' said Keenan and Dad simply replied, 'I am with you.'

Dad was still worrying about the law but, for one reason or another, the case against him for breaking a contract (What contract? The whole thing was a misunderstanding.) was dropped. But the problems were far from over. Toweel had a clause in his contract for a return fight but no such clause was in Keenan's paperwork. Toweel's people wanted to take no risks in case the wee man from Glasgow came to their mountain lair and destroyed their meal ticket. Dad was not having that and, after much argument, the return clause was dropped. Vic Toweel came to our camp himself, fed up with all the haggling and said that they should just get on with the business and that he did not care if there was no return and that they should just let the boxers settle it in the ring.

Despite risking jail for him, despite keeping the title fight and despite getting rid of the return clause, Keenan still wanted nothing to do with my old man. He brought along his trainer Alex Adams to Dad's hotel room days before the fight. He asked for his contract back and was told he could get it if he handed over £3,000. They stormed off. Adams, who later became PK's manager, said, 'He wants to know if you will want more for the contract if he wins the title.' – a no-brainer as they say these days. He was told, 'Naturally.'

At the weigh-in Keenan glowered at Dad and told Solomons he did not want him in his corner. So The Starmaker had travelled thousands of miles to sit in a seat and watch the action unable to do anything about it. Keenan lost the fight on points. Later on, he made much of the problems of fighting at altitude and alleged that he had not had enough time to acclimatise – a debatable point. But my dad told me that, if he had been in the wee man's corner on the big night, the result might have been different.

Back home, all the contract stuff went to a lengthy British Boxing Board of Control inquiry. Dad enlisted the help of Jack Solomons who knew the background to the dispute. In a letter to the London promoter, Dad complained that some newspapers were siding with Keenan and presenting the whole affair as if he 'took a liberty in matching him with Toweel and getting him so little money. And that the public were saying no wonder Keenan wanted rid of Gilmour.' For a time, as The Starmaker put it himself, his 'name was mud'. In the end, the facts of what was much more complicated than had been made out in the press emerged. It was a worrying time for the Gilmours but a field day for the lawyers. In the end the Board of Control inquiry came down heavily in favour of The Starmaker.

Nonetheless wee Peter, a complex man, did a lot of bad-mouthing of my father in the wake of the Toweel fight. A man who knows more than most about this stramash is boxing historian Brian Donald. Back in 1991, Keenan asked Brian to write his biography. Brian agreed and was given access to much original material. The historian liked Peter a lot but told him he reserved his right to draw his own conclusions to anything controversial after he had researched his claims. Brian Donald was not going to write a hagiography of the wee man and, in the event, the book was dropped. Here, however, is what Brian had to say about the relationship between PK and Dad:

Peter was very bitter about Tommy Gilmour Sr and made all sorts of allegations such as he only got £400 in 1952 for challenging Vic Toweel for the undisputed world bantamweight title in South Africa. Mind you, £400 net in 1952 was a fair sum of money but I will talk about that later. Peter also alleged that he had been forced to fight a Glasgow flyweight called Joe Murphy against his will. Murphy had been Peter's best man at his wedding to Cissy. In my researches for the book, I found no evidence at all for this in contemporary press reports. And it is also significant that Peter did not bring this up in his evidence to the Board of Control at the 1953 hearing in his attempt to break his contract with Gilmour Sr.

I had given Brian a transcript of the whole inquiry which, as I mentioned, came down firmly in our favour. Of course, the actual payments for the fight are on record and the £400 claim is nonsense. The Board also pointed out that many of the boxer's complaints were trivial and that many more of his allegations were without foundation.

Brian tells an amusing tale told to him by Keenan in 1991 when they were working on the abortive biography. It was not a story that PK mentioned to the Board inquiry but it shows what a difficult character he was. It seems that, back in May 1951, after Peter had won the British bantamweight title at Firhill, Dad went round to the dressing room and presented the wee guy with a huge celebration cake. Peter proceeded to punch it to bits and leave it lying on the floor. Brian's researches also turned up an interesting cutting from the *Daily Express*. In the same month that Peter was punching cakes as well as bantamweights, his mother was praising The Starmaker's skill in managing her boy.

An entire chapter in the book was to be devoted to the Keenan-Gilmour dispute. In it, Brian came down heavily in favour of Dad. Indeed, he says:

I came to virtually the same conclusions as the transcript of the PK v Tommy Senior hearing before the Board of Control. And that was years before I had seen the transcript. My conclusions

135

were that in 1952 very few British fighters obtained world-title fights as there were only eight world-title holders. The American mob-run International Boxing Club had a strangle hold on most weights between 1946 and 1963 so it was a remarkable feat for Tommy to swing a world-title fight PK's way.

Brian went on to say that PK's moaning about being paid low purses doesn't stack up when you examine his fifties' lifestyle – large houses in upmarket areas of Glasgow, including a mansion in the Charing Cross area, complete with private gym, his son Peter Jr being privately educated at St Joseph's in Dumfries, the cars and many other trappings of success that Peter provided for his wife Cissy and his family. Brian's considered conclusion was that PK and Dad were simply two people who were personally incompatible. He told me that Keenan 'hated taking orders from anyone' and that Dad also liked to be in charge, remarking, 'What manager in any walk of life doesn't?'

Brian says Peter gave much of his attitude to life away when he told him a story from his early days. His ability as a boxer helped present him with the opportunity of a good-paying job as a chauffeur to the chairman of the NB Loco company. Peter would not touch it because, in his words, 'it meant wearing a uniform and I was nobody's flunky'. Brian Donald says:

Peter was a supreme individualist and no one managing him would have had an easy time as he loathed authority figures, something Tommy Sr increasingly came to become in PK's mind. All this despite the fact that his manager steered him to British, Empire and European titles at a time when many top quality boxers, with loads of bouts and successful records, never even saw an Area title fight. PK just ignored this. Even so I cherish his memory and have a huge admiration of his feats in becoming Scotland's first and thus far only double Lonsdale belt outright winner. But I equally feel that Tommy Gilmour Sr did a marvellous job of managing him throughout his career.

It's all a bit sad when you think back of the early days of the Gilmours and the Keenans and my own great relationship with Peter, a relationship that survived the ups and downs of big-time boxing in and out of the ring. In the end, they started talking again and, in 1974, they both helped publicise a Bill Bryden play about Benny Lynch's tragic life. Lynch was Scotland's first world champion but he could not beat the bottle and died at thirty-three. His ability in the ring was matched by his talent for self-destruction. The play's programme notes remarked that 'maybe his boxing will not be matched but when they buried Benny they did not throw away the mould'. Sadly the tragic ends to successful careers in the ring of some modern Scots have shown that to be a remarkably perceptive comment.

It is also interesting to recall that, despite the ferocity of some of the disputes between Dad and PK, Dad always insisted that Peter was the best boxer he ever had. And, whenever there was any argument about who was Scotland's top wee fighter, Lynch, Keenan or Jackie Paterson, Dad always came down for Peter – no argument, he was the best. The feud was, in reality, a clash of personalities though there is no doubt Keenan did not enjoy paying his 25 per cent to Dad. I have had similar complaints from some of my own fighters from time to time. There is a way to silence them. I say OK, you promote instead of me. I take the 25 per cent and tell them: 'You pay the hall, the boxers on the undercard, give them as much as you like, all the associated expenses like advertising, programmes etc. I get my percentage if the show makes money – if it loses money you pay it all.' I get a lot of wry smiles from the moaners but no takers for the proposition.

11

A 'PULSATING STRUGGLE FOR SUPREMACY'

My father liked to reminisce when he had the rare chance to put his feet up and when the worries of days at the gym and betting shop had slipped away – perhaps eased into the background with a wee cup of tea or maybe a dram. He had stories galore about old Jim and his own early days in the east end, a place rich in characters. One of the most memorable of these was Mattha Gemmell who trained Bridgeton and Rutherglen's football team, Clyde, for many years.

Dad blamed old Mattha for making him utter his first swear word. The eye problems that kept Dad out of the ring did not stop him being a bit of a track athlete. Still at school in Bridgeton and aged only fourteen, he entered Clyde's sports day. At this time, most football clubs had an annual open sports day in the close season. One year, Dad won twenty-six of the twenty-seven events he entered – things like sprinting, the high jump, tug o' war, five-a-side football etc. On this occasion, he took a bad tumble on the gravel track, badly cutting knees and hands. Mattha appeared and carried him bodily into the inner sanctum of Shawfield stadium, to the treatment room beneath the stands, and set about him with an old scrubbing brush and a bucket of water and disinfectant to remove the stones and gravel from the bleeding wounds. This was done energetically. The old man who had never sworn in his life at that point cried out, 'Mattha, you old b*****!'

If you got him with a moment to spare, Dad told entertaining stories of the game. Remember he had 'managed' his first boxer in 1924 when he was only fourteen. This was before the Board of Control was founded and the sport was much less regulated than it is today. One of his best tales was about his first legitimate boxer, a wee fellow called Paddy Docherty. Dad told Malcolm Munro of the old *Evening Citizen* that 'Paddy was so slight that 'you could pick him up with one hand'. He weighed 7st 4lb when dripping wet but had beaten Benny Lynch three times as an amateur and he had a great following in the city. Publicists these days think they are big shots when they come up with titles like The Thriller in Manila (Ali v Frazier) or The Rumble in the Jungle (Ali v Foreman) or even The Midnight Maelstrom (Watt v O'Grady in downtown Glasgow) but copywriting skills have been around for years in the fight game.

In my archives, I have a programme for a Premierland promotion of my grandfather in Main Street, Bridgeton. In it Paddy is described as 'a boy with pep, punch and personality, now back to his best form'. His opponent 'Ginger M'Leod (*sic*)' is called 'a rugged two-handed fighter who has fought all the best boys in England'. Fans are urged not to 'miss this pulsating struggle for supremacy'. That night, 9 September 1932, featured ten boxers and showed how local the fight game was at that time. All stayed not far from Premierland. The farthest travelled was 'Seaman' Nobby Hall, all the way from Peebles. The others listed their bases as Glasgow, Glasgow south side, Whitevale, Clydebank, Shettleston, Townhead, Hamilton and Parkhead. Doors opened at 7.30, which seems early nowadays for a Friday night, and the boxing started at a quarter to eight. Admission, 'tax included', was seven pence or one shilling and thruppence.

Boxers like young Paddy fought many times a week in the ring or at the booths in Glasgow Green and elsewhere. Boxing booths were a big part of the showground scene in those days and, in the summer, the boxers travelled to the seaside resorts with the showmen as they moved round a regular circuit. There was even booth fighting as far north as Wick. The boxers themselves often transported and erected the ring and frequently slept under its shelter when on the road in the summer. A great character from these days was Puggy Morgan who managed Lynch after he had left managers Sammy Wilson and George Dingley. Puggy was weel kent, as they say, in all the many gyms in Glasgow in the great old days before the Second World War. At an early age I used to sit on his knee at the shows.

As well as keeping the late Malcolm Munro in touch with what was happening in boxing on an almost day-to-day basis, Dad also told him a few home truths about boxing managers. Munro was a larger-than-life character who made his name with the old *Evening Citizen* where he was dubbed 'The Heavyweight Champion of the Fans'. In those days, Glasgow had three evening papers, the *Evening News*, the *Evening Times* and the *Evening Citizen*. It seemed that every street corner echoed to the newsvendors' cries of '*Times, News* and *Citi-zeen*'. All the evenings had Saturday sports editions and the *Citizen* was printed on green paper on Saturday nights while the *Times* was on pink paper. Back then, I, like every other kid on the street, waited patiently at around half past five or a quarter to six for the vans carrying the papers to pull up outside the newsagent shops where the bundles of papers were thrown on the pavement while the vans accelerated away to the next stop. The 'green un' and the 'pink un' as those editions of the *Citizen* and the *Times* were called, were packed with the Saturday afternoon results, columns and analysis and speculation about the sporting week ahead. Football was king then but boxing, too, got massive coverage and I devoured every word. It is worth remembering that, at the time, there were around twenty regular venues for boxing in and around Glasgow.

It was also fascinating to remember that the Saturday afternoon football games all ended around 4.45 and, just three quarters of an hour later, you could buy a paper with up-to-date results and tables. It was some achievement for the old-time journos and print workers, considering this was long before the days of computerised typesetting. The hot metal journalists and printers had tremendous skills. This was the sort of environment that guys like Malcolm Munro worked in and the big names in the papers were celebrities every bit as much as the folk they wrote about. Malcolm was a fine writer but a bit of a gambler and a man who would have fitted neatly into a Damon Runyon storyline. His eccentricity ran to a habit of seldom wearing a raincoat, even in the heaviest of downpours, and arriving at fights or football matches without the must-have spiral reporter's notebook carried by his rivals. He would plant himself down on the press benches and ask whoever was seated beside him for a few sheets to be torn from their notebook. Then he borrowed a pen or pencil and he was ready to file some of the great copy he was known for in his early days.

The old-time sports writers had the ear of the football and boxing managers and they worked together. The managers gave the writers the inside stories for the readers which helped sell papers and the stories helped sell tickets so it was to their mutual benefit to be cooperative – it also meant that both sides kept their jobs. So Dad always kept big Malky well informed and sometimes he explained his deepest thinking about the game. Dad told big Malky that he always tried to get the best deal for his boys – as I continue to do. In one big interview with Munro, he emphasised that he was opposed to the idea of boxers hitting the big time and deciding to manage themselves. He put it this way:

> A manager is, or should be, the protector of his charges. He is the buffer between the boy and the press and the promoter and the public. If a lad is asked to fight so-and-so and refuses, he may be goaded. Are you afraid? And the reply is that he is afraid of no one and the result is that he ends [up being] over-matched.
>
> No boxer of any standing admits to anyone, least of all himself, that he is frightened. Sometimes though he is pleased to have a manager who can make excuses for him. In the long run it is worth the percentage he pays.

Maybe Peter Keenan could have reflected on that.

Dad didn't do too much philosophising but, when he spoke, there was a lot to learn. He taught me that hype plays a large part in the boxing game but, even more importantly, he told me that, in promotion and management, your word must be your bond, no matter what. I found out what he meant when one of his fighters tried to hold him to ransom at the last minute for more money. Rather than break his word to the promoter, my dad offered to forgo his commission. The fight did not take place because of illness and this was the last time my dad had any association with this boxer.

143

Dad was the best fight manager I ever saw. I was always picking up good advice from him. For example, he told me to beware of talking too much to a boxer between rounds. Pick out the most important points of advice to give your man and keep it short. Sometimes he'd just say, 'Breathe.' And, between rounds, it's gulps of air that a fighter needs more than anything – not a lecture. Dad was a great teacher and would even go into the ring with a fighter to show him how to improve his technique. A remarkable man.

12

CIGAR SMOKE, BURGUNDY AND BLOOD

When your dad is a famous manager with his face in the papers on a daily basis, even a kid can understand that there is not too much time to play Ludo or Snakes and Ladders at home – especially if, as well as being Scotland's Mr Big in boxing, you know he has a few bookies' shops to take care of as well. Tommy Gilmour Sr was a busy man. But we did play one little game together – one that was rather different, I expect, from the games of Monopoly or whatever that my pals at school would play with their parents.

Our house was always full of newspapers and racing papers but pride of place went to the magazines *Boxing News, Boxing Illustrated* and the beautifully produced glossy *Ring* magazine, which also featured quality writing on the sport. I digested the magazines down to the last item, as did Dad and my brother Jim. I suspect even Mum had a quiet look at them. A major component in such magazines is the ratings given to the best boxer at each weight and the best boxer in each country or continent. It was a big excitement to watch the changes daily and monthly. If you got a good, stylish points' win or a quick KO against a quality opponent, you went up the ratings but, if you lost a couple of bouts, you'd be on the slide. And it was fun to disagree with the ratings – especially if a favourite wasn't given the respect you thought he deserved.

From the earliest days, along with my dad, I used the magazine ratings to play an imaginary role as matchmaker. I would peruse the various lists and speculate about putting Boxer A against Boxer B in fights that would pull the crowd and give a real show of boxing skills. Dad would play along and give me his comments on my suggestions – sometimes dismissing them and sometimes agreeing that so-and-so against so-and-so would be some fight. If he disagreed with me, he always told me in detail why a suggestion was not a good match. From an early age, I was honing my skills as a matchmaker and that would serve me well in the future. What's more, I was learning from a master without realising it.

So it was really no great surprise that, all through my career as an engineer, I harboured the notion that, some day, I would be a promoter myself. Dad had, of course, been everything in the game – cornerman, trainer, cuts man. He could do all the jobs himself but, as his career grew in importance, he gradually distanced himself from the hands-on role of trainer to concentrate on matchmaking and managing. Latterly, the training of the biggest names in the stable became the responsibility of Dunky Jowett.

Legendary is the most overused adjective in sports writing but it really is the only one that properly describes Dunky. In my schooldays, I met him on an almost daily basis and learned so much from him. It wasn't like learning at school – there were no long sessions of tuition. I just watched the man in action, asked the odd question and had fun. But it was also an education – you can't buy something like that.

However, I think that maybe, at an early stage, I had a

slightly flawed conception of what a boxing manager did – and I think the same could be said for my brother Jim too. During a bit of social chat between more important matters, he was asked the question that's always thrown at kids: 'What do you want to do when you grow up?' This when his feud with wee Peter Keenan was at its height and my dad exploded at the answer. Jim wanted to be a boxing manager like my dad 'and not work'.

But, of course, I worked for almost twenty years in the printing engineering game. Dad had had lots of cash through his hands in his days at the top. In the bookie business, it comes across the counter fast but it can also go quickly. And boxing promoting can be a big gamble. Towards the end of his life, Dad had to face up to both a slump in boxing's popularity and big changes in the betting industry. We had gone from the days of back-street betting and raids by the police to a time when the local bookie was part of the city streetscape. Glasgow had a goodly share of bookies, each with a handful of shops, stands at the dog tracks and racecourses. There were household names with loyal punters – people like John Banks and Tony Queen – but a big squeeze was to come and the national groups like Ladbrokes and William Hill and the Tote began to open flashy places in every city and town. Gradually the Gilmour betting empire shrank under the onslaught of such big-timers. He also had the inevitable wrangles with the taxman but, even when squeezed by the authorities, he retained his natural cheerfulness and good manners.

After his death, we even got a nice wee letter from the tax folk saying what a great guy he was to deal with and passing on their condolences. We were never on our uppers but, by the time I was ready to leave school, a regular job was a must.

When he died, Dad was no longer a wealthy man, the battles with the taxman and the changes in the bookmaking and boxing scenes saw to that. But he was an open and generous man who had enjoyed a full life with huge memories of the fun days and, to the end, he loved life with his family. Even in the sadness of his death, the notion to getting into boxing promotion in a serious way was always in the background of my thinking.

I had, of course, never left the game. I was always about the gym when not at work or courting Veronica. Boxing is much more tightly regulated than those outside the sport understand and rightly so since it is a contact sport where the participants risk serious injury or even, sadly and very rarely, death. You need a separate licence for every job – the second, matchmaker, manager, trainer etc. I was a mere eighteen years old in April 1970 when I got my first licence as a second. This little piece of paper opened up a new world to me. I even got to go to London and the famous National Sporting Club when one of our guys fought there.

Maybe that is where I got the bug for club boxing that led to me owning the St Andrew's Sporting Club later in life. The National in London was an institution. If you took away the boxing nights, it was similar to many of the other places in London's famous club land. Good, simple food – the sort its members had got used to in public school. The Gordon Ramsays of this world would disparagingly call it nursery food but it can still be sampled in such as Claridges if you ignore the blandishments of the modern menu designed to attract the 'foodies'. The National had the obligatory huge leather armchairs and was well heated on a winter's day. The broadsheets were at hand and an array of waiters armed with silver trays were ready to bring you a whisky and soda or perhaps a port or brandy.

On boxing nights, the members ate under chandeliers amid the highly polished wood and brass of the dining room and then proceeded into an anteroom set up for boxing. They sat in comfortable chairs with little tables at their side to place the port on. In the National, the tradition was that they watched the fights in silence, only breaking into applause when the bell to signal the end of a round had echoed round the smoke-filled arena (most of the smoke coming from expensive Cuban cigars). The action could be fast and furious. I remember hearing of a regular reporter there, Bill Brown, London editor of the old *Evening Citizen*, who told the desk back in Glasgow that he was filing some great copy after a night when so much blood flowed at ringside he 'had to change his white shirt three times'. On nights like that, the members would show their appreciation of the boxers' efforts by throwing 'nobbins' (coins and notes) into the ring. Excitement there may have been but I also saw for myself many an old member of the club nodding off during a bout after a port too far and a tiring day of watching his investments grow.

My part in this 'glamour' included washing out the gumshields and generally assisting the other more experienced cornerman who sometimes would be Dunky Jowett. We worked hard in those days. The boxers all had other jobs and took the minimum time off to maximise their earnings. It was normal to take an early train from Glasgow Central to Euston in the morning and pitch up at the Regent's Palace Hotel – a place much beloved by the Tartan Army of football supporters on their annual trek to Wembley to see Scotland take on England (though in those days the term Tartan Army had not been coined and the supporters themselves were a bit rowdier than the modern lot who live their theme song 'Que Sera, Sera'). Rooms for the afternoon and early evening had been booked.

We then took the fighters out for a light lunch, steering them, sometimes with difficulty, away from steak pie or sausage and mash in favour of a small portion of chicken or fish. Then it was back to the hotel for the fighters to have a snooze while the trainers, seconds etc. went to the pictures. After the fight, we'd head for the station and the sleeper home. It was tiring but we had a lot of fun on those trips south.

We also got into a few scrapes. I remember one of the afternoon trips to the cinema vividly. We were watching a Bruce Lee movie. There was lots of noise and lots of violence but that didn't stop Tommy Sr doing what he often did at the cinema – falling asleep. And, once he'd dropped off, boy, could he snore. I'd have to keep nudging him but no sooner had I woken him than still he fell asleep again. On this particular occasion, he annoyed the punter in front of him so much that he turned round, chinned the old man and ran from the theatre. It didn't stop future visits to the cinema – he just took a headguard and gumshield with him!

On another occasion, we took our boxer to Topo Gigio's, a favourite Italian restaurant in Soho. Getting there involved a stroll through the streets of the notorious red-light area. The girls were gathering for long hours of work and, during our stroll, they often approached us. When this happened, Dad kept them away from the boxer and spoke to them himself as our lad was naive and on his first visit to the Big Smoke. During lunch, he remarked to Dad that he must be very well known in London judging by the number of folk who spoke to him.

We did not explain what was going on. Why spoil a reputation for popularity?

We were always exhausted on our return to Glasgow but, during this time, I was lucky indeed that, at the print works, I had a wee cubbyhole where I could catch up on my sleep as the guys looked out for me and covered up. I thank them yet again! Happy days. Mind you, these wee sleeps at work were snatched and likely to be interrupted. I envied the guys at places like the Rolls-Royce plant in East Kilbride where I was told some crafty engineers on night shift managed to have real beds hidden away in the factory. Skivers, yes, but crafty with it. Money lost by me on days off to do some boxing business had to be made up with nights of overtime at time and a half.

It was almost nine years after getting my second's licence before I got my licence as a matchmaker. I think I am a pretty good one and all that fantasy matchmaking from the lists in the boxing mags with The Starmaker helped. One of the promoters I was involved with was a friend called Philip McLaughlin. I had helped him with various bills in venues throughout Ireland. This was in the late seventies and the early eighties and I did all the arranging from my Glasgow base. Like a lot of folk, I found many an excuse not to travel to Ireland during those troubled times. Although I was heavily involved in the matchmaking, I did not see the contests. But, in May '81, Philip was moving up a class or two in the promoting game and he had a big event arranged for Dublin's Dalymount Park, home of the Bohemian Football Club. This show was the biggest Philip had been involved in and top of the bill was a European championship lightweight fight between Charlie Nash from Derry and Italian Joey Gibilisco.

Philip needed all the help he could get for this show which was in the open air, always a problem in these rainy isles of ours. It was scheduled to go out on the BBC and was also on Italian TV live. It was a big deal. Phil Coulter, the Irish songwriter, performer and music producer, had even come up with a specially written anthem for the occasion. Coulter, a good pal of Philip, comes from Derry where his father was a policeman. He knew a thing or two about life in Northern Ireland during the Troubles. Indeed, in one of his most popular songs, 'The Town I Loved so Well', he talks about that troubled city and 'that dammed barbed wire'. Philip wanted it to be a really special night.

Troubles or not, I had to go over. My brother-in-law Richard went with me to Dublin and he was pleased to do so as he had many friends in the area. A limo picked me up at the airport and I was taken to the Gresham Hotel. I seemed to be important enough to have a nice large suite in this Dublin landmark, opened in 1817, in O'Connell Street. A place of grandeur and elegance, with Waterford crystal chandeliers and a massive grand staircase to greet the guests, Philip was doing things in style.

As I worked on the details of the show from the luxury of the Gresham, in the background, there was tension in the air. Bobby Sands was on hunger strike in jail up north and, in many parts of Ireland, there were marchers on the streets demanding he be freed. It made me and most folk connected with the show feel uneasy. The atmosphere is hard to describe but it was scary and, to make matters worse, the rain had started to pour down – just what you don't need for an open-air show. I did what was asked of me and was just beginning to feel happier about the whole thing when I arrived at the stadium on the morning of the fight. I was checking out seating and other details when I glanced at the ring itself and asked the guys building it when the canvas would arrive. I was told that what I was looking at – the worst sort of painter's dustsheet – was it. I have never seen a canvas on a ring in worse condition – it was dirty and full of holes. A nightmare. We had a problem. I asked when the last professional show in the city had been staged and was told it had been nine years since a big event. In July '72, Muhammad Ali had fought Al 'Blue' Lewis. I asked the obvious – where was the canvas for that fight now? One of the builders working on the ring thought of someone who would know. And sure enough, when we tracked this fellow down, there was the canvas neatly wrapped up in his garage. The show was saved.

It was a historic night in one sense for one of Ireland's greatest fighters, Barry McGuigan, made his professional debut against Manchester's Selvin Bell and won in the second round. But that was really the only bright spot. Just before the gates opened, I'd gone back to Dalymount, this time in my dinner suit, white shirt and bow tie, for a final check. I was still pretty edgy about the tension around as a result of the ongoing Bobby Sands story and because the papers seemed full on nothing else but the Troubles. As I was checking one row of ringside seats, there was an almighty bang in the background. I threw myself full length on to the rain- and mud-soaked seats and lay there waiting to see what happened next. After what seemed like minutes, I got to my feet to see a group of Irishmen laughing their heads off. They had set off some firecrackers. I felt daft but better safe than sorry. My clothes were ruined but I managed to borrow a new suit and the BBC's famous boxing commentator, Harry Carpenter, was able to lend me a bow tie.

The rain still continued to pelt down, as it can in Dublin, and the misery of the night went on. The gate receipts were poor, the crowd small and Charlie Nash lost. What an experience.

13

THE SKIPTON WEASEL,
THE PLAZA AND A PEASOUPER

The Starmaker and old Jim Gilmour usually promoted under their own names but I started out with something called H and G Promotions. No prizes for spotting where the 'G' comes from but the story of the 'H' is interesting. In the old Bridgeton print works, I had, as I explained, somehow or other, found myself in the shop steward business – maybe it had something to do with my tendency to be a bit of a control freak. Our wee works in the east end was small beer to some of the other big engineering places in what they call Greater Glasgow. Out on the motorway to Edinburgh, at Holytown, the American corporation Terex had a massive facility for the manufacture of giant pieces of earth-moving equipment. They employed hundreds so a place that size needed good union representation and good leadership. The shop-floor boys out there were looked after by a really smart operator called Henry Hoey. When not talking union business and comparing our problems we talked boxing. Henry had an interest in the sport as a former pro who now trained Willie Booth, an up-and-coming lightweight from Airdrie managed by my dad. He had the ear of his bosses who had thoughtfully provided the workforce with a large canteen – an ideal place, thought Henry and I, for a boxing show. The Terex top brass were up for it as a good night out in the canteen after work would, no doubt, they thought, help keep the employees in the right frame of mind for churning out bits and pieces for earth movers and the like the next morning. I suspect they did not think through the Scottish working man's good night out and its inevitable result – a stinking hangover which was not the best aid to production.

Be that as it may, our first promotion as H and G was a great success. Willie Booth topped the bill beating a north of England fighter Don Burgin on points. Neither were classic stylists but both were known to give value for money and the audience in the Terex canteen that night liked what they saw. And the success of the occasion encouraged Henry and me to go on to other promotions. We also did some shows with Eddie Coakley before we all just decided to go our own ways. Eddie was a pal of Jim Watt and was in the motor trade, working for motor-racing star Ninian Sanderson who had a Citroën franchise in the city. Ninian was a bit of a maverick. He had won Le Mans and he liked practical jokes – his idea of fun ran to sticking a fire-cracker up an opponent's exhaust. His death from cancer in '85 was big loss to Scottish sport. I was, by this time, still match-making, managing, training and promoting and had plenty on my hands. Co-promoting can be problematic but I have been very lucky in my partnerships – especially with Barry Hearn. Even when my son Christopher started out as a promoter himself, I limited myself to advice and guidance when asked. There can only be one boss in a promotion and you have to make your own decisions. Of course, sometimes you also make own mistakes but you learn from them. The Terex show and others like it made, say, a few hundred pounds – not big money even then but it was enough to keep us going. It all led to those chicken-in-a-basket nights in places such as the Plaza.

At this time the big-time boxing was in decline in the city – the days of huge crowds in stadiums for fights starring Jackie Paterson and Peter Keenan were now history. But there would be a revival years later with people like Ken Buchanan, Jim Watt and Pat Clinton and national TV interest. But, for now, it was a slog round small halls where five or six hundred people made up a good crowd and you had to work your butt off getting a little publicity in the papers, sticking up posters and generally trying to create interest.

It was during this period of learning how to squeeze profit out of small shows that I began to realise the value of sponsorship. And one of the first to back us was that remarkable Maryhill figure, Peter Ferguson. Peter was the king of the carpet business in Glasgow. Until he and a few other smart entrepreneurs figured out there was big money to made selling carpets, the folk in Glasgow tenements generally got by on some old lino to cover the floors of their flats. Peter and a few others got rich on the changing trends as tenement dwellers were decanted to new flats in housing schemes and carpets rather than lino became a must. It was a no-lose situation because the folk left in the tenements suddenly all wanted carpets to keep up with those in the new flats. Peter was just one of many huge characters who seem to come out of Maryhill all the time and, as a boxing fan, he put his money where his mouth was and helped the game over a rough patch. Peter was not alone. Other fans, who had, say, lorries for a building business or whatever, would let us use them for transporting rings etc. And income from adverts in the programmes was also useful. There was a hard core of businessmen who could be relied on to take out an advert even for small promotions. The love of the game shown by such folk helped keep things turning over till the new era arrived and boxing, other than in the sporting clubs which seemed immune to the turndown, made a comeback.

During this time, I was still doing some matchmaking and one of the guys I depended on a lot for help on what was going on south of the border was the man they call 'The Skipton Weasel'. If you wanted to keep up to speed, you needed to talk to Graham Lockwood, aka The Skipton Weasel. Boxing is rich in characters but one of the most memorable is without doubt Graham, a man not too well known to the fans but genuinely legendary with the insiders. When I think back on the last thirty years or so and remember the people who have worked with me and helped me, his name leaps out. I first came across him when he was working with a former heavyweight from Yorkshire called Ken Richardson. Ken was a joiner who managed a few boxers and Graham Lockwood and his friend Jim Devaney Sr worked with him. Ken often brought fighters north for my shows. One night (I was still an engineer for the day job at this time!) after a fight had been arranged, I got a telephone call to say that Graham Lockwood didn't think it was a good match. That got my blood pressure up a bit and I demanded to know who the hell Graham Lockwood was. Over the next twenty-five years, I found out. During that time, Graham became one of the busiest and best matchmakers of his era – perhaps any era for that matter.

After their association with Ken ended, Graham and his pal Jimmy Devaney moved camp to work for another former heavy-weight from Yorkshire, John Celebanski, who was a very active promoter and manager in Leeds and Bradford. Big John was the brother-in-law of Richard Dunn who boxed Muhammad

Ali for the world title. Boxing is a contact sport and, in the ring, there is no quarter given or asked but boxing folk themselves, in their private lives, can find it easy to form life-long friendships. John and his wife Jean became very good friends of Veronica and myself. At this time, Graham was making a bit of a name for himself and helping John to groom his stable of boxers. He was making regular trips north to the St Andrew's Sporting Club for fights arranged by matchmaker Les Roberts, another great character. Anyone who ever met Les would, I suggest, agree with me that, if Hollywood ever embarked on a remake of *Grumpy Old Men*, he would have been a shoo-in for one of the lead roles and he would probably win an Oscar. I was now extremely busy matchmaking myself as well as running the odd show but I had all the time in the world for Graham. We gradually created a great mutual respect as we helped each other building up our careers.

At this stage, I was working for four or five promoters while Graham, at busy periods, was working for as many as fifteen, five of them in the north-east of England alone. As one season followed another, we were beginning to work more and more closely. Graham and John Celebanski were bringing along a British super-featherweight champion John Doherty and they needed help to secure a shot at the European title. I bid for the fight and won it but, due to injury, John Doherty didn't box. That though was the real start of our long and fruitful relationship. Now I was managing and promoting and I used to speak with Graham on the phone every night for at least an hour and a half. The only exception was when Graham was just in from work and 'going t'bath' or on a Saturday night when he was 'going to t'pub' – he sounded like an early version of Peter Kay. During these marathon conversations, we discussed

159

matches we might make and exchanged gossip about the boxing world and the events of the day generally. I was, of course, still an engineer and Graham's day job was as a gravedigger – an ideal job we used to joke when we were trying to dig up an easy opponent. Graham built up great confidence in me and was always ready to tell others to seek my help to move their fighters on.

One of the first fighters Graham got me involved with was Derek Roche who was managed by John Celebanski. Derek boxed out of Leeds but was Irish and proud of it. I became his joint manager and he went on to win a Lonsdale belt outright and box for a world title – not a bad start for so early in my career.

How Graham got that nickname of The Weasel is a good tale. As I mentioned, he and I were great natterers on the phone and it was during one of our long chats that I heard about something he had learned regarding one of the boxers I was associated with. I took it upon myself to speak to the boxer concerned who immediately said to me, 'Who told you that? Was it that weasel Graham Lockwood?' It was said in a more amusing fashion than it sounds when written down. In fact, it was an acknowledgement of how good Graham's networking was. Whatever went on in boxing, he knew about it. Graham's home base was Skipton in Yorkshire and, from then on, his nickname – The Skipton Weasel – stuck. It really became a term of endearment and I think he secretly enjoyed it.

One of my other true friends in the boxing world from this time was Tommy Conroy from Sunderland. Like the Lockwoods and the Hearns, we became friends with Tommy and his wife Annette, attending weddings and family functions. Tommy and I worked together from the early eighties when he used to bring boxers up to my shows in the County Inn, Cambuslang, which, like the Plaza, has been swept away by the wreckers' ball and replaced by housing. Tommy was now handling a tough Geordie called John Davison. His reputation was such that it was becoming difficult to get him fights and The Weasel suggested Tommy and I become co-managers. It was a typically wise Weasel suggestion. We won the British title with John and he went on to box for the European title and lost a split decision to Steve Robinson (more about him later in the book) for the world title.

By now Graham and I were working closer than ever and he was always on the lookout for boxers. He took the view that, if I went full-time, it would benefit boxers and managers as there were only a few full-time promoter/managers around. Most of the other managers had businesses to run and their love of the game had them involved as a hobby. Graham was working with Jack Doughty who also ran a successful family business that took up a lot of his time. The Weasel suggested a co-management arrangement with Jack. This was another of his good ideas. We got a big purse for a Derek Wormald fight against Ritchie Woodhall for the European title. Incidentally Ritchie went on to be a successful BBC commentator.

This bit of co-management was a good fit. Jack trained the guys and I went on the hunt for opportunities for them. It was very successful with Adey Lewis, Bobby Vanzie and Charlie Shepherd. Adey won a British title and fought for a world crown. Bobby won a Lonsdale belt outright and was Commonwealth champion. But it was Charlie who exceeded all our expectations, winning British, Commonwealth and world titles. And, in 1999, along with Barry Hearn, I promoted Charlie in a world-title bout with the American Tom Johnson. It was another version of the fever that gripped Glasgow for the Clinton fight against Perez. In some ways, it was even more intense because Glasgow is used to hosting huge sporting events. The city is home to two of the greatest football teams in the world who play to crowds of around 60,000 week in and week out. And Glasgow has spawned a truckload of boxing legends. The city is no stranger to big-time sport while Carlisle, on the other hand, is the sort of place where people drop in to see the castle or snatch a cuppa in the station when changing trains for the lakes or whatever. The venue for Charlie's attempt on the world title was the Sands Centre and, within forty minutes of the seats going on sale, every one was gone. It was amazing. The tickets I had held back for an emergency were sold in the initial rush and I even had to sell the seat held for John McDonald, the MC.

Charlie had a huge following in Carlisle and, not surprisingly, this was the first world-title fight in the border town. The whole community got right behind us, not only snapping up the tickets at high speed but helping with sponsorship. For example, a great guy called Roland Stanwix, who ran a holiday park company at Silloth, stepped in to sponsor Charlie. The feeling in the town in the run-up to the fight was electric; there was an enormous buzz about the place. And when the MC announced that Charlie had beaten Tom Johnson to take the title, I would not say the roof of the Sands Centre was in danger in the same way as that of the Kelvin Hall when Clinton won but it was certainly given a good old rattle.

The Skipton Weasel was the man responsible for mapping out good careers for hundreds of boxers. He brought me in to form a co-management agreement with Chris Aston and, this time, the main boxers were James Hare, Mark Hobson and Dale Robinson. James Hare and The Weasel had a real rapport and

Hare won a Commonwealth title as well a version of the world title. He was also a success in tournaments promoted by Barry Hearn's Ringside Promotions' agreement with Naseem Hamed and his brothers. James was very popular in and around Huddersfield and was what every promoter looks for – a good ticket-seller. Our MC John McDonald, a colourful Londoner, often worked a nickname or so into his introductions. He labelled James 'Lord of the Manor' which somewhat embarrassed the boxer but he took it in the good fun that was intended by John. Mark Hobson also won British and Commonwealth titles and had a world-title shot in his time with me. Wee Dale was a 'cheeky chappie' and he signed for Chris and me. Before he signed, we met his parents and I still have a note from them thanking us for 'making it easy' to make a decision on a management team.

Our success with James and Mark led to us being approached with a view to speaking to Jawaid Khaliq. 'Jav' had only lost once as a pro and was looking for a new manager. We took him to Commonwealth and IBO world titles. He was one of the nicest people you could meet and we became close. He left the ring as an undefeated world champion and, in retirement, was awarded the MBE. He was the first boxer I had been involved with to gain such an honour. In sport, there is an old saying that the 'first' leads to repeat success so I was really pleased later when John McDermott who had trained Pat Clinton for me was awarded the MBE in 2006. John is responsible for many of my young boxers, including my heavyweight hope Ian Millarvie. Ian could be something special – indeed, he could make history. Despite the successes of all the wee guys, Clinton, McGowan, Paterson and Lynch and others, Scotland has never had a heavy fight for the British title. That's a target.

Incidentally, although wee Walter Gans was not one of Dad's boxers, his father, the legendary Joe Gans, had worked for the Gilmours at one time. But, when Walter started to chase a world title, old Joe was the man at the helm working with promoter Jack Solomons. But the two families always remained close.

All this success – it included co-management with Steve Woods of Jamie Moore, a British titleholder – was, in a large part, down to the skill of Graham Lockwood. As well as making good matches in the ring, he was an expert in bringing interested parties together. In addition to matchmaking for me, he worked for Barry Hearn's Matchroom Boxing. This linked him closely with Barry's director of boxing, the quiet and unassuming John Wischhusen. The name was a bit of a mouthful so he became 'Johnny Wish'. Fair dealing is at a premium in boxing and Graham Lockwood, a true friend and loyal associate, never once asked for more, or would accept more, than his matchmaking salary for anything else he had sparked off by way of introductions, meetings etc. Graham has now retired and I, for one, believe it is a great loss to boxing. I am glad that writing this book has given me a chance to publicly thank him for all that he did for me.

The early years promoting in Scotland was a time spent dodging about such places as the Plaza and Govan Town Hall. I will never forget one night at the Plaza. In his time, Dad had had thirty-nine Scottish champions and longed to make it a round number of forty but the final victory was proving elusive. Eventually it happened when Willie Booth took on popular veteran Tommy Glencross – it was a great night and it's a record that will probably never be beaten.

THE SKIPTON WEASEL, THE PLAZA AND A PEASOUPER

Glasgow's weather can play havoc with outdoor promotions and, on one occasion, we even found it could hit an indoor show. Dad was in the old Mearnskirk hospital (now swept away and replaced with flats) and missed out on the action. So did a lot of fans! We had decided to put on a show in Govan but our luck ran out. The show coincided with a bus strike *and* a peasouper of a fog. The area on the banks of the Clyde was prone to heavy fogs and they often threatened football matches at nearby Ibrox. In these days of central heating and smoke-less fuel, folk just can't imagine what a peasouper was like. People had to abandon cars and you often could not see one side of the street from the other. You'd see folk walking along the tram rails to guide them. This reminds me of an amusing story told by one of my newspaper friends who phoned Ibrox one morning, when visibility in town was poor, to enquire how bad the fog was down in Govan. The then Rangers manager Scott Symon, a man notoriously wary of the press, replied, 'No comment.' – very funny but our night in Govan was no joke. The promotion lost £800 which was a lot of money almost thirty years ago.

14

SLUGGING IT OUT IN COURT

There really is something special about the Kelvin Hall. I can never hear its name without having flashbacks to that night in 1992 when Pat Clinton lifted the world title. That was the peak but I have other memories of the place and not just the trips to the circus as a kid with the family. When I was still toiling away in the day job in Bridgeton and acting as a matchmaker for promoters up and down the country, Dad produced a rare touch of the old pals' act. He asked Mickey Duff to appoint me matchmaker for Jim Watt's defence of his European title in the Kelvin Hall. Dad proudly told Mickey that 'our Thomas is up to the job'. Mickey, who had known me and my family since I was in short trousers, granted the favour.

This was a major step into the big time. As well as making the matches for the undercard, Mickey used me in many other tasks to ensure the success of the night. Jim won his fight against Antonio Guinaldo on a stoppage. Working on this promotion gave me an insight into the problems football schedules can cause boxing. Rangers were playing at home on the night of the fight and the crossover between fans of both games could have hit our attendance. Mickey and his partners Mike Barrett and Terry Lawless think fast and they came up with a brainwave

– lay on transport from Ibrox stadium to the Kelvin Hall. This win preceded Jim's successful battle against Alfredo Pitalua for the world title which had been vacated by Roberto 'Hands of Stone' Duran as they called him. Mickey must have liked that first big job for he paid me well and gave me the job of match-maker for all Jim's title bouts in Glasgow. I was on a high, working for the man who is probably the world's number one matchmaker and getting my name on the poster!

During the time I worked for Mickey, I learned a tremendous amount and it was an experience that helped me immensely in my career. There was even talk at one point of me moving to London to work with him. Mickey could zero in on the crux of any argument. He asked me the question often asked of Scots, in any business, thinking of going south. 'Did I want to be a big fish in a small pond or merely another fish in a big pond?' More importantly, as he well knew, I was Scottish through and through – a Glaswegian and proud of it – and I wanted to make a mark on my home turf. I stayed in Scotland. The right move and Mickey gave me the right choice. The night Jim Watt MBE won his world title was memorable.

Mickey asked me to arrange the undercard. It was one of those boxing nights, though, when only the big match really mattered. There was more excitement about Jim's bid for the title than there had been in the city for years. The boys on the undercard, some managed by my dad, gave their best but everyone was really just waiting for the big one.

Watt, who had spent his early years not far from me in Bridgeton before moving to Possilpark, did not let the fans down. Early on, he was hit by what he has since called the 'single hardest punch I have taken in the ring' but steadied himself and went on to win an epic battle. He was a worthy world champ who successfully defended the title four times. Jim often reminds me that, on the night he won the title, my old man congratulated him and, with a tear in his eye, told him how delighted he was. Incidentally, this match in the Kelvin Hall made a bit of boxing history as it was the first title fight in Scotland where an American referee, Arthur Mercante, was in charge.

Jim's record is remarkable – before he lost the crown to Alexis Arguello and retired, he had a great run of defences beating Robert Vasquez, Charlie Nash, Howard Davis Jr and Sean O'Grady, with three of the fights taking place in the Kelvin Hall and one on a June night in the open air at Ibrox, home of Rangers.

The defence against American Sean O'Grady was called 'The Midnight Maelstrom'. This was controversial and still talked about today. Jim fought very cautiously early on in the fight where much blood flowed. Jim sustained a bad cut and the Scottish doctor at the fight was called to have a look at the injury. He took some time to get to the ring to do his examination. The delay did no harm in that it gave Jim a breather should the fight restart and everyone there still remembers what was called Dr Shea's slow walk. Jim was cleared to fight on and, in the end, he won when O'Grady was so badly cut that the cornermen could not stop the bleeding. Another memory of that night in the Kelvin Hall was the fact that the fight did not start until the wee small hours to accommodate live TV back in Sean's home state of Oklahoma. In the run-up, Jim was asked if fighting at three in the morning was a problem. 'Not a bit,' he replied, 'doesn't everyone in Glasgow do that?'

Nonetheless the starting time was a bonanza for the restaurants and pubs near to the venue. Fans with a bit of cash in their wallets had a late dinner and more Burgundy or Chardonnay than they needed before joining the hordes streaming up Argyle Street for the fight. Those in the cheaper seats tended to while away the hours to midnight with a pie and a pint in some crowded howff. It led to a bit of a charged atmosphere in the arena and lots of nice overtime for the cops. The 'polis' in Glasgow can spot trouble a mile away and, for this fight, at an unearthly hour, almost in the city centre, they were deployed in strength. Apart from keeping peace in the streets they were stationed round the turnstiles and were instructed by the top brass to make sure no drink was taken into the arena. This could have been embarrassing for a nameless editor of one of the city's top papers. A boxing fanatic, he was really looking forward to the battle and he was not going to be beaten by some silly police ban on drinking in the stadium. In what you could call a sleekit move, he filled a tonic water bottle with more than tonic. Anticipating trouble at the door he asked his girlfriend, now a top magazine editor in London, to slip the wee bottle of G&T into her handbag. They arrived at the turnstiles and while the drouthy journo walked straight through – after all he was not carrying the booze – his girlfriend ended up in a back room having her handbag searched and with some explaining to do. Her illegal wee bottle removed, the girlfriend eventually got into her seat. It could have provoked a battle between editor and moll but it was soon forgotten as the real-life fight got into action between the ropes with Jim and O'Grady putting on a great show.

The O'Grady fight was a good win for Jim but, in the end,

he lost his crown to Alexis Arguello at the Empire Pool, Wembley, London. This was no disgrace as Alexis was something of a 'ring legend' and a great fighter. Jim went on to be a perceptive and entertaining TV commentator on the sport, travelling the world to the big fights and giving millions the benefit of his inside knowledge. Jim's commentaries are succinct and knowledgeable and there are never any of the hysterics you get from some guys who go into overdrive the moment a mike is in their hands and they try to make a couple of journeymen slugging it out sound like a world-title fight. That is not Jim's style.

And he had a lucrative sideline as an after-dinner speaker. His secondary success out of the ring is no surprise to a journalist pal who told me a fascinating story. He was flying down with Jim on the Glasgow–London shuttle to attend a function at which the boxer was the star speaker. Up until ten minutes out of Heathrow, they laughed and joked. Then Jim asked for a moment's peace. Out came a piece of paper and a pen and the champ set about writing his speech. It was finished just as the wheels hit the tarmac and, when he delivered it later that night to a dicky-suited audience of hundreds, it was a great success. Jim Watt, a natural at more than boxing.

Around the time I was doing the matchmaking for Mickey Duff and running my first promotions, I was also doing a bit of work as an agent. It was another string to my bow and I was tutored in this by another cog in the boxing network, Dennie Mancini, a man much used by the big London promoters to handle all the form-filling, all the details of work permits etc. Dennie steered me on the right course for this and, despite much contact with the men at the ministry in

Ebury Street, London, I never had much trouble. But I often wonder if the fans have any idea of the paperwork involved behind the scenes. It is especially complicated when foreign fighters come here.

It was one of the busiest times in my life and it got more and more complicated after Dad had his stroke and died the day after our Plaza promotion. The family was devastated. But there was also an extended family who depended on the Gilmours for employment – boxers, trainers and all the rest. And Dad, as I have earlier explained, left little or nothing. There was a mighty lot of sorting out to do. Up to this point, I had concentrated on lots of skills other than pure management, though that was my ultimate ambition. I felt there was not much point in being second best. And The Starmaker was the best.

Others too had to decide what to do after his death. Dad had about eleven fighters in the stable at that time and six or so decided to stay with me and Dunky Jowett who was an immensely respected cuts man and second, a man with an encyclopaedic knowledge of boxing and ring strategy. He has saved the careers of hundreds of boxers threatened by cuts. Dunky is an amazing man. For donkey's years, he took his place in the corners of hundreds of boxers and even the guys fighting away down the bill got every bit as much commitment, expertise and care from him as the big names. And there were plenty of big names and big-time televised fights. One Glasgow reporter said the phrase 'and there is the instantly recognisable Dunky Jowett in the corner' became a cliché for TV commentators.

Dunky was to my mind simply the greatest cuts man in the world – a calming figure with his ice bag and sponge in the midst of the wildest of ring action. What do you need to do that job well? Have ice running in your veins. Picture the scene. Your man comes into the corner for the mandatory minute between rounds. You have only a few seconds to dry the wound and apply adrenaline to staunch the flow. After a bleeding wound has been dried, really dried, it can be sealed in a mere seven seconds. Seven seconds to dab away gently with a sterile pad, apply your adrenaline in a solution of one in a thousand. Surgical skill is needed to get the balm deep into the wound, to the heart of the bleeding. Any careless handling can widen the cut and make matters worse. And often the referee is nosing around over your shoulder to assess the extent of the injury. That's where the ice water in the veins kicks in. I have watched in amazement as Dunky, oblivious to the noise around him in the arena, unconscious of what is going on the opposite corner, went about his business. He didn't have medical qualifications but he had all the skills and mindset of a top surgeon. Cuts above the eyes, the most vulnerable area of the face, have ended many a fight and many a career. How they are treated at the time is as important as is healing time before the next fight. In the old days, men like Dunky would do a bit of stitching at the end of a contest stopped by cuts. A wag remarked that a good cornerman could stitch you up like a good suit. These days, though, with sometimes millions of pounds in future purse money at stake, a plastic surgeon is called in to save a career. And maybe good looks, too.

Dunky grew up in the Gorbals in a house a few streets way from Benny Lynch's and did his war service with the Royal Army Service Corps, boxing in Palestine and winning a couple of titles before becoming a trainer in charge of the army boxing team. After the war he boxed in Glasgow Green booths for £3.50 a fight – hard-earned corn. But, for all his years in the tough so-called 'leather trade', Dunky had a soft side that extended to him sometimes taking boxers into his home to be looked after by him and his wife Jenny. I loved the story they tell of one boxer subjected to this routine in order to hone his fitness. He complained he was being starved but Dunky simply pointed out he had a couple of lettuce leaves yesterday! Another boxer trained by Dunky was caught buying himself a sly pint of milk and a couple of pies at a railway station. His punishment? Hours of running the weight off pounding up and down the terracing stairs at Ibrox.

Dunky was integral to the team I inherited. My early days of managing after Dad died in 1979 were far from easy. I was on a learning curve and grateful to have this great friend and close confidant of The Starmaker as my right-hand man. I was now in charge of the gym in Ingram Street, just round the corner from the City Chambers and George Square. Many champions had trained there, including Calderwood, Watt and Buchanan. The place could be costly to run and it was not unusual for Dunky to dip into his wallet and pay the odd bill to keep the place going and not look for the cash back. Dunky had watched me grow up and looked on this as a chance to help Tommy Sr's son and keep the dynasty on track. Loyal supporters at that time included Chic Brady, Frank Hislop and Johnny Bell. Johnny ran the Glasgow Corporation amateur boxing club and had been a great pal of Dad. He would send me any of his boys with the talent and desire to try their hand at the pro game.

One of these was Peter, Harrison, father of former world champion Scott. Peter was at the top of the amateur game and had boxed in the Commonwealth Games. He was my first champion when he beat Willie Booth to become the light-weight titleholder in the St Andrew's Sporting Club back in February 1981. At this time, I had been managing for less than eighteen months so I was pretty excited at the success. I was even more pleased when Peter retired and decided that he would work for me as a trainer. Eighteen months was pretty quick going but, in the aftermath of that success, I would never have believed that it would take me another seven years to get my first British champion. The man who did it for us was Steve Boyle, trained by Peter Harrison. We had other successes with Paul Weir, Drew Docherty and Wilson Docherty but that wait of almost nine years for my first 'British' was frustrating.

Each year since 1979, I had a fighter boxing for a major title but success was minimal and I was beginning to doubt myself. A big disappointment came after Ray Cattouse had beaten Dave McCabe. Terry Lawless, who trained and managed Cattouse, took me aside after the final bell and, in the depth of my disappointment, gave me some sage advice. It came from one of the most respected men in the game, a guy who had been round the block more than once and usually ended up in front of the pack. He told me to think positively and said I was doing well for my boxers in the opportunities I was getting for them. The old fox said that, even if my man lost, it did not reflect the effort I had put into making the big fights happen for my stable. Nice but I still wanted a champion.

The night it happened was at the Scottish Exhibition and Conference Centre – I wish they had given it a snappier name – and Steve Boyle was the man who did it for me. He fought

174

another Scot, Alex Dickson from Larkhall, who had been a top-class amateur while Boyle had, at best, had a mediocre career in the amateur vest. Boyle had one major advantage – he was a ferocious puncher while Alex was your classic boxer rather than a fighter. On 28 February 1988, that long, agonising wait was ended for me. Steve Boyle knocked Alex out in the second round and I had my champion. I was so proud that one of my fighters had won a British title and a Lonsdale belt. I took that belt home with me and, that night, it slept between Veronica and me. During the night, my mind full of the excitement of the fight, I got up a couple of times to dance round the bedroom floor, singing.

During those early days in management, I learned quickly that you need a good team around you and I had one. Boxing can seem like a one-on-one sport but no boxer – or manager – ever did anything in the ring without a team behind him. It includes youngsters with the energy to go through the routines of rattling the speedball, sparring and skipping with their charges and sometimes old-timers whose gift is to pass on their experience. A gym is a great place for teamwork. I loved the old days at the Olympia but, likewise, I remember great times at the east-end gym of the Glasgow Transport Amateur Boxing Club or at my place in Ingram Street. Gyms are sporting heaven to me, evocative places where the smells of sweat and embrocation mingle and where down from the wall gaze faded or fading portraits of the greats of the past and posters for long-forgotten promotions. Even the clock on the wall which operates on three-minute cycles underlines the timelessness of it all. And, above all, there is the optimism of the fighters. The next bout is the one that will launch them on the road to greatness.

Another vital member of my team as I built the Gilmour stable back up after Dad died was my pal Benny 'The Bandit' King. Benny was almost as good a cuts man as Dunky and a great pal as well. Matchmaking and promoting keeps you on the road for weeks at a time – Manchester, Nottingham, London, Wales, you name it, somewhere someone is promoting a boxing tournament away from the bright lights of TV. Both boxer and manager have got to go where the money is. I was clocking up thousands of miles a month. And that brought me a couple of frights. Twice on the motorways I nearly killed myself by nodding off after fourteen-hour days. You read all the signs on the gantries across the motorways warning that 'tiredness can kill'. But, like the Formula One driver with his foot permanently on the floor, an accident is something that happens to someone else. If it happens once, you get a real scare but still think that it is a one-off thing – at least I did. But, when it happened twice, I began to be more than a bit worried. The next time could be the last. But I was not as scared as Veronica. She insisted I got a driver and Benny The Bandit was selected to add that job to all his other roles. It did work although I have to admit, on occasion, I took the wheel while the 'driver' had a wee snooze. But it was a whole lot better than driving home, mile after mile, in darkness and maybe waking up in an ambulance or worse.

It worked and Benny and I survived motorway madness though I often still arrived home in Glasgow to a house full of folk sleeping dreamlessly while I made a cup of tea and felt like Motor Mouse. Benny and I did, however, have the odd adventure on the road – like the day we were heading south, weaving our way in and out of the artics that clog up the roads these days. Of course, my own experience leaves me with nothing but admiration for the guys who drive these behemoths day in and day out in all weathers for a living. They get good money and they deserve it. This particular day was wild with rain and the lorry driver's worst fear – a strong crosswind. We were on the tail of one particular artic and were a bit wary of it as it was swaying a bit and moving from lane to lane and seemed to be having problems with the wind. We hung back and were in a good position to get a close-up when it finally toppled on its side, metal crunching, sparks flying. It was really scary. I pulled the car into the breakdown lane and Benny jumped out at the double to help the driver's mate pull the lorry man from the wrecked cab. Everyone had stopped and someone was on the phone for emergency services. Benny didn't wait. He got out the cornerman's kit and set about sorting out the driver who was covered in blood and cuts. Benny did such a good job that, when the ambulance men arrived to take the accident victim to hospital, having heard that there was blood everywhere, they were dumbstruck. One turned to me and, indicating the driver, said, 'This guy looks like Rock Hudson.' The old cuts man's magic had worked again.

There is no getting away from the fact that, in the ring, blood can be spilled. Usually, though, there is no permanent damage and the injury is slight. But at times it can be more of a problem. I remember being with Benny in the Bellahouston Sports Centre when Craig Docherty fought Abdul Malik Jabir, for the Commonwealth super-featherweight championship, and was cut. It looked bad and someone remarked that there 'was blood coming out of blood'. Benny went to work. The blood stopped and Craig won. Sometimes, though, you can have a cut that is deep but doesn't immediately bleed. I remember being in Belfast when Damaen Kelly was defending his British and Commonwealth title against one of my boxers, Keith Knox. Knox was losing and I was considering pulling him out of the fight as he was taking some punishment when there was an accidental clash of heads just on the bell. I shouted to the referee that Kelly was injured but in all the confusion the man in the middle thought I was just indulging in one of my ring-side 'rants'. But in actual fact Kelly was so badly cut that it was some time before he started to bleed. It was a deep wound and the referee stopped the fight in Knox's favour. At the time, the cut was so bad that, if you had asked me, I would have said Kelly was as unlikely to fight again. But he healed perfectly and he went on to win a world title with me as his manager.

One of The Bandit's tasks was to pick up people at the airport and bring them to my office in the Albany. You could get the occasional surprise. On one particular occasion, Benny was despatched to the airport to pick up a guy called Nelson Vasquez who was to officiate at one of our world-title fights. I had known and worked with Nelson before and was looking forward to seeing him again. Nelson was a policeman in San Juan, Puerto Rico, but Benny had never met him. But since they both had Hispanic looks, including the Zapata moustache (the reason for that 'bandit' nickname), it occurred to me that Nelson might recognise Benny as a bit of a soul brother. Anyway, Benny headed out to the airport. My office in the old Albany was on the mezzanine floor at the end of a long corridor. My door was usually left open and I could see anyone coming to see me making their way along the corridor. That day I was giving one of my boxers a bollocking for some misdemeanour or other and, as I sat at my desk, I could see Benny making his way along the corridor with his charge in tow. When I looked at Benny's companion, I got a shock. 'Who the f*** is that?' I asked and Benny said, 'It's Nelson.' It was not the Nelson I knew. Sometimes officials are changed at short notice and replacements sent and I wondered if that was what had happened here so, just in case it was, I made a few phone calls. But, no, Nelson Vasquez was our man.

I tried a word or two with the chap Benny had wheeled in. No joy. He was lost and bewildered and jabbering away in a language I did not know. We searched the hotel for staff to speak to him in various foreign languages but no one seemed able to get any sense out of the guy. We were in the final preparations for a big show and this was something I did not need. My temper was not improved by all this. Veronica suggested giving him a coffee. I said, 'Give him nothing!' or words to that effect. Everyone but me seemed to be feeling sorry for this lost soul but all I wanted to know was who he was. I took the law into my own hands and started to search him and eventually found a passport that said he was a Brazilian from São Paulo. 'How did his happen?' I asked Benny and he told me honestly that he had been a wee bit late getting to the airport and went straight to the information desk and explained he was looking for a foreign gentleman who had just arrived. The girl behind the counter pointed to our lost soul and said he had just arrived and was waiting for someone to meet him. That was good enough for Benny.

Nelson eventually arrived under his own steam and the luckless Brazilian was shunted back to the airport. The incident came to mind a few years later when we were visiting Rio and Veronica remarked that she hoped our Brazilian was not an immigration official or it could be payback time.

All this was pretty light-hearted stuff but the life of a boxing promoter can be traumatic. Your emotions, rather like shares in the stock exchange, can go down as well as up! I have had plenty of high points and some desperately worrying times. One of the lowest involved that tough Welshman Steve Robinson mentioned earlier. It is the only time I have had to take a boxer to court on a contractual issue. The background may sound intriguing in retrospect but, at the time, it meant months of worry for me. Boxing folk are no strangers to fallings-out – they happen all the time and are in the nature of the business – but this was different. It was really serious stuff – a case heard in the High Court of Justice in London. It goes back to 1993 when my friend Tommy Conroy and I were co-managing the exciting little Geordie featherweight John Davison. At that time, the world champ at that weight was Ruben Palacio from Columbia. Barry Hearn and I were keen to promote John in a bid for the title. The promotional rights for Palacio were held by Frank Warren so Barry came to an agreement with Frank that we would give him an agreed fee for the rights if we could use Palacio against Davison in Washington in the north-east of England. Everything was settled and Frank would be paid after the contest, which was to take place on 17 April 1993.

As the date of the fight neared, it was time for Palacio and his party to come to England. In rules that apply to all boxers, he had to bring his documents giving him medical permission to fight and a current HIV blood certificate. But, when Palacio arrived in the UK, he did not have his blood certificate. We didn't panic as years of experience had shown that boxers are not necessarily the most careful keepers of paperwork. We would just send him to the local hospital and get some tests done and presumably, with the new certificate, all would be OK. Then came a bombshell. Palacio failed the blood test. As far as I knew this was the first time a world champion had failed such a test. We needed a second test for confirmation. He failed again and we had a problem as the fight was in the television schedules.

Barry and I worked long shifts into the night trying to get permission to stage the vacant title fight and to find an opponent for Davison. Barry, at this time, was doing a bit of business with Welshman Dai Gardner who was the manager of Steve Robinson. Steve was a good, fit guy. A critic might have labelled his record as merely OK but he had boxed in good company. We had to work hard to get the fight officially recognised as being for the vacant title and show that Robinson deserved the opportunity. Tommy Conroy, who co-managed Davison with me, was doing the rounds of local TV, radio and newspapers to raise the profile of the fight. Tommy was on the telly one night and he made much of the fact that Robinson had recently travelled to France where he fought and defeated the French champion Stéphane Haccoun. He said on air that 'Robinson had beaten Haccoun in France'. After the broadcast, he went home to Sunderland where his wife Annette and his father-in-law, a fine old cockney gent, waited. As you do, the first thing he asked was how he had done in the interview. His father-in-law floored him by saying it would have been better if he had simply said Robinson had beaten a coloured guy. These were the days before political correctness had really taken hold. When it was explained to him, the old guy took it as a laugh.

Barry agreed the purse for Davison v Robinson but I insisted that we needed options on future fights for Robinson and this is what landed us in court. The actual contest was hard and competitive with Davison stealing an early lead and Robinson coming on strong in the later rounds. At the bell, I thought that Davison had shaded it but the decision went to Robinson though it was a close call. This was a Cinderella ending for the Welshmen – having been called in at short notice, he'd now won the world title.

But there was to be no quick fairytale ending for us. Robinson's first fight under our option agreement was against Sean Murphy in July of that year. He duly won it but then decided to dispute the option on further fights. I thought that we must seek legal advice and I was fully backed in this by Barry Hearn. The snag here was that I was based in Scotland, Robinson was Welsh and the dispute would be heard under English law. I needed the very best of legal advice. Andrew Sleigh was recommended to me and I took to him immediately. He listened carefully to what I had to say, explained the implications and his advice was forthright. He explained the cost and value – and the risks – of taking the matter further. He was a hugely well-qualified top corporate lawyer, an expert on contracts. He was also lawyer for the Scottish Football Association and knew sport and sports people well. I suppose Jack Solomons would have called him 'a diamond geezer'! He was the best.

I had never been in this position before but, from day one, I fully trusted everything Andrew advised. I quickly discovered the hard fact that litigation is expensive. We had to employ the services of a London solicitor and a London counsel. The costs were racking up and the hope was that some out-of-court agreement could be reached. It didn't happen and a date was given for a court hearing. If you haven't been in a similar position, you can't appreciate the sleepless nights and the endless

A night to remember. Boxing fans thronged the Holiday Inn to celebrate the thirtieth anniversary of the St Andrew's Sporting Club. These black-tie nights are hugely popular and the club has done much to raise the profile of boxing and help it through the occasional bad patch … and, of course, to raise large sums for charity.

Bottom middle picture: Blood and guts – Craig Docherty defending the Commonwealth Super-featherweight championship.

One of my world champions … Jawaid Khaliq MBE, one of the nicest men in sport.

I have heard it said that boxing is show business with blood. And maybe there is something in that. When STV wanted to film a series on boxing featuring Dirty Den, Leslie Grantham, from EastEnders, they turned to me for help. The whole Gilmour team had a lot of fun with the Luvvies.

Glasgow has officially honoured my services to boxing and charity more than once. Here I am with Midge Ure after receiving the Lord Provost's silver medal, the first time it had been awarded to boxing. For his services to music, Midge Ure, of Ultravox, also got a silver.

I travelled to San Juan with Barry Hearn to collect an award as WBO co-promoters of the year. We met up with Jose Torres, by now a respected writer and commentator, and my old pal Ed Levine from Miami.

One of the proudest days of our life as Veronica and I, with the help of one of the pupils, cut a ribbon to open a sensory room at Craighead School in Blantyre to help youngsters with autism. Much hard work and fun on the fundraising side went into this moment.

Graham Lockwood ... one of the most remarkable matchmakers in boxing.

Even a world title promotion benefits from some fun advance publicity. My daughter Stephanie spotted this papier mâché Mexican on display in Princes Square and *el bandito* was soon helping us in the build-up for the fight in press conferences and TV shoots. Pat Clinton gives him a right-hander, a punch that 'Sid' Perez was to feel himself in the Kelvin Hall.

The most emotional boxing night of m[y]
life as Pat Clinton of Croy takes th[e]
world title in a packed Kelvin Hall. Yea[rs]
of struggle had brought the ultima[te]
accolade – a world champion an[d]
a win on his home tur[f]

Benny 'the bandit' King and George Peacock.

Cassius Clay, as he then was, with the men from Miami Chris Dundee (left) and Angelo Dundee.

Me with my first British champion, Steve Boyle, Dunky Jowett and Peter Harrison.

A Burns Night spectacular at the Club ... former Tennants lager lovely June Lake with me and Barry Hearn complete with kilt. June was the St Andrew's resident numbers girl for many years.

Some Dynasty glamour - in Scotland not US - as my son Christopher marries Tracey. Stephanie and Veronica have appropriately spectacular wedding hats though my kilt is not as eye-catching as Christopher's!

Young Max, my grandson ... could he ensure that a fifth generation of Gilmours go into boxing management?

Awards galore as some of my champions, in formal gear, gather for the photographers.

hours of going over the whole thing, your mind swirling with a myriad of possibilities. Veronica and I talked it round and round for days. Barry and I also discussed it interminably. Never having been involved in anything similar before, I felt I had to talk to Andrew Sleigh about it again on an almost daily basis. He was invariably sympathetic and understanding but, more importantly, reassuring. Our relationship became close and developed into friendship. Later, when Andrew changed firms, I followed him. We still have a pizza lunch to set the world to rights but, at the time of the court hearing, it was all pretty tense.

When the day for the court hearing arrived – two long years after the Davison fight – I was pretty nervy and my stomach was churning. This battle with the law was affecting me like a contender taking on Tyson or Ali! But I knew I just had to tell the truth and explain the situation and leave it to the judge. It all seemed to go pretty well but it would be another month or so before we would hear the verdict. Eventually the day came when I answered the phone and the London lawyers broke the good news. We had won and had been awarded £100,000. The first person I phoned was Barry Hearn. He was delighted at the outcome but, more than that, I think he was delighted that he would no longer have to listen to me going over the same ground on the telephone night after night. It was costly for Steve as he had to pay us over £130,000 and he had his own legal costs. It was a long worrying episode in my career and the feeling of relief when it was over was immense.

Boxing, as I have said, is a great place for feuds and rows but some of the toughest 'wars' inside the ropes end with the contestants showing a surprising degree of friendship. A minute or two before the final bell, they are hammering each other and then, when it is all over, they shake hands. I am glad to say that I still see Steve Robinson from time to time and he even trained one of my champions Dazzo Williams. That's boxing.

Around this time, Davison's biggest rival in the north-east was Billy Hardy who had been a British champion and who came close to winning a world title in Sunderland. He was managed by Dennie Mancini and promoted by Mickey Duff and his partners. He defeated a couple of my boxers, Brian Holmes and Ronnie Carroll, but, despite this, we became great friends. Eventually he wanted a change in management and asked me to look after him. He went on to be my first European Champion when he defeated Mehdi Labdouni in Paris. I was not in his corner that night as I was looking after another couple of boxers in the UK but Billy had an expert at his side – Paddy Byrne. Billy was the only one of the three from the Gilmour stable to win that night. Paddy does mention it from time to time.

15

BLAZING CARS, A BULLET AND LIFE WITH THE LUVVIES

I don't need many reminders that, in Glasgow, you need your wits about you at all times. I learned that the hard way as a kid in my dad's betting shops and gyms. There are citizens in this great city who like to turn a furtive dollar or two at every opportunity. And it is undeniable that there are some characters in or around the fight game who are unlikely candidates for Sunday School teaching jobs. I still laugh at that warning given to me by Paddy Byrne in the run-up to the Perez fight to count my fingers after shaking hands with some of the Puerto Ricans in the fight scene on the other side of the Atlantic. In certain regions of Africa – where boxing is immensely popular and where I have travelled a lot – there are also folk who will take any liberty going, especially a diabolical one, to score off you. In any big-time sport where large sums are involved, it is inevitable that some people do stray from the straight and narrow. All this sort of stuff is entertainment when you're sitting in an armchair with a dram, watching *Goodfellas*, *The Sopranos* or a DVD of Marlon Brando using cotton wool to great effect in *The Godfather*. It is not much fun, though, in real life, to be even occasionally on the periphery of such action.

But it has to be repeated that, thousands of miles away from San Juan, Miami or New York, there are people near to home on the lookout for easy money. And my fellow Glaswegians can be imaginative in their scams. You have got to stay one step ahead. But, after a spell when everything goes smoothly, you can get complacent at times. I did get a wake-up call in the days before the Eubank v Ray Close fight at the Scottish Conference and Exhibition Centre in 1993. As I mentioned earlier, I have always had good relations with both Rangers and Celtic and there is a great crossover between football and boxing fans – as there is between the boxers and footballers themselves. So it was quite natural that the Rangers shop was selling tickets for the big night. Sipping coffee and nibbling a biscuit in my city-centre Albany HQ a few days before the fight, I was indulging in that feeling we all have from time to time that everything is going swimmingly. Three title fights on one bill, tickets selling well and the newspaper back pages full of the promotion on a daily basis. I should have known better. The phone rang and the voice calling from the Rangers shop asked when they could expect their 'comps' for the fight. What comps I asked. 'The ones your people who picked up the ticket cash told us you would be sending over to us,' said the caller. I should not have been as surprised as I was! The cops were called in and the papers made a big fuss with pre-publicity that helped to scare the villains and anyone they had sold seats to away. But the simplest of scams had got someone a bagful of the folding stuff and reminded me that you never take anything on face value in this enterprising city.

If you want an easy well-regulated life, take a job as a bank clerk. If you want a little fear and worry thrown into a mixture that can include triumphs, disasters and a genuine sense of achievement, then try your hand at boxing promotion. It can be as hard outside the ring as inside and sometimes you don't know your opponent. In the ring you can see 'the enemy' dancing towards you, intent on landing as many telling blows as possible. Outside the ring 'the enemy' can take on mysterious, shady shapes. The tales that follow are the exception rather than the rule in a professional sport. I think boxing is much cleaner than some cynics suggest – especially nowadays – but, in the past, there were scary moments.

In the eighties, we were living in Cambuslang and I was in the early stages of my career as a manager, running boxers and promoting the odd show or two. I was beginning to be something of a fixture on the sports pages but I was still working at the day job as an engineer in nearby Bridgeton. Our kids Christopher and Stephanie got into the habit, at this time, of collecting the mail from the front door for us – because of the boxing, there was usually plenty. And with me at work, they sometimes opened it on their own to save us the bother. The opened letters would then be given to me to deal with when I came home. It didn't always happen that way, however, and, on one occasion, I was hugely relieved the kids had not got hold of the mail first. I opened an innocent-looking letter, never giving a thought of anything untoward happening, only to discover it contained a bullet. There was no message, no letter, no written warning or anything – just that single scary bullet.

Whenever such things happen, I have always had a policy of getting the police involved from the start. They investigated but such an incident is hard to deal with and nothing ever came of it. But I got the message that someone somewhere did not like me. For the rest of our time in Cambuslang, there was to be no similar nonsense and gradually the incident receded. But, at the time, it was no pleasant occurrence.

It was years on, in the early nineties, when another worrying incident happened. One night Christopher and I were on a routine visit to the gym in Fordneuk Street in the east end, ironically just round the corner from London Road Police Station, one of the busiest in Glasgow and well used to trouble, much of it coming from a couple of pubs in the area which were what the Glaswegians tend to call Stab Inns. You watched your step in such places. I always like to have a nice car and the one I was driving at that time was a cracker, a 420 Merc SEC in gleaming black and with nice grey leather upholstery. By this time, the engineering days were over! We were all going about our business in the gym when a youngster burst through the door to announce that there was a car on fire in the street. Surely not, I thought, my lovely Merc. But outside in the street our worst fears were confirmed – the motor, as they say, was a blazing wreck nearing complete extinction. It was not far to go to inform the police. But again nothing came of the investigation. Scary again as well as annoying.

This was not to be the only time I lost a car to fire although, on the second occasion, the police investigation put it down to a mysterious 'electrical fault'. This time it happened during one of the televised promotions that Barry Hearn and I ran in Musselburgh, East Lothian. As well as being a lot of fun, these nights were profitable and often featured Willie 'The Mighty' Quinn. On the night it happened, I had driven through via Edinburgh in my black BMW. It was another unsettling happening. Now you will understand why, these days, I have a strictly no-smoking policy in my car! Again we told the cops right away and the electrics officially took the blame. Around this time we were being plagued with nuisance telephone calls and the police were brought into this as well. We were not the only target for this – Dunky Jowett, that master cornerman, and various others around the Glasgow boxing scene were getting similar calls. It all went away in time.

However, one telephone call that I will not forget was not anonymous. It came from Arthur Thompson, the Glasgow Godfather. Thompson walked in the footsteps of the original city Godfather, Walter Norval. A bank robber with a talent for organising gangs, Walter loves sport, especially watching Celtic. In his youth, he was a good footballer and could have been a pro if he had kept out of jail. In fact it was when Walter was doing a long stretch in Peterhead that Thompson stepped in to run the Glasgow crime scene. He became pre-eminent in his day and in turn was followed by big-time gangsters like Paul Ferris and Tam McGraw who, ironically for a man of violence, died in his bed, like old Arthur, of a heart attack in the summer of 2007.

Arthur and I had known each other for many years but it was still a shock to get a call from him one Friday night, as I was about to leave work and head home. He did not mess about and told me he had been asked by a friend to try to sort out a problem regarding a contract that I was involved in. I should point out right away that it was not the sort of 'contract' that was more commonly associated with the gangster's name in the papers in his days as a crime lord. This was, by contrast, a simple business matter. I told Arthur my side of the story and said I would get in touch with his lawyer Joe Beltrami to verify what I was saying. Joe, a legendary courtroom lawyer and known variously as The Great Defender or the Sage of West Nile Street, had been the legal eagle for the Thompsons for many years (in between his courtroom dramas he found time to write some great books on his career). A remarkable character, Joe had taken over from Laurence Dowdall as the most successful and in-demand pleader of his day. He has been followed by Donald Findlay QC in that role. Joe Beltrami had been involved in drawing up the disputed agreement mentioned by Thompson and he could verify everything I said and, by the Tuesday of the next week, all was well again. But it can be bad for the blood pressure to find a real life Godfather on the end of the line when you pick up the phone!

There have been major downsides to my life in boxing as well as good memories. My great love in boxing is the St Andrew's Sporting Club and my passion for it and what it stands for cost me many sleepless nights and a long-standing friendship. For years, Gerry Woolard had handled my father's accounts and, in turn, mine. And at one stage, he was a top dog in the Board of Control in Scotland. After Dad's death, Gerry and I became much closer and it was because of him I eventually acquired the club. He arranged everything for me in my initial purchase of shares when Moss Goodman, the early driving force in the club, died. He also helped later when I bought the remaining shares from Les Roberts and Gloria Kitty Goldstein, the final purchase happening on 7 June 1987. Newspaper pals tell me the most dangerous two words in the English language are 'I assumed' and, sadly, I was to find out that was right. I had left all the paperwork to Gerry assuming that, as a pal, he would see that there were no problems. But the friendship between him and me and my family went seriously pear-shaped when Gerry had a heart attack. Naturally my business life went on as usual and Gerry's partner Brian McAllister took over my accounts.

One day, Brian and I sat down together to go over things. I told him, 'Gerry says this and that etc.' I am very good with figures but I am not a professional accountant. I had just given my paperwork to the accountants and let them get on with it. Early in that meeting, Brian said something along the lines of, 'Sorry, Tommy, Gerry has not done it the way you thought.' Alarm bells started ringing for both of us and Brian decided to look through everything Gerry had done with regard to my business affairs. As I have said, I paid for the shares and everything went through Gerry's office and this, together with the close friendship of our families, had caused a complaint from another Boxing Board of Control licence holder. The Board held an inquiry to ask if Gerry had any involvement in the St Andrew's Sporting Club. The answer was a definite 'no'. I was the St Andrew's club.

This was underlined by the fact that Gerry had his lawyers send a statement to the Board to say that that neither he nor any member of his family had any shares in the St Andrew's Sporting Club – all the shares were held by the family of Thomas Gilmour Jr. It was a statement I thought was perfectly true. Then the bombshell came. When Brian started to go through everything Gerry had done for me, it emerged that he had not registered the shares in my kids' name as he was supposed to! Looking back, I realise I was foolish not to have seen everything in black and white but this man was a mentor and pal so I'd assumed – that dangerous word again – that there would be no problems. The affair became public and it all caused a huge legal stramash that kept investigative newspaper reporters busy for weeks. Gerry, a major local personality with a high profile in the papers, had featured in all sorts of controversies in the past, some of a financial nature, and he took a lot of stick. I was devastated. With the help of Gerry's partner Brian McAllister and my lawyer, the ever-perceptive and efficient Andrew Sleigh, the problem was unravelled in time. There had been a lot of acrimony swirling around the affairs of Gerry Woolard but, at the end of the day, the club was mine.

At times like this, your true friends emerge. I would not embarrass them by naming them in a list but the folk involved know how much I appreciated their letters and words of support in a difficult time. The saddest thing to happen during my falling-out with Gerry was that it meant that my kids, particularly Stephanie, lost the close relationship they'd had with Gerry and his wife – people they had looked up to as the grandparents they'd never known.

But, when I look back, I prefer to remember the good times rather than the bad. And there were a lot of good times outside the immediate world of pro boxing. Some folk call boxing show business with blood and there certainly are similarities in the two worlds which sometimes come together in TV commercials, plays and photo opportunities. I enjoy my boxing and I also enjoyed a little foray into the world of showbiz back in the eighties. It started with a call from Scottish Television producer Robert Love who was looking for advice and help in a new production called *Winners and Losers*, a three-part TV series. This was big stuff and it would feature no less than Leslie Grantham, 'Dirty Den' from *EastEnders*. It would also star our own great comedian and character actor Jimmy Logan.

My remit was to provide rings, equipment, some folk to act as extras and to help with the script. I sat down with Robert and the STV people and easily agreed most of the deal, including the fee. But there was one sticking point. I wanted my name on the credits – just in case it was a major success. I dug my heels in on this and in the end I got it. The 'glory' of an on-screen credit for a top TV show was nice – as was a fat fee from STV. Now I could visualise myself swanking around the BAFTAs. You know how your mind jumps into overdrive at these times? Well, I could not help thinking that maybe Cecil B. de Mille started that way!

The whole shoot was to take place over the summer, which was ideal for us as it was boxing's close season. It was all great fun and an eye-opener with regard to the hours worked by film crews. We had plenty of early rises. Everyone in the business, as the luvvies say, needs an assistant and why not me? That role fell to my trusty buddy, Benny 'The Bandit' King. I also managed to get one of my boxers, Steve Williams from Grangemouth, a leading role. He was not, till that point, an actor but he seemed to have what was required for the small screen. In addition to natural acting ability he was blond, blue-eyed and handsome. The only snag in this arrangement was that he enjoyed showbiz so much that he quit boxing to become a full-time thespian!

Making the series meant that the boxing crew had to work closely with all the various TV departments to get an authentic feel to the drama. The wardrobe department was, of course, important and one of the women in that department had the apt name of Binky Darling. Add in that the man in charge was Robert Love and you can see we were in real show business. It caused a few laughs.

One day after filming, Veronica and I were sitting with Benny and his wife Vina in their flat in Nicolson Street, Greenock, when the phone rang. This was near the start of filming and Veronica and Vina did not know who was involved or their names. Vina answered the phone and said that it was Binky looking for him. Now, for some reason, we had got into the habit of calling our thespian friends by their surnames, never using the Christian names. I watched Vina's eye balls roll around her face as Benny chuntered on, 'Yes, Binky Darling – don't worry I will sort it out Binky Darling.' Veronica and I were in hysterics. The Bandit would have to do some explaining about his 'darling'. He survived.

Another personality to be involved in the series was the comedian Alex 'Happy' Howden who had also been a top-flight amateur middleweight. He must have been good in the ring as Dad, at one time, tried to sign him as a pro. Happy was great company if we were ever sitting in the trailer waiting for the rain to go off. He played the role of a trainer and, in the big fight scene, he was supposed to shout encouragement to his boxer. He was doing his best but it seemed a little more enthusiasm was required. The director was a fellow named Roger Tucker who was a very fussy guy, a perfectionist. In true Hollywood style, he was forever shouting, 'Cut!' and 'Action!' After a few efforts by Alex, Roger shouted a very firm, 'Cut!' He took Alex aside and explained to him that this was supposed to be a world-title fight and he had to put more passion into his shouts of encouragement. Alex listened, nodded sagely and said he had taken on board what was wanted. The set was told to go quiet. The next cry was 'Action!' and, at this, Alex started screaming at his boxer, 'Belt the f*****!' Roger was on his feet and he, too, was screaming – 'Cut!' It took a few more takes before the right mixture of passion and language was achieved.

Happy Howden is some guy. He is a member of the St Andrew's Sporting Club and his most famous film role was that of the assistant hangman in *Gangs of New York*. All his

Hollywood experience made for good stories when he was hanging out with boxing pals in Glasgow. One night, he went on and on about his experiences with Leo and we managed to guess that he meant Leonardo DiCaprio. Then it was on to another pal, Marti. This time we had to ask who he was talking about. Who else but Martin Scorcese? The heavyweight champion namedropper was in form that night. I look forward to the time he brings Leo and Marti to the club.

Winners and Losers got us out and about. The boxing training camp was set in Rothesay and it meant countless crossings of the Firth of Clyde for everyone involved. I used to love the place as a kid for holidays and days out but I have not been back since we put *Winners and Losers* in the can, as they say in the business! One of the most satisfying parts of this excursion into TV was the fact that the fight scenes were shot at the St Andrew's in the Albany. We put the fight into our brochure for one of the regular club nights without pointing out to the members that it was to be staged, as that would have taken away the authenticity of the scene. Jimmy Logan and Leslie Grantham were ringside and the club members, being well used to having celebrities in their midst, joined in and created a real big-fight atmosphere. The whole episode was, I suppose, another string to my bow but I don't think Marti has anything to fear.

16

THE FIGHT AT SALCEY GREEN AND AFTER

Now for a look at that great love of mine – sporting clubs, a somewhat different world from the mainstream promotions. Maybe I first got a taste for club fighting years back during the trips to the National Sporting Club in London. But the St Andrew's club has been part of my life for around a quarter of a century. Even my car carries the number plate STA for St Andrew's. Boxing has a curious mix of aficionados. Working-class folk always enjoyed a night out in places like Bridgeton's old National Sporting Club (not quite the same sort of place as the London club with its crystal chandeliers and polished mahogany) or, in later years, at Glasgow's football stadiums like Firhill, Ibrox or Hampden or indoor arenas like the St Mungo Halls in Gorbals or the Kelvin Hall or the old south-side dance hall, the Plaza. There was no dress code for the fans in such places in the early days. Often a slunge under the cold-water tap in a chipped sink in a shared tenement toilet, just to wash the grime of the mine or steelworks off the face, was all that was required. Some fans may have changed their bunnet or put on a clean shirt but that was about it. But the sporting clubs of London, Glasgow, and many of the cities of England, where the smell of expensive aftershave mixes with a whiff or two of embrocation and where the shirts are crisp white linen and cufflinks tend to be gold, are not the recent phenomenon some would have us believe. Growing up in a boxing dynasty, where the fight game is talked about twenty-four-seven, as they say these days, gives you an appetite for the history of the sport.

I found it revealing to read in the archives of the match that became known as 'The Fight at Salcey Green' in Northamptonshire in 1830. The story of the match and the men involved is a fascinating, sometimes horrific, insight into the roots of the fight game and a dramatic example of how things have changed down the years. The match was made between Alexander McKay, said to be the champion of Scotland, and an Irishman Simon Byrne. The arranging of the fight took place at a 'sporting dinner' in the Castle Tavern and the stakes were £100 a side, a huge amount in these days. There was a lot of money around that night, both from the gambling fraternity and from the patrons of the match who included Gentleman Jackson, Tom Cribb and Tom Spring, the landlord of the tavern. Jackson and Cribb were famous figures from the bare-knuckle days. Reports of the time say London society and local gentry were well represented. It was a boxing match all right but not as we know it. I am glad that our family dynasty began when the bare-knuckle days were over!

There were no twelve rounds of three minutes each round in 1830. There was no fixed time to a round at all – when one combatant had floored his opponent, the fallen fighter was given half a minute to lie and recover and, when he was on his feet, the next round had started. In the event of a fighter's seconds not being able to bring their man up to 'scratch' – the centre of the ring – after the half a minute he was deemed to have lost. This fight went to forty-seven rounds but others went for many more rounds. It ended with McKay, a Glaswegian, unconscious and, following some apparently ham-fisted efforts by a local so-called surgeon, he died not long after. His gravestone carries a poignant inscription:

> Strong and athletic was my frame
> Far from my native home I came
> And bravely fought with Simon Byrne
> Alas but never to return
> Stranger, take warning from my fate
> Lest you should rue your case too late
> If you have ever fought before
> Determine now to fight no more

The story was not over, however, as Byrne was eventually charged with murder. The big-money aspect of the fight was underlined by the fact that he was defended by 'three learned counsel and five solicitors' and that twelve witnesses travelled up from London and stayed locally at great expense. The case was further muddied when a Glasgow paper alleged that McKay had been nobbled by a sleeping draught that had been slipped into his water bottle. But the jury took only ten minutes to arrive at a not guilty verdict, a decision well received in the town and in the capital. Byrne's ugly triumph became tragedy when he himself died some years later after a fight lasting ninety-nine rounds and taking three hours sixteen minutes. Thank God boxing, these days, is a much, much safer sport though like many others, such as mountain climbing and motor sports, there are occasional tragedies. Some say the sport goes back 5,000 years though the literature shows that it was in the early 1700s when it began to be organised, however roughly, in Britain.

Right from the start, it appealed to folk across the social range. Salcey Green showed the involvement of the top of the social scale, almost two hundred years ago, in following the 'fancy' as some called it. This continued right up to the modern era. In the research for this book, I came across a Board of Control licence granted to my grandfather to promote at Paisley Ice Rink in the early sixties. The president of the Board then was the legendary J. Onslow Fane Esq. and the vice-president was Col. Viscount Scarsdale TD. Twenty-one stewards were listed on the Board's official notepaper. Of these, there were three lieutenant colonels, one colonel, a major, two judges, an MP, three QCs and an assortment of other ennobled members of the hoi polloi.

This yellowing document produced two other points of note. One was that the fee, for the year for licence no. 76984 (reg no. 36), was seven guineas. The other was the name of W. Barrington Dalby on the notepaper as a steward. This is a guy with a special place in Glasgow folklore. Along with Raymond Glendinning (and latterly Eamonn Andrews), he commentated on the big fights of the fifties and sixties – in those days, radio was king and battles between the likes of Americans Gus Lesnevich and Joe Baksi and Britons Bruce Woodcock and Freddie Mills attracted huge audiences. We often listened to boxing on the radio up that close in Rutherglen Road. The two commentators were known as The Terrible Twins and had a regular routine. Raymond did the blow-by-blow stuff and Dalby, an ex-referee, was the inter-round summariser. It was his job to score the round and analyse what had happened so far and what was likely to happen next. The two of them were great old pros and the word 'Dalby' slipped into the Glasgow patois and is still heard occasionally when older fans meet. Glaswegians like to drink in between rounds but sometimes, for some thirsty folk, the next round at the bar can't come fast enough so they slip away from the group and sneak in an extra drink – an 'inter-round summary drink' or, as it became known, a 'Dalby'. Funnily enough, the name of Joe Baksi also lingers on as Glasgow rhyming slang for a taxi.

After Salcey Green, the game gradually became less savage. But it was 1867 before the Queensberry Rules were codified. The basics are the same today: three-minute rounds with a minute's rest in between; after a knockdown, the fighter gets ten seconds to get up; and you don't whack a man who is down on one knee. These immensely sensible innovations and, of course, the modern rules on medical matters have made the sport much safer. After they were introduced, keep-fit clubs and other sports clubs sprang up in many cities. I know from experience that, to this day, such clubs are a source of community good especially in areas of bad housing – they offer a chance for young folk trying to escape from poverty and unemployment. A youngster with nothing much going for him grows in self-confidence when he take up the game, keeps himself fit, stays off the drink and channels his energy and perhaps his aggression into what some call the 'sweet science' of boxing.

I defy the critics of the game to deny the good effect of a well-run boxing gym or club. The benefits, both physical and mental, are obvious and, these days, safety is paramount. I can show the critics hundreds of men who have changed their lives for the better because of an involvement in boxing. The 'antis' can and do make their own case against the game but there is much that is positive in it. Boxing is a mixture of athleticism, technical skills, strategy, bravery and sportsmanship and, at the highest level, it can be beautiful to watch. Men like Sugar Ray Robinson, our own Dick McTaggart, Sugar Ray Leonard and, above all, Muhammad Ali were awesome in the ring. Of course it is an aggressive sport – aggression is part of human nature – but, if you do not show *controlled* aggression in the ring, you are finished. Lose your head and, nine times out of ten, you lose your fight. The dedication needed to succeed is huge. When I watch films like the *Rocky* series, I may think that some parts of it are on a different planet from reality but one aspect is right (and it is a lesson for teenage tearaways watching the DVDs) – you cannot succeed in boxing without the sweaty slog of mile after mile of roadwork and hour after hour in the gym, working the bag or running through a regime planned to the last detail by your trainer.

The outsider is not aware of the pre-fight regime of a boxer. And many a youngster, when he faces the reality rather than the fictionalised version you see on films or television, gets a shock. Training for a fight requires a controlled diet – taking out some of the things youngsters love like steak smothered in sauce, beer, greasy soup and bread. Still water, fish, fresh fruit and chicken can have limited appeal to teenagers. Incidentally, despite the health columns and huge sections in newspapers devoted to medical matters and the current 'five-a-day' campaign, not everyone has taken healthy eating on board – even some fighters ignore dietary advice. I remember one who had trouble making the weight so we asked him to run through his diet. He went into great detail and all seemed well and we were puzzled. What was the problem? We suggested he may have had a sneaky glass or two of milk, maybe even some sweet tea. No, he denied it all. It was only after further probing we discovered he was slaking his thirst with cans of sweet lemonade. We remonstrated with him but he insisted, 'You said no tea, no milk, no beer. You never mentioned lemonade!'

People can be selective about what they tell you about their diet. A friend told me of a doctor who had a patient with stubbornly high cholesterol. He was made to write out his intake of food and drink every day. Again it was a mystery as to what was causing the problem. Knowing the guy was a sales rep the doctor asked him to describe his daily routine which involved many stops at petrol stations to fill the tank of his repmobile. Each time he did this, he added a bar of chocolate to the bill paid for by his employer. It was an automatic reaction to buying petrol. He just never gave it a thought. When he stopped the chocolate habit and stuck to the diet he had been given, down went his cholesterol reading.

The run-up to a fight can last five or six weeks with full training every weekday involving at least a minimum of five miles running a day at a pace that brings you home in around thirty-five minutes. And you do not run at an easy constant pace. Every few hundred yards, you break into sprint pace, then slow almost to a walk and then back to a fast run. This makes the different muscles work to their maximum. After the roadwork, most fighters will pull off the sweaty hooded tracksuit and take a nap before going to the gym in the afternoon. There they go through a punishing regime of exercises designed to strengthen the parts of the body that need building up. The modern gym is a place of hi-tech training machines to torture the body into peak fitness. There are hours of endless sparring, not something I fully support, with an opponent who can mirror the style of the guy who you will be fighting. I also like to have a boxer do a lot of shadow boxing in front of a full-length mirror which shows the fighter his own vulnerability and allows the trainer to work on points of technique and study the results.

It is not quite the easy life some aggressive young bucks think it is. The reality is far removed from their notion that you just climb into the ring and knock the hell out of the other guy. And I find it hard to get over to novices that your feet are as important as your hands. Footwork can win a fight just as surely as a big punch. And it can get you out of trouble. There are many ways to get off the ropes and back into the centre of the ring but they all involve footwork rather than bish and bash. And the truly great boxers have an attribute they all share – balance. Many of the greats are up there with Fred Astaire when is comes to grace, effortless synchronised movement and aesthetic appeal to an audience. Try watching a Sugar Ray Robinson video to see what footwork and balance are all about.

The 'good thing/bad thing' debate on the sport is never going away. Recently, I was called to defend it on radio in an interview which included Sam Galbraith, a noted ex-neurosurgeon and successful politician – and a nice guy! He made much of the fact that, in boxing, the brain can be pushed around violently in the hard confines of the skull, causing damage. But boxing is not the only sport where that happens. In jump racing the shock of repeated landings after clearing high fences jerks the brain around in similar fashion and that can happen ten or twelve times in one race. And a jockey can take part in four or five races in an afternoon five or even six days a week. And there is evidence that some veteran jockeys show signs of what is loosely described as punch drunkenness at the end of a busy riding career. Modern boxing submits the contestants to regular scans so that their brain patterns and eyesight are constantly monitored. They are assessed medically before every fight. And they can fight only once a week or so at the most. Fighting for a championship means that the twenty-eight-day rule comes into play although a fighter going for a title would normally have even longer fight-free. And the top exponents of the game often fight only a couple of times a year. Compare this with jump racing, just one example. I don't recollect the anti-boxing fraternity leaping to the barricades to demand an end to racing. Or to even some stringent health checks on jockeys who, apart from any possible damage to the brain, can have suspect diets, sometimes existing on toast and cigar smoke for years on end to make a weight.

Nor is there much of a fuss over footballers, especially those whose careers spanned the forties and fifties. Repeated heading of heavy wet footballs can cause brain damage, something I believe that has been the subject of medical research but not much publicised. I can think of at least a couple of old-time footballers, strikers famed for their heading skills, who, after retirement, showed classic signs of the brain damage that is so often wrapped up in the phrase 'punch drunk'. More than the fight game causes brain damage to sportsmen but it is boxing that always takes the big hit, no pun intended, when the subject is debated. But I passionately believe, if we took all risk out of all sport, we would be the poorer for it.

In my experience, those who want boxing banned have not thought through what would happen: the game would go underground and would no longer have the medical input and supervision demanded by the British Boxing Board of Control and other organisations. It could popularise what we term today unlicensed shows and that is a real danger. Incidentally, a ban would also be bad news for writers. Prize fighting has been around for thousands of years and the way it encapsulates much of the human condition has stimulated many great writers. No, a well-run safety regime with maximum care for the boxers is the best we can hope for and I think it is a duty for those of us in modern promotion to keep the game as clean as possible and prevent a return to the old days of marathon battles over many rounds with little in the way of safety. Some people, even some in the sporting clubs, hanker after longer rounds and more rounds and find the modern concern for safety over done. Occasionally, from the ringside, after a nice steak and with a glass of red at hand, it might look that way but those in the gyms, the promoters' offices and in the game on the medical side thankfully don't see it that way.

Many of the lads who begin by boxing at local gyms and keep-fit clubs graduate to turning pro and boxing in venues like my St Andrew's Sporting Club, now based in The Radisson SAS hotel in Glasgow, and go on to stadium and arena fights and the riches that accompany them and the associated television coverage. The clubs themselves – usually male only – are interesting places with a body of dedicated supporters who love their monthly night at the boxing. With recent legislation, it looks like we might have to admit women in the future but would they want to go and be a minority at tables full of guys who have been attending the fights for years? We'll see how it pans out but, for the moment, the members and guests at the St Andrew's get a good dinner, drinks, an amusing speaker and the guest chairman, often someone from the media, is always a well-known figure. Some of the names we have had in the chairman's role and as guests would produce a list that looked like a Who's Who in Scottish sport. The list of chairmen alone includes Jim Black, Dougie Donnelly, Alistair Alexander, Alistair Murning, the late Jim Reynolds (not fond of public speaking, he dreaded the call from me but was always a success) and Archie McPherson. The Ladies' Night, too, has had names like Shereen Nanjiani, Jackie Bird and Louise White from TV. And there is always a sprinkling of sports stars, many from football and rugby, to introduce from the top table. Glasgow journalist Ron McKenna got a lot right when he visited the St Andrew's Sporting Club in the Holiday Inn (the old Albany, as was, at the top of Bothwell Street) in 2005. He had never seen live boxing before and had some of his preconceived misconceptions shot down. Writing in his column in *The Herald*, he made several confessions. One was that he had been a tad disappointed with the clientele. He had hoped for a whiff of gangsters and gloves. As he put it:

> An air of menace, *Goodfellas* in the heart of the city, gentlemen in the ring, ruffians in dinner suits. It is just not like that. In fact some of the boys [club members] look like the only thing they will batter out is your tax return . . . Boxing, then. What can I say? You come for a bit of wooh and wah, some raw testosterone, and what do you get? An evening where even the bouts are held in dignified silence. Where the only sounds are fighters gulping oxygen, muttered instructions of cornermen and that whack whack of leather hitting damp flesh. No jeering or cheering, lager louts, or even strutting around the ring.

But, in the true tradition of the writing trade, Ron had one moment of fear. The boxers were throwing themselves about with a brute force that made the wine bottles on the ringside tables tremble. The urbane and perceptive Mr McKenna feared the drink might topple and spill! Surely not?

17

BLACK TIES AND BELTERS

After Dad died, it took a lot of cash to keep the team together. It took even more to finance my dream of owning the St Andrew's Sporting Club.

The St Andrew's can lay claim to be the premier organisation of its kind in the United Kingdom. It was vision of a businessman called Moss Goodman who started it. 'Mister' Goodman, as everyone called him, had the idea of setting up a gentleman's sporting club in 1972. It came at a vital time for Scottish boxing. After Peter Keenan retired in 1959, the professional game went into a slump for a numbers of years only to be revived eventually for a golden age that produced stars like Chic Calderwood, Cowboy McCormack, Walter McGowan, Ken Buchanan, Jim Watt and John McCluskey. Mister Goodman knew what was required during the bad days and he had the contacts – the early patrons of the club included the Earl of Roseberry, the Earl of Elgin and the then Provost of Glasgow, John Mains. The chief aim of the original project was to 'foster the interests of Scottish sport and those who patronised it'. The early club director was Les Roberts and the aims of the launch night were maintained by him and, I like to think, by me after I bought control.

BLACK TIES AND BELTERS

After our monthly shows in the wintertime, I get letters from visitors from all over the world praising the organisation and atmosphere. Our reputation is so high that we were chosen to present the centenary show of the National Sporting Club in London – the same venue where I had taken boxers all those years ago and where I watched the occasional gent fall asleep under the chandeliers. No one slept when I returned for that centenary. At the St Andrew's, Moss Goodman set out to provide top-quality entertainment in an atmosphere of welcoming surroundings where friends could meet, relax and enjoy good food, hospitality and companionship. And I think, down the years, we have achieved that and are still achieving that at our current home The Radisson SAS hotel in Argyle Street. And I believe it will never change. The club is undoubtedly the most successful of its kind in the UK. My pride in the St Andrew's was such that, along with John Quinn, I was delighted, in 1988, to produce a lavish leather-bound souvenir book of the history of the first twenty-five years of the club. All club members got a free copy of this limited edition which is a great keepsake.

One of the attractions of the club was the chance for businessmen and their pals and the real boxing enthusiasts to rub shoulders with famous sportsmen. We never put on a show without stars ringside as well as stars and potential stars in the ring. Some came from the world of boxing – like Lennox Lewis and Henry Cooper, the man who is forever remembered for decking Muhammad Ali (as well as his aftershave commercials). Allan Wells who won Olympic gold in Moscow in 1980 attended a show as did George McNeill of Tranent, the former world professional sprint champion and Powderhall legend. Football and boxing have an affinity (though hopefully not during actual games!) and nearly all the Glasgow greats have turned up at one time or another for our shows – John Greig, Billy McNeil, Walter Smith, Tommy Burns and more. Scott Hastings came from the world of rugby, Stephen Hendry and Ian Doyle from snooker and Jimmy McRae and his sons Colin and Alistair from rallying (I was saddened to learn of Colin's tragic death in September 2007 in a helicopter crash which also claimed the life of his young son). Barry Hearn also brought along the seven times world snooker champion Steve Davis and world darts champion Phil 'The Power' Taylor.

Having some big names always helps to create a great atmosphere on club nights. It was the same from the first night. A really big match was needed to catch the imagination of the press and public. Les Roberts was matchmaker for the first night and he used all his skill and knowledge to get a bout that would make a spectacular start. He wanted Ken Buchanan v Jim Watt for the British lightweight title. He made a bid of just over £7,000 for it – not a large figure by today's standards but big enough, he thought, to get the fight. He was right.

Now the owner of the club and intensely proud of it, I often think back to that night. It was a wonderful bit of boxing and I was in Jim Watt's corner holding up the water bucket and washing the gumshields. I was paid £3 by Les Roberts. The sum seems tiny but should be put into context. In the old days, the boxer would often tip the guy who handled the spit bucket a quid or two. With the fees and the tips it could all add up to a decent amount of money for the night. And you got to see the fights ringside.

The club was well and truly launched on the Scottish scene thanks to the foresight of Moss Goodman and the shrewdness of Les Roberts. The background to the fight was that Buchanan had won the world title against Ismael Laguna in searing heat in Puerto Rico a couple of years before, only to lose it in Madison Square Garden to a series of low blows from Roberto Duran. Ken needed a few good results to force a rematch. Jim Watt, for his part, had prospered domestically while Ken was away fighting on the international scene. Buchanan seemed to regard the fight as a minor inconvenience as he traipsed round the world and that proved to be a bit of a mistake as Watt was, by now, a real player. Buchanan duly won but not without an epic battle that left both boxers with cuts.

Ken was big in spirit and, after the fight, he told the press:

> I have fought a lot of great fighters in my time, in America and round the world. Jim Watt came in here after only seventeen contests against my forty-seven. He proved in this fight he is a man, not a boy. I think he is a great fighter.

Buchanan never did get a return with Duran but he was inducted into America's Boxing Hall of Fame. And Jim went on to win the world title himself.

It was a night few would forget – certainly not reporter John Quinn and Ken Buchanan – and not just for the boxing. In our history of St Andrew's, John tells how, after the fight, Ken was making his way to his room in the penthouse suite when the lift stuck. John was in the lift as well, heading for an interview with the champ, and so was Ken's dad Tommy. After the lift stopped it was like one of those comedy scenes in a sitcom. The trapped passengers joked and laughed but, as a few minutes dragged on to quarter of an hour, the cramped space and the deteriorating air began to take their toll and, when eventually, after forty-five minutes, the lift began to inch slowly to safety, as the engineers manually wound in the cable, tempers were as foul as the air. Just as the lift and its wretched occupants reached the level where they could get out, the doors were prised open an inch or two. On the other side was James 'Solly' Sanderson, the *Daily Express* sports writer, sometime referred to rather cruelly by his peers as Hans Christian Sanderson because of his tendency to take 'fliers' in stories. John Quinn says that the bold Solly, notebook and pen in hand, asked him to shout out a few quotes from Ken that he could use in a story about to be filed in a couple of minutes. John is an easygoing guy but, on this occasion, he records, 'I obliged. But I kept it short – only two words. The last was "off".'

Club fighting is part of the hospitality business and I am always conscious that the entire package, including the food and drink, has to be right to keep the members and their guests happy. This is not an inconsiderable task, as John Major might have said using his favourite adjective, and, down the years, I have been greatly helped by hotel top brass, chefs and countless cheery and efficient waiters and waitresses. Glasgow is, I may say, a great place for producing waitresses well able to cope with the crowds at functions, to weave around the tables with a succession of courses, plates delicately balanced on their arms, and distribute the fine wines and malts with a smile. The patter between them and the dicky-suited punters can raise more than a few laughs. They are a valuable part of the show. The trade magazine *Caterer and Hotel Keeper* did a 'special' on one of my fights that emphasised the scale of the operation. Alberto Laidlaw was the Albany General Manager at the time and he told the magazine reporter he was delighted every time a 'fight' broke out during dinner – it gave the staff a break as the boxers went about their business! The match the night the catering mag put under the journalistic microscope was a WBC international bout between Steve Boyle, then the UK champion, and Pedro Gutierrez, champion of Argentina. It took place in front of 865 dinner-suited men and was the biggest ever event in the hotel (in the catering business, they like to keep the numbers accurate) and on hand were 120 hotel staff. Eight hundred and sixty-five haggises were cooked and countless bottles of wine bought to wash the food down. This was no ordinary club night but a special event. Money is the bottom line in a hotel, as elsewhere, and it was pointed out that the St Andrew's provided the Albany with around 5,000 covers a year in a suite that would be otherwise difficult to sell on a Monday night.

The hotel itself, on this occasion, became a co-sponsor with Younger's Tartan to provide the £40,000 needed to stage the evening. The hotel gave free accommodation to the Argentinian boxer, his connections and the referee and WBC officials. It was 30 January 1989, not long after our traditional Burns Night, and a four-course Burns menu was laid on. Our normal nights ran to four to five hundred in those days but this one had the hotel's then banqueting operations manager, Pedro Gomez, crawling around the banqueting suite on hands and knees using a yardstick to calculate a table plan that would fit the extra seats needed in. Because of the number of covers and the television coverage, everything in the kitchen had to be timed to seconds and chef Frank Boggie worked out a time chart for everyone to follow. It began at 5.45, when the boxers had barely woken from their afternoon naps, with the almost a thousand haggis ready to boil. Earlier, the ring had been erected and the tables stocked with drink. The fact the championship ring was larger than our normal one meant that I had to take thirty-two seats off the plan – if that had not been the case, the audience could have been 897. Sales manager Bernadette McKenzie recalled that this 'was all pretty basic stuff'. Wine, water, whisky – what else do you need for a drouthy boxing crowd?

The hotel's commercial interest in keeping the St Andrew's members is obvious. This was back in the late eighties but even then Alberto Laidlaw could tell *Caterer and Hotel Keeper* that the boxing nights were worth around a quarter of a million a year to the hotel. There was more value than just the cost of the dinners and the drink sold. Then, as now, the club members are senior city businessmen who use the night to entertain corporate clients and fill other functions rooms as well as the main dining space. Laidlaw also pointed out that, almost every day for a month, the hotel got a mention in the papers in the build-up to a major fight. This was high visibility that you just could not buy.

The night was a great success though the winner, Steve Boyle, complained about the effect of the cigar smoke on his breathing. This caused an investigation by the Board of Control into Boyle's health. He needed medical tests to prove that he was fit to box and did not have an asthmatic condition. It kept him out of the ring for some time till he got the OK. Away from the actual boxing, Alberto Laidlaw had an interesting final quote, 'The biggest advantage to the hotel is the PR spin-off. And the long-term aim of taking the financial risk is to ensure the St Andrew's Sporting Club is still going to be around in fifteen years' time.' It is but, sadly, the Albany isn't.

This was far from the only time I featured in leading magazines. The German edition of *GQ* sent a reporter over to interview me and he produced an eight-page glossy coloured spread on the Sporting Club. It was great to think that I was now known in Berlin if not in Bellshill.

The eighties and nineties provided many memorable nights and a great favourite of the members was wee Paul Weir from Irvine who had made history by taking part in the first world-title fight to be held in a private members' club. Paul had won the WBO straw-weight title in only his sixth fight. And he went on to become the first Scot to win two world titles at different weights. Hughie Smith was another great favourite though he never won a title. He was the master of the old-fashioned left jab. He deserves his place in the St Andrew's roll of honour as the man with a record number of appearances in front of the members – seventeen. With, as I say, no titles won but, at one stage, a string of eight wins in a row, he was named as our boxer of the year. He and I go back a long way and I am one of his greatest admirers. He never put on a poor show, always gave value for money and is a genuinely nice guy as well as a fine boxer. I have many happy memories of Hughie and he holds a special place in my recollections as he is the first boxer I managed after the death of my dad in 1979. I had been his trainer but, when Dad died, Hughie asked me to manage him and I consider it a privilege I was the first one he asked. He used to call me Joe Lampton (from *The Man at the Top*). He said it was important to maintain the family connection. I get annoyed when I think of the word 'journeyman' used to describe a boxer such as Hughie who never reached the status of star. A good journeyman is the backbone of the sport. With Hughie, I would use the word as a compliment. A manager, a trainer and a punter buying a ticket for a show could rely on Hughie Smith – you can't say better than that.

Terry Lawless, that famous Essex man, is a great fan of the club. He particularly remembers his man Jim Watt, who he was nurturing and steering towards a world title, stopping

Frenchman André Holyk in the club. This was a vital win that led to Jim moving into the top flight. The world-title win against Pitalua, in the Kelvin Hall, which followed is something that greatly affected the much-respected English manager. He says:

> When we made our way from the dressing room deep in the back of the hall to the ringside, there was bedlam. The bagpipes were playing, the fans, around 10,000 of them, were going berserk in their acclamation of their man and the hairs on the back of my neck were standing to attention. I remember thinking, 'My God, this is terrifying for me – what is it like for Pitalua?' I have heard a lot of noisy support in rings round the world but that display of partisanship beats them all.

The sort of Scottish support – the football team gets the same sort of buzz from the Tartan Army – is something that brought Terry north on a regular basis and left him always looking for an excuse to come back. It is interesting how the club builds great loyalty. Not all the members are huge boxing fans – some, indeed, would be unlikely to attend shows in stadiums and sports halls – but they all like the formula of a good dinner, good entertainment and a bit of boxing. A regular night out at the St Andrew's is a must – the mixture is right.

It is always great for the fans to see famous faces at first hand and, at Morley's Nitespot in a show run by Henry Hoey, Eddie Coakley and me (the club was operated by the legendary show-business figure Eric Morley of Miss World fame), we had Harry Gibbs along one night. Harry is perhaps the most famous and respected referee of recent times. He must have appeared in televised big fights hundreds of times and is a familiar face to fans. He also played the ref in *Winners and Losers*. Harry has refereed most of the post-war greats in British boxing. But he was not too 'big-time' to come up to Glasgow and put something into the grass roots of the sport by refereeing a couple of youngsters slugging it out to take the first steps to get them on the ladder of success.

I remember that night in Morley's watching Harry at work. I like to think I can score a fight with the best of them and, as I watched one particular battle, I had it down as a foregone conclusion for one of the boxers – it was just so one-sided – but, when the final bell went, Harry took his time to examine his card ultra carefully. I expected him to raise the winner's arm with not a moment's hesitance but no – this fight was being given the respect due to a world-title eliminator or, indeed, a title fight itself. Eventually Harry announced the winner – the right man of course – but he had the loser within a point of success. Over a glass of wine later, I asked Harry what he was playing at? There was only one winner and even the newest guest at the club who knew little about the game and less about the exotic scoring methods would have got that one right. 'Tommy,' said Harry, 'that little guy who lost will go home believing that, if the great Harry Gibbs had nearly made him a winner, all he had to do was run a little further and faster in his road work and sweat a little more in the gym and he could be a success.' It was a kindly and accurate assessment. And the right boxer did win.

Incidentally, Harry would not accept the lavish fancy food on offer in the hotel and insisted on going to a chip shop under the Heilan' Man's Umbrella in Argyle Street at the entrance to Central Station. A man of the people, Harry was always proud to talk of his affinity with the Scots which stretched back to the time he served with them in the war.

Len Mullen, who came into this story early on as a boxer in the Gilmour stable, became a referee when he retired. Like Harry, he could show a lot of humanity in this hard, hard game, always putting the boxers' welfare first. But he was a stalwart in the Scottish area in the seventies when we didn't have all that many refs. We used to run a number of charity shows where, as part of the fundraising, the patrons had to predict the winner of three of the fights. There was no room on the slip for a draw – you had to pick a winner. It was not unusual on these occasions for Len to declare a draw. This meant all the money wagered went to the charity. This I think, more than anything, showed Len's honesty in scoring as he saw fit. Nobody lost and the charity got a bit of extra cash. Harry Gibbs and Len Mullen – two great guys. And it is nice to be nice for a change when talking about referees. I am not, generally, noted for my high opinion of the third man inside the ropes. I have a touch of the Alex Ferguson in my nature. I like to shout and moan and point out, every chance I get, what I see as bad refereeing and by that I mean anything that goes against my boxer. Even after fights, I like to grumble Ferguson-style about the actions of the ref. It is my nature. But, when seriously questioned about the skill and intent of the men in the middle, I have to say that they get it right more times than they get it wrong. But there have, I must say, been occasions in the past when I feel the decision has gone against me and my boxers for reasons not apparent in the ring. But that is me. And don't ask me to be too specific. Maybe it is all in the mind. And, when I begin to think like that, I can put a little humour into it by reminding myself of the old saying: 'Just because you are paranoid it doesn't mean they are not out to get you.' And it has now become a bit of a joke in Scottish boxing that you have not made it until you have been at the receiving end of one of my rants.

Despite all the recent furore and legislation about men-only clubs, the fact remains that the only women around on normal monthly shows were those hardworking waitresses. Even Veronica and Stephanie did not attend although some months they had been up all night sorting out place settings and attending to all sorts of vital details the night before. However, there's one exception – the annual Ladies' Night. Veronica and Stephanie play a major part in this glamorous occasion that has become a winter tradition. When I think of Ladies' Night, I can almost smell all that top of the range perfumery that hangs around the tables – quite a change from the men-only aroma of whisky and perspiration. The two hotels the club has been based in have always been appreciative of the business it has brought to bars and dining table. On Ladies' Night, I have often thought that similar appreciation should come to us from such as Frasers and John Lewis – their perfumery counter takings must rocket. The cabaret for this much-looked-forward-to event is always top notch. Big-name Scottish showbiz stars have provided the entertainment and some, like Brenda Cochrane, have starred for us several times. The event has real glamour, pulling in big names like Hazel Irvine, Kaye Adams, Shereen Nanjiani and Jackie Bird to name just a few.

A backbone of the club has always been a core of boxing-loving city businessmen and, in the souvenir book, I mention just a few of the most solid supporters. People like Patrick Farrell, who had a successful career in the steel business and was one of the first to sign a membership cheque. And Gerry Woolard, John Smith, a haulage contractor, Geoff Fleming, a great friend of the late Dunky Jowett, Douglas Gillespie, a plant hire supremo who also loves golf, John Cooper and Gerry Lipton. Now, more than thirty years after the first night, I look back at good memories and forward to good times to come.

It is sad that my dad never lived to see me running the St Andrew's. I always like to put on record that I am deeply indebted to him for my upbringing and apprenticeship in this tough business of boxing promotion. I would have amounted to nothing had it not been for him. But the St Andrew's is a team. Boxers, doctors, paramedics, chefs like Frank Boggie, also new Radisson SAS executive chef James Reid and the members themselves have made the club a Glasgow institution. I am proud of that – and so would Tommy Gilmour Sr have been.

18

DEATH IN THE RING

I consider the world-title win of Pat Clinton as the highlight of my life in boxing but there were many other great occasions that could challenge for the next most memorable moment in my career. However, there are no challengers and there is no argument about the lowest point – the death of James Murray in October 1995. It is amazing how often folk who have been involved in a tragedy talk of, if not a premonition, a feeling of tension, bad vibes or whatever, before the event. Somehow or other, I was tense about this one from the start. My boxer, Drew Docherty, from Condorrat, was the British bantamweight champion and the Board of Control ruled he had to make a mandatory defence against Jim Murray, the Scottish champion, from Lanarkshire.

I knew it would be a tough one but Jim deserved his chance. He went into what was to be his last fight with a record of fifteen wins (five by knockouts) and two losses. He was managed and promoted by Alex Morrison and I knew there was little chance of us doing a deal to promote the fight as we both wanted it for our own promotions. In a case like that, the Board calls for purse offers which clears the way for any promoter to bid for the rights to stage the fight. The English promoter Frank Warren won the bidding and set up the fight for Glasgow's Hospitality Inn, to run as a Morrison/Warren promotion.

The fact that this battle between two local lads was to take place in the city added to the tension round the promotion. Everything went well at the weigh-in but, for some reason or other, I still felt tense. For the night of the fight, we had a room to change in and prepare that was well away from the hubbub of the arena and its charged atmosphere and, as far as we were concerned, everything seemed to be OK. Drew was well trained for the fight, he knew what he had to do and we had talked endlessly about strategy and he had performed really well in his gym work and out on the roads. He was confident but quiet which is his normal approach. He is a deep and contented person who had no problems with his own thoughts and his own company – rather different from many who make a success of life in the ring. He even enjoys the contemplative sport of angling. He seemed to take this difficult period, before the fight starts, well.

Eventually the waiting was over and we went down to the foyer, just outside the banqueting hall where the ring had been built, to wait for that march through the noisy crowd, up through the ropes and into the ring. Unlike Drew, I was tense and my mood was not helped by the noise of the crowd watching the fights on the undercard next door. There was a feeling of aggression that seemed to seep through the walls and out into the foyer.

Alex Morrison, I suspect, also felt some extra tension for one reason or another round this fight. He approached me and asked if I would be going into the ring with my boxer, something that is customary in the game. I said yes and we agreed that we would both go in the ring with the boxers and that we would publicly shake hands. This is exactly as it should be and, since I think Alex was also aware of the tension in the air, such a public handshake would make sure that the fans knew that all everyone wanted was a good clean contest.

Jim Murray started very well and, despite my man being on the wrong side of the score sheet, I was not my normal self, screaming advice and encouragement from the sidelines. I was edgy in the hostile environment. But, as the fight went on, Drew kept his cool and began to come back, boxing skilfully, and, in our corner, the feeling was that he was beginning to edge it and was gradually becoming the stronger fighter. Up to the last round, an objective observer would have seen a great display of boxing with two little fellows determined to win and drawing deep on everything they knew about fighting and ring craft. But the last round never really ended. Shortly after it began, Jim Murray collapsed and fell to the canvas and was stretchered from the ring to an ambulance and on to hospital. This was Friday 13 October and Jim, just twenty-five, was taken to the nearby Southern General Hospital, a nationally renowned centre for neurosurgery. He died two days later after an operation to remove a brain clot.

At the hotel, the end of the fight provoked a riot at the ringside with fans having to be treated for cuts and the police making several arrests. It was a horrible night for boxing. In the hours after the fight, we were in constant touch with the hospital hoping against hope that it would all end well. It was not to be and, of course, everyone's sympathies were with Jim's parents. Drew and I did not know them but we knew we had to meet. It could have been difficult but we had to do it and the arrangements were made. We worried how they would feel towards us. We needn't have. They made us genuinely welcome, handled the whole affair with great dignity and showed wonderful compassion to Drew who was in a terribly difficult position. The Murrays, naturally deeply shocked by the unexpected accidental death, took comfort from the fact that Jim had loved boxing and had been so successful. Indeed, he was buried in his ring kit. Their kindness to everyone else sucked into this tragedy was as remarkable as it was admirable.

The emotional impact of this shocking event was such that I flirted with the idea of quitting boxing. My boxers told me to forget that – to a man, they asked me to keep going and pointed out that I was the best person to look after their interests. They urged me to stay on. I appreciated that reaction.

The days after the fight were filled with a media storm. I sent Drew and his wife Caroline abroad to escape what I can only call a frenzy. The press wanted to speak to everyone concerned and they gave no quarter in the hunt for a new twist in the story. I have worked with the press and I am a close friend of many in that game but I have never experienced anything like what happened in the wake of the death of James Murray. Much of this was because the story was now front-page news and the sports journalists, men with a feeling for the game and its history, had been roughly elbowed aside by the hawks from the news desks – in many cases, they were reporters without any sensibilities who were driven to wring the maximum news value out of tragedy, be it a car crash, a mining disaster or an accidental death in the ring. I did not like that. The boxing writers themselves were a different matter. For example, the late Jim Reynolds of *The Herald* was personally close to the Docherty family but he never took any underhand advantage of that relationship. He, and others like him who had spent their lives in the sport, behaved with true professionalism but they had colleagues who were less fastidious.

Everyone felt for the Murray family. And I was determined that everything should be handled sensitively. In an attempt to control the press and TV feeding frenzy, I called an early-morning press conference at which Drew and I would try to provide straightforward and honest answers to legitimate questions. The sports guys were good and so were most of the news reporters present but one went right over the score. This man, not from Glasgow I am relieved to say, waded in with the most insensitive question I have ever heard. I won't quote what he asked here but talk about ghoulish . . . I reacted with anger I must say and said I had no intention of answering such objectionable questioning. I gave this guy a hard time and, I am glad to say, so did many of his colleagues. The Murray family deserved to be treated with dignity and allowed to grieve in privacy. This sort of question was out of order at a press conference. Even worse was the behaviour of some reporters and photographers at the funeral. It was a very sad occasion and the way some sections of the press carried on was nothing less than a disgrace.

Such a tragedy is hard to get out of your mind and, although my own fighters had convinced me that I should stay in the game, you can't help doing some deep thinking. My friend Jim Watt got it, I think, pretty right in his comments in a newspaper feature looking back at the Nigel Benn v Gerald McClennan battle in 1995, a fight of astonishing ferocity that left McClellan partially blind, confined to a wheelchair and needing twenty-four-hour-a-day attention from his sisters. Twelve years after the event, Jim was quoted as saying that when 'these things happen you are shocked and appalled and question what you do'. He went on:

> I have seen this with Michael Watson, McClellan and others. When young James Murray died his parents took that decision to bury him in his boxing gear because he had died doing what had made him something in life. Boxing has stood the test of time. It is exciting but it can be cruel, brutal, dangerous and sometimes tragic.

Jim is right. Despite the danger and the occasional tragedies, boxing is still around after hundreds of years and it is not going to go away.

Drew Docherty went back into the ring – after all, that was what he did for a living. Frank Warren played his part in rehabilitating Drew after such an emotional ordeal by offering him a crack at the WBO title against Daniel Jimenez in Nottingham. As Drew's manager, I was criticised by some for letting him take such a high-profile contest as his first fight after the tragedy but I knew my man well. Throughout his career, I found him to be the sort of guy who rose to a challenge. Offered what, on paper, looked like 'easy' fights, he struggled but offer him a real challenge and he prospered. I knew what Warren had offered him was right for him and he took it, losing on points. He fought on a handful of more times before retiring, managing a successful defence of his super bantamweight crown in one of his last contests. Drew retired to his family and his hobby of fishing. Some boxers can handle retirement, others can't. But we see the same sort of thing in other dangerous sports. How many motor racing drivers have changed their mind on retirement when they sit at home, missing the adrenaline rush that comes from competing at the top?

It is no secret that Ken Buchanan fought a tough battle with alcohol but, in the end, he won and is now a popular after-dinner speaker. What he has to say on the subject is interesting:

> It is hard to go to the top of the world and come back to live in the real world. I never missed getting punched in the face but the moment you throw your hands up in celebrating being the best in the world is irreplaceable. Remember that we – boxers – come from the working class. We are from the streets and success can turn your head very quickly. Fortunately I have found a way of staying in boxing without being hit.

I understand the boxers' difficulty. I know the rush I feel taking a boxer into the ring. I do get excited ringside and my own adrenaline kicks in. I have even got myself into such a state of excitement that a medic or two asked if I was OK. What must it be like for the contestant? I am sure that it is not money that lures sportsmen in dangerous events out of retirement. It is the rush you get from the adulation and the glamour. It is more than money.

There is no doubt that an accidental death in the ring always produces a flurry of examination of the sport. All sorts of people, in the media and outside, many of whom have never attended a fight and have little or no understanding of the plus points, throw themselves into the argument with a fury of criticism that is seldom, if ever, used against other sports where there is loss of life. The tragic death of James Murray even provoked a lengthy debate in the House of Lords in that October. Two Scottish peers, Lord Taylor of Gryfe and Lord Carmichael of Kelvingrove, were questioning the future of the fight game.

I found the various comments of the noble lords, for and against, made interesting reading for boxing people. Lord Taylor initiated the debate by asking Her Majesty's Government 'whether, in the light of recent tragic events in the boxing ring, they will consider appointing a Royal Commission to examine and report on boxing?' Lord Inglewood, the Parliamentary Under-Secretary of State, Department of Natural Heritage, replied by expressing, on behalf of the government, their deepest sympathies and condolences to the family of James Murray who 'recently died so tragically'. Lord Taylor immediately went on the attack. He said:

> While I appreciate the sentiments of the Minister, I recall one or two tragic incidents which prompted this Question. Michael Watson is paralysed and in a wheelchair; Gerald McClellan is permanently paralysed; Bradley Stone died eighteen months ago in the ring and James Murray died three weeks ago in the ring. How many cases of death and how many cases of brain damage have we to witness before the government consider an independent inquiry into this matter?

Not much doubt on what side of the for-and-against debate Lord Taylor stood. Lord Inglewood replied to his question by pointing out that boxing is 'an established and lawful sport' and that the government believed the appropriate course was to ensure that safety is paramount. He went on to point out that the British Boxing Board of Control had just announced the provisional conclusions of its medical revision committee which the Board proposed should be introduced as soon as possible to improve the safety of the sport. Lord Renton then put the question:

> Is my noble friend aware that violence has increasingly become part of the way of life of too many people in our country and that boxing encourages that attitude? Would it not be better if we were to stop boxing just as duelling was stopped some years ago?

The minister swatted this one away with the remark, 'I am grateful to my noble friend for drawing that comparison to my attention but I do not think that it is directly comparable.' (A sentiment that the majority outside the gilded circle of the Lords would no doubt agree with!) He went on to say, 'In any event, one of the tenets which is, I believe, accepted by both proponents and opponents of boxing is that it imposes a form of discipline. In a violent world, that, in its own way, is an important safeguard.'

Lord Avebury introduced what was, to my mind, a note of reality. 'Does the minister know how many people have been killed and seriously injured in the Isle of Man TT Races and the Grand National? Why does no one ever call for these sports to be stopped?' he asked. This allowed the minister to point out that boxing is not the only sport which is considered dangerous and in which injuries occur. He said that, in 1991, the Great Britain Sports Council conducted an analysis of sports accidents based on general household surveys and concluded that boxing was the least risky of the categories it identified.

However, the notion that there should be some kind of official inquiry still had its supporters and Lord Carmichael said:

> This is not an appropriate place to discuss the nature of boxing or some of the other sports that have been mentioned but will the Minister consider if the government will not set up a Royal Commission, setting up a Select Committee of the Lords to look into this matter and report on it?

The minister again swatted the suggestion, succinctly pointing out that this was an idea they had not considered and had no plans to do so.

Lord Taylor was not to be silenced and he continued his attack:

> Does the Minister agree that, in comparison with other sports, boxing is the only sport in which an individual enters a ring to inflict damage on his opponent? Would not these two individuals in the ring be arrested if they did the same thing out of the ring?

Lord Inglewood replied that 'it is the nature of the so-called sportsman's defence that, in a whole variety of circumstances, activities that might lead to criminal prosecutions outside a sporting occasion are defences in the event of some accident or injury occurring'. He went on to agree that Lord Taylor was right to say that the position of boxing is anomalous. However, he pointed out that it was not unique in as much as the same applied to martial arts.

230

DEATH IN THE RING

The penultimate word in this intriguing bout of verbal sparring went to Lord Donoughue:

> My Lords, does the Minister accept that there will be widespread sympathy for the approach of my noble friend because of the fact that one of the prime objectives of boxing is to render damage to an opponent? However, in the light of what has been mentioned in relation to other sports and the fact that, for instance, motor sports and mountaineering result in ten times as many deaths as boxing and rugby and horse riding many more, does he agree that he would have support in taking the view that any attempt to ban a sport which is entered into voluntarily and willingly by the participants needs very careful thought?

And the minister replied that Lord Donoughue was right to place the matter in context. I agree – long-winded but right!

The comparison with motor sport is interesting. No one knows the risks taken here better than neurosurgeon Professor Sid Watkins. For years, he ran the fast-response medical team at Grands Prix, arriving at the wreckage seconds after a crash and desperately trying to extricate drivers and, if they were still alive, giving them immediate treatment on the way to the hospital. He saved many lives and was one of the first on the scene when his friend Ayrton Senna died at Imola in 1994. 'The Prof', as the drivers called him, led many changes in his sport in an effort to make it safer. Now retired, he says, 'Of course motor racing is dangerous but I have always believed people should be able to do what they want. Life is full of risks and man has always strived to defy natural law.'

The Internet does not quite have the class or appeal of the ermine-clad Lords but it is a great place for debate. A few years ago, I was impressed by some of the opinions expressed in a flurry of 'for' and 'against' after another tragedy in the ring. A guy (I assume it was a guy) called Splodgethecat – where do they get these names? – gave a very fair and detailed analysis of the arguments on both sides. As in the Lords, the main case against is the matter of 'intent' and the classic defence is that it is less dangerous than other sports and that boxers are not forced to box. Splodgethecat said he had come into the debate believing the sport should be banned. After research and reading what other bloggers had to say, however, he reached the conclusion that banning is in no one's interest. To do so would simply drive boxing underground. Like me, he seemed to think that, as I have said on many occasions, a well-controlled sport with rigorous medical constraints is the best we can hope for. Like me, he also acknowledged that this is a debate that will never go away.

And realists, be they boxers, managers, promoters, doctors, cornermen or whatever, know that the sport, like others, has a history of fatalities. Even Barry McGuigan took part in a contest that resulted in a death. An opponent, Young Ali of Nigeria, went into a coma lasting months. Barry, an intelligent and sensitive man, resumed his successful career. And, just before the death of Jim Murray, another bantamweight, Bradley Stone, died after a contest. The list is a long one but, compared with the list of boxers who have fought down the years and the numbers of fights fought, it is short. The sport can be cruel but not as cruel as some others. In the debates and blogs on the Internet, the anti-boxing fraternity always criticises the sport for the fact that there is 'intent' to hurt your opponent.

That intent always, but always, falls far short of serious injury or death. Death in the ring is always an accident in the full meaning of that word.

19

HIGH JINKS IN THE BIG TIME

I consider myself a pretty good self-publicist. With tickets to sell and club members to recruit, you can't hide yourself away. But even I was never in the same class at banging the drum for myself as one of Dad's old colleagues in the promoting game, the truly legendary Jack Solomons. Jack, with his sleeked back hair, sharp dark suits, permanent grin and trademark cigar – along with George Burns they must have kept half the factories in Cuba on overtime – was a fun guy who enjoyed the good life to the full. He had a close working connection with Tommy Gilmour Sr and not just at the time when Dad managed Peter Keenan. They got together for all sorts of boxing ploys. They were both showmen supreme.

Jack had started out as a fish importer and I believe he was the first to bring carp to the dinner tables of London. This was in contrast to Dad who, of course, came into the game by following in the footsteps of The Auld Yin. But Solomons soon stopped importing fish and turned to importing boxing champions, especially from America. Jack was, without doubt, the number one promoter in the early years after the Second World War. He staged hundreds of fights including twenty-six title fights and, at that time, when boxing was booming, his name was known the length and breadth of Britain. Some say he was responsible for the boom and reviving the sport after the dark days of the war when fighting meant something rather different. Radio was king in those days and it would have been difficult, in the late forties and early fifties, to find someone who did not recognise his name. Such was his fame – and his own high opinion of it – that, when he staged the still-remembered fight between Sugar Ray Robinson and Randy Turpin, he put his own photograph on the cover of the programme rather than one of either of the great champions who would do the actual boxing!

Jack had started out before the war as a manager of Eric Boon and he owned the Devonshire Club in London; this was a popular venue for young fighters, and it also helped him build a network of the movers and shakers in the capital. He also worked as a manager and matchmaker before moving into promoting. It is a career path with a familiar ring. Another similarity is that Jack also ran the private World Sporting Club in London. His breakthrough fight as big-time promoter came when he put Bruce Woodcock and Jack London in for the British heavyweight title.

And the war was still fresh in everyone's memories when he brought light-heavyweight American Gus Lesnevich over to fight Freddie Mills. There was a lot of enthusiasm for all things American at this time and Jack liked to take advantage of that and, as master of publicity, his doings with the American champs he imported filled the airwaves in the days before TV stole the big fights away from the live audience. In Solomons' day, thousands paid top dollar to see his promotions but hundreds of thousands, if not millions, listened in to the fights on the radio. The list of champions he brought to Britain is impressive – Robinson, Jimmy Carter, Dado Marino, Chartchai Chionoi, Ike Williams, Archie Moore, Joe Brown, Emile Griffith, Joey Maxim and Sugar Ramos. After the Robinson–Turpin fight, Solomons' empire started to decline but he was still promoting until his death in December 1979. It was he who staged the Cassius Clay v Henry Cooper fight in 1963.

There is a story is that emphasises his high opinion of himself. It may or may not be true but it is certainly worth re-telling. The Duke of Edinburgh liked a night at the boxing and knew Solomons well. Who in the London establishment didn't? And, when Jack was awarded the MBE for his charity work, the Queen's husband noted the award and wrote to pass on his congratulations. Rumour in boxing has it that the great promoter wrote back thanking the duke for his kind words but remarking 'the people of the East End thought that the honour was long overdue'. The promotional ability never left Jack. He was known as 'The Sultan of Sock' though whether or not he came up with that himself or not I do not know.

He had many connections with Scottish boxing. One of his famous fighters was Rinty Monaghan of Belfast who lost his first fight after a winning run to our own Jackie Paterson. The Sultan of Sock called Rinty 'a leprechaun with fists of steel'. Many years later, the same theme was attached to Roberto Duran nicknamed 'Hands of Stone'. What a fight that would have been, Hands of Stone v Hands of Steel! Two boxers from different eras and different weights – it could not happen but what a promoter's dream.

Incidentally, I am proud to say that, as a school kid, I held up the ring cards for 'Jolly Jack' at Kelvin Hall promotions.

I suppose the successors to old Jack would be Barry Hearn and Frank Warren. Frank had, of course, been involved in the tragic Docherty v Murray bout. And I was grateful to him for the world-title offer to Drew. It eased his way back into the ring and paved the way for a good few paydays for him until he retired in his own time. My relationship with Frank has always been on a professional level but Barry Hearn and I have grown to be friends as well as colleagues. At the start of his career, Barry did what I had always wanted to do – he qualified as a chartered accountant. All these years later, I still regret that I took my eye off the ball in my final years at school. If I had not done that, I could have been up there with Barry as a boxing promoter who can add the magic letters CA after his name. But, in any case, we are now best friends as well as colleagues and we are at ease in each other's social circles, enjoying the odd holiday break together and going to family gatherings south and north of the border. Like Veronica and I, Susan and Barry have two kids, a boy and a girl.

We did not, though, start out as natural friends or business partners. After one of Steve Boyle's fights, Barry got in touch with me and came to see me in my office in the old Albany. There was an odd family connection. Barry was, of course, the Tsar of Snooker and was Steve Davis's manager. Now the other top manager in that game was Ian Doyle who looked after Stephen Hendry. Ian's father had boxed at one time and had been managed by my grandfather, Jim.

With Barry sniffing around on the fight scene in Scotland, I phoned his snooker rival Ian Doyle to do a little research. He is a straight kinda guy, as Tony Blair would say. Now that we are mates, Barry and I laugh at the conversation that followed. Ian Doyle said to me, 'He is a bit slippery. But one thing is for sure, don't worry about your money.' That is the highest compliment you can hand out in sports promotion business. Barry wanted to stage Boyle against Carl Crook but I didn't fancy the match. Barry let it go but told me, 'It will happen.' It didn't happen when I was Boyle's manager although, later in his career, he lost to Crook.

Barry had come into boxing after a spell as a finance director for an investment firm and time in the fashion industry. It was way back in 1976 that he struck up a friendship with Steve Davis, the ginger one, and got into the snooker business. He went into boxing promotion at the deep end with a Joe Bugner–Frank Bruno fight that attracted 30,000 to Tottenham Hotspur's White Hart Lane ground. The sort of guy he is can be illustrated by the way he dealt with the first contract we were involved in. We had agreed terms for the contract verbally, subject to each receiving a typed copy. During the intervening time, some points had changed so I contacted Barry with my concerns. He simply told me to make the changes. When we next met, I gave him the altered contract to look at and approve. He went to the signature part, signed it and gave it back to me. I remarked he had not read the changes and he said whatever I had done was OK by him. He trusted me and that is the way our relationship developed. Any promoter–manager relationship can generate a huge trail of paperwork and no doubt ours did but we worked a different way. Whenever we had a business meeting, the conversation would go along the lines of 'You owe me X grand and I owe you Y grand and difference is Z grand to you'. The required chequebook was then produced and the appropriate cheque signed and handed over. A chartered accountant and a wannabe chartered accountant could do business the easy way.

We first really got together when Barry took on the managership of Chris Eubank from '89 to '95 and he was promoting his man against Tony Thornton, known as 'The Punching Postman from Philadelphia'. After he decided to bring his man north to box in Glasgow, he spoke to a Manchester friend called Jack Trickett who knew me well and who had been a friend of Tommy Sr. Jack told Barry to 'do it with TG'. Barry was less than keen, saying that I was a nice enough fellow but 'hard work', which is a sort of Scottish kind of comment. Maybe that is why we get on. Trickett pointed out that, in his opinion, I was the man in Scotland with the know-how and the contacts. I was flattered to hear his comment and Barry took the point and came to see me and we had that discussion on the contract, mentioned earlier, that sealed our relationship and trust of each other.

We quickly moved our relationship from business associates to close friends. These days, I tend to call him at least four times a week. If I have a problem, he is there for me. And mixing with him in the big time let me loosen up a bit and become a more accomplished entrepreneur. We have travelled the world together and had fun together as well as making a bob or two. One of the nights I remember best is being with Barry in Sun City, South Africa, having a nice meal out. When it was over, the chef popped out of the kitchen and we went on talking for ages over a glass or two about what was the most expensive spice in the world. I don't blame the wine but, for the life of me, I can't remember what conclusion the three of us came to. But it was fun.

That wee bit of socialising was not really the norm for Barry. Here is what he told one interviewer of our relationship:

Gilmour is a bleeding tourist. Always on holiday, jumping on to a plane with Veronica at any excuse for a break. Me, I like to go to the airport, get off the plane and into a limo and off to a nice suite in a nice hotel. Then I do the business and its back to airport by limo, onto the plane and home for the next deal. I could not believe it on one of my first trips abroad with Tommy when he actually knocked on my door and asked if I wanted to go for a walk. He wanted to do some sightseeing. Sightseeing! I am a promoter not a holidaymaker!

Barry went on to be a little more serious and spelled out why our relationship worked so well. He pointed out too that, when I play the tourist, it is only after the business has been done. It is my way to relax after work, if not his! Our relationship is a bit like a marriage where opposites attract and different personalities complement each other. Hearn went on to say I was a penny-pinching nitpicker who worries about where the last cent was going. True! On the other hand, he pointed out that he was a big picture man – a showman with flair and imagination who did not mind taking a risk. I, though, was so obsessed with detail that I would apparently spend a million suing for a penny's damages. All true but Barry also pointed out how much he likes working with me since, especially, he has never lost a penny in any of our joint ventures.

Barry loves his trips north and, on one occasion, he asked me to get him kitted out in full Highland dress. This I did and I must say he looked the part. He enjoyed it all so much that he said he felt like a star in *Braveheart* and asked us to 'find an Englishman to kill'! Not all his visits went so smoothly. My attention to detail backfired one night when Barry turned up at one of our ventures, a show in Irvine, without the correct identification, no tickets, no lapel badges etc. He was paying for everything. It was his show. But he was refused entry at the door because 'if anyone got in without a ticket, Mr Gilmour (who had arranged the security) would go mad'. It was Barry Hearn who went mental. To be fair to the security firm, as I explained to Barry later, I had told them that, if anyone without the right tickets etc. was found in the hall, the firm would not be paid a penny. Hearn told the interviewer about this as well maintaining that neither Don King nor Bob Arum would have the nerve to treat him like that. It was a difficult moment but it did not spoil our friendship. In the same interview, he went on record as saying I was one hundred per cent straight and loyal, a man of principle. I look forward to many more ventures with Barry. But I promise to use my talent for nitpicking to ensure that he never turns up at a show without the correct paperwork!

One time, a visit to Puerto Rico on behalf of Barry led to a worrying happening. I was flying out to make an offer for a fight for our old friend Chris Eubank. The procedure on such occasions was that you had to have all your paperwork and documents on hand plus a 10 per cent deposit of the amount you were bidding. I flew down to London and met Barry's accountant Steve Dawson who handed me the cashier's draft for the deposit and any other necessary documents. I then headed out to San Juan. This meant changing planes at Chicago O'Hare. It is worth pointing out that I have travelled to the States frequently. As I noted earlier, I had started crossing the pond by air at the age of three months. Business and holiday trips and visits to my sister Rena in Detroit added up so I was not exactly a rookie or naive about international air travel. My passport was OK and I had a full American visa. The flight across the pond was pleasant – a meal, a movie and a glass of wine – but I was counting my chickens too early.

When we touched down in the windy city, I was one of the first to reach immigration. It is easy when you travel up front, first class, courtesy of Barry Hearn. I handed over my passport to the officer behind the desk in the immigration hall. He was unusually friendly and, during our chat, he asked where I was going and why. A mention of boxing made him even friendlier. He was a fan. But, out of the blue, there was a slight change in the atmosphere. He asked me my middle name despite the fact that the passport said clearly that I was plain Thomas Gilmour. I explained I had no middle name and the small talk and form filling continued. The next thing he said surprised me and I began to feel just a little edgy. 'Sorry, what did you say your middle name was?' Again I told him I had no middle name and he carried on looking at the passport and the forms. I was now getting agitated. He asked again and I said I had already told him three times that I had no middle name and asked what the problem was. He explained the database on his computer said Interpol were looking for a Thomas 'Something' Gilmour with the same date of birth as mine. I know the Gilmours are a dynasty but I didn't know anyone wanted by Interpol! The uniformed officer didn't tell me the missing middle name but he at least wished me a safe onward journey. It was unsettling to say the least. Now there was the problem of customs. You can't take more than $10,000 into the country and my cashier's draft was for a lot more than that. So I declared it to the customs, now feeling a bit shaky but it was all OK and I headed out to the San Juan plane.

A few weeks later, I was going through O'Hare again – this time on holiday with Veronica – when it looked like it might be starting all over again so I hastily pointed out what had happened before and we got the OK. I never heard if Interpol did get the mystery Thomas Gilmour but no one has asked me my middle name recently.

Barry Hearn, like Solomons, is the eternal showman. He has great charisma and I learned an enormous amount from him about presentation. We have lots of arguments but we have confidence in each other and a great rapport. Mind you, we are not peas in a pod. Barry has all sorts of interests outside boxing. His Matchroom Sport organisation does not concentrate just on boxing and snooker. He promotes the world's richest coarse fishing match, Fish'O'Mania, on Sky and is involved in televising marlin fishing from Mauritius. Pool, too, has experienced his magic touch. His own sport is golf and his clubs travel with him. And, to make him the complete sporting polymath, he also took a big financial interest in Leyton Orient.

Chris Eubank's appearances in Glasgow – he boxed twice at the Scottish Exhibition and Conference Centre against Tony Thornton and Ray Close – gave us a lot of laughs. The great eccentric famed for his jodhpurs, tweed jackets and bowler hat, not to say the occasional use of a monocle, was larger than life out of the ring. He turned up at one press conference we ran immaculately dressed but carrying a Louis Vuitton bag. I rather naively asked why he needed such an expensive and showy item at that time. 'So that I can change for the conference,' he said. And he indicted that he now needed to do just that. I asked my wife Veronica to arrange a room for him but he interjected to say that a suite was required. Veronica got him a room and off he went. He then reappeared looking much the same fellow who had gone upstairs. I said I thought he had gone to the room to change and asked him what was different. 'My tie, of course, my dear fellow,' he said with a straight face. He had indeed changed his tie and, in that expensive holdall he was carrying, there was little else but the tie he had taken off and his mobile phone. He proceeded to give a virtuoso conference for the boxing writers, living up to their expectation of him as an eccentric.

After the conference in the hotel in Bothwell Street, he announced he needed cash and said to me in his upper-class lisp, 'Tommy, can you give me a grand?' Not surprisingly, I do not carry such sums about me and I thought I would cash a cheque at reception since Barry Hearn had told me just to give the money to Chris and we would sort it out later. The reception did not have the cash either at that point in the day so we had to scuttle around to the bank.

Then he announced that he wanted to go into town to do a little shopping. He had taken to my son Christopher, then a teenager and enjoying a day off from his legal studies at university, and he was to be allowed to accompany the great man on the shopping trip. I told Eubank to stroll down the street towards the Central Station. This advice took him aback – walking, it seems, was not a word in his vocabulary. So a car had to be arranged and it had to be one that suited his stature. I offered Veronica's but, stylish as it was, a BMW 5 series did not fit the bill. Eventually he was transported to the shops in a 420 Merc. He dragged Christopher into one expensive gents' outfitters and started to look at silk ties. He immediately told the awed assistant that Christopher was to get the 'same discount as you will be giving me – 50 per cent'. Such was a close-up of the life of a great of the ring.

I reckon Chris Eubank was remarkable in that he was a boxer who was as well known to the general public as he was to fight fans. And it wasn't just his clothes that were eye-catching. When he was ferreting around for a suitable car to take him downtown from the Albany, he was just indulging in his passion for top-of-the-range transport. He had his own customised

Harley Davidson, drove a huge American Peterbilt truck and, at one time, he owned the only Hummer in Britain. At my press conference, he had only changed his tie but that was all he needed to do as he was always well dressed – indeed, he won the award for Britain's Best-Dressed Man twice. Quite a contrast from some of the boys I have managed who needed serious arm twisting to drop the jeans and T-shirt for a suit for big occasions.

Chris could even take a joke about his lisp and, when he was made a puppet in *Spitting Image*, he took it in good part and had as big a laugh as the TV audience. He also had a generous streak. In 1994, he took over a site in the Brighton area and knocked down part of a listed building, keeping the façade intact, and sixty-nine flats were built for the homeless. Much of his own money went into this charity project which provided homes at very low rates. In my opinion, Chris was really good for boxing. The youngsters who fought on the under-cards for his fights benefited from the publicity he generated. He brought money into the game. He was an oddball but he was also a good fighter from a boxing family. His twin brothers, Simon and Peter, fought professionally as did his cousin Bobbie Joe Edwards.

One of my biggest nights in the early days of my association with Barry Hearn took place at the Scottish Exhibition and Conference Centre on the banks of the Clyde in May 1993. Eubank took on Ray Close for the world middleweight title, Pat Clinton was in against Baby Jake Matlala to defend his world flyweight title and Paul Weir took on Fernando Martinez for the world minimum-weight title. The Glasgow press was in its usual form when Ray Close was introduced to them and it was announced that he was a Mormon. A reporter, whose name I prefer not to mention, though perhaps he should be named and shamed, asked, 'A Protestant or a Catholic Mormon, Ray?'

Three world-title bouts on the same bill – what a great night for Glasgow boxing. There were around 8,000 in the hall and the show was on TV. Only Pat lost.

Baby Jake was one of the most interesting boxers I have met. At four feet ten high, he was the shortest world champion in the history of the sport. In fact, when he retired, he said it was because he had run out of wee fellows to fight. Nelson Mandela and actor Will Smith were ringside to watch his final fight back in South Africa and, after the final bell, Baby Jake gifted his world-title belt to the President of the Republic. It was a great honour to be introduced to Mandela. I remembered that meeting a few years later when I met Bill Clinton who was at a speaking engagement in Glasgow. It all seemed a long way from life up a close in Rutherglen Road.

20

NO FINAL BELL

The dictionary has it that a dynasty is any sequence of powerful leaders of the same family. It certainly applies to the Gilmours. I think it is totally fair to say that the words 'leader' and 'powerful' apply to Jim Gilmour, Tommy Gilmour Sr and, with suitable modesty, I suggest perhaps to me. And, in time, these words will also, I am sure, apply to my son Christopher who already has his promoter's licence and has run his own shows. And when his toddler son, Max, sits on my knee smiling and happy, hugely loved and without a care in the world, I cannot help but wonder if there is a fifth generation to come in this boxing dynasty. That really would be one for the *Guinness Book of Records*.

But the word dynasty can also conjure up the wrong impression. The transition to leadership and power as one generation succeeds another is often not as seamless as it can appear to the outsiders. A wee study of history can confirm that dynasties have peaks and troughs, successes and tragedies. Readers of this book will know that I spent almost twenty years as a printing engineer and, during that time, boxing and the boxing business were things that were done in the evening or in the lunch break. Deals were made from those old red public phone boxes that used to stand at almost every corner. Conversations were held as the coins tinkled into the little black cash box one by one. I seem to have spent my working days weighed down with loose change. The wonder is that today I don't walk with a list. Mobile phones, credit cards and faxes were all a distant dream in the beginning – I operated by the public call box and the first-class stamp. Leisure time that my east-end engineering colleagues spent at home with their families watching the telly or going to football games was used by me to fulfil what I knew from my early days in Oatlands was my ultimate destiny – to follow old Jim and Dad into the top level of sports promotion. The whole family, Veronica, Christopher and Stephanie, all contributed to that destiny and, although our lifestyle was a bit different from those of the nine-to-five neighbours, we all enjoyed what was in the early days a struggle. It was a real family thing.

I may have been born with what would appear to be the Glasgow version of the silver spoon in my mouth. The early days of holidaying by private plane, of flying the Atlantic, of meeting the greats from the boxing world and of having a free-spending dad are testimony to that. It is staggering when I think back of all the boxing folk, some the biggest names in world sport, who had a cuppa and a scone up our close in Rutherglen Road. And I will always be grateful to my parents who gave me a very special and, in some ways, privileged upbringing but, above all, kept my feet on the ground. When I look back now I realise how shrewd they were to get the fun out of the big money and newspaper headlines that occasionally swirled around us but, at the same time, keep us all in total contact with our working-class roots and friends. It was no easy trick to pull off but they did it. How I wish my mum had not died so young, how I wish she could have seen how well it worked out for me and my family.

When Dad died, much of his wealth was gone and he was doing a fifteen-round world-championship-class bout with the taxman. At his death, boxing in Scotland, always a cyclical business, was in one of its downturns and was only kept going by faithful fans and trainers, managers and promoters to whom the game was a hobby, a way of life, as well as an occupation. Outsiders and those who criticise the fight game, and they are entitled to their opinion, never get to see the upside of boxing. Camaraderie is an over-used word in this context but it is real when you talk of fight-game folk – they are a special breed. In the ring, your fortunes can change over the period of a three-minute round. Outside, it is much the same – great victories can be quickly followed by devastating losses. Nothing is for sure, nothing totally predictable. It is an emotional and financial roller coaster. You need to show courage and you need to be able to take knocks and get up and carry on with your life. It is the same inside and outside of the ring.

And the criticism the game gets from those who are antagonistic to it just adds to the feeling of 'we are all in it together'. Sure, there are feuds and sometimes shady characters attracted to the game and, at times, things that are indefensible do happen – especially at the very top and mostly in the States. I always take rumours of fixing with a huge pinch of salt and always remember an embittered and cynical old sportswriter's observation that 'the only sport on the level is mountain climbing'. You get allegations of bad practice in all sorts of sports, especially where gambling is concerned. Just think of the rumours that swirl around cricket, big-time soccer matches, motor racing, horse racing and even tennis. The fight game is not alone in having an occasional scandal though it seems to be badmouthed more than most. Some of the talk may be true but the bad eggs are a minority and tend to be exposed in time. The fact is that, if boxing is in your blood, you take all that on the chin and keep going, concentrating on the good things in the game.

When I first made moves in the promoting business, I was easily angered by suggestions made in the some papers and by some sports writers that I was a front man for Tommy Sr or that I had success handed to me on a plate. That was far from the case. Obviously I learned much from Dad but, as I have said, he did not actively encourage me to follow in his footsteps. And everything I did in the fight game – from holding spit buckets for fighters to arranging accommodation for big names or overseeing the boys fighting in the St Andrew's Sporting Club – I did by myself and properly. The advantage I had was mixing with mentors like Dunky Jowett and learning how, in fact, you did do things properly. I was proud of my heritage and proud of my name but I valued my independence too and hated the tag 'junior'. My attitude was that of, say, an actress who disliked being called the new Marilyn Monroe and just wanted to be known as herself. As much as I respected him, I did not want to be the new Tommy Gilmour Sr – I wanted to be Tommy Gilmour pure and simple. These days, I have been in the game so long that, sad to say, I now meet folk who have never heard of Dad or old Jim. And of course I am immensely proud to use initials after my name now – Jr has been replaced by MBE.

I reckon I have seen more boxing than most of the population of Britain. And, when you are in that position, one of the favourite questions of the scribes who interview you ask is, 'What is the best fight you have ever seen?' It is also a question that you get asked over the steak and red wine at the dinner table and over a pie and a pint in a pub. My answer always tends to shock the listeners. I have seen the greatest in action. My own Pat Clinton was the most naturally gifted boxer I have managed. My boyhood hero Chic Calderwood was a great scrapper and watching wee Peter Keenan could be a delight. I could list dozens of top names, including the American legends like Sugar Ray Leonard and Sugar Ray Robinson, Archie Moore and a host more. That is not the question. What was the best fight I ever saw? Few will remember the names of the two boxers in question – a Glasgow lad called Robert Harkin and a youngster from Liverpool called Sugar Gibiliru Jr.

It was not a contest that had much in the way of pre-publicity – on paper, it looked like just a run-of-the-mill fight in St Andrew's Sporting Club on my stomping ground of the Albany – but no one who was there, back in November '87, will ever forget the epic battle. They went at it from the first bell to the last with both boxers fighting their hearts out. In those days, you could gauge how good a fight was because the paying customers would throw money into the ring after the final bell. There were only 600 black tie guests there that night but they threw so much money into the ring that there was more than twice the actual purse lying on the canvas in readies. The 'nobbins', as such cash was called, were massive. There was way more money chipped in by the punters than had been raised by good fights in front of six or seven thousand people. When it was all over, everyone drew breath, not just the boxers – it was as exciting as that. The result, a draw, was as immaterial as it was fair. There was no rematch of this one-off fight that still stays strong in my memory twenty years later. The fight had taken so much from the boxers that neither could face doing it again.

The dinner table is a great place for reminiscing. But it is pointless to pitch heroes of different eras into imaginary fights with rivals from the past or the future. The best a boxer can do is beat the guy who is on the stool in the corner diagonally opposite him and keep on doing it fight after fight. To be the best around when you boxed is enough. But it doesn't stop fans or promoters imagining. One of my regrets is that Chic Calderwood never made it into the ring with Archie Moore, unquestionably one of the best of all time. But, of course, at the time when they could have met, Moore was in decline and Chic on the up and up. It never happened but it would have been a great fight.

If asked who is the best boxer I have ever seen, the answer is not an obvious one – not one of the American greats who got massive coverage on TV and in the papers and glossy sports mags. But many folk who know boxing would agree with me or certainly put my man on their short list. Quite simply, the best boxer I ever saw was Alexis Arguello. His performance against Jim Watt in 1981 in London was masterly. I was mesmerised by the way he could cut the ring off and manoeuvre Jim into position for his punches. It was sheer technical brilliance.

The Mexican Julio Cesar Chavez was another magical fighter who could do it all. He could box when it was called for and he was able to rough-house it when that was the correct tactic. Of the Scots, I particularly admired Jim Watt and wee Walter McGowan and Ken Buchanan. Of boxers I handled, Pat Clinton, of course, would be high on the list. Wee Danny Flynn was a man with everything but self-belief and that failing cost him a lot. I remember the night he fought Hugh Russell for a British title and, in the dressing room before the fight, he said to me,

'I'll try my hardest, just for you.' – not the sort of remark a man sure of himself and his ability would make. Yet wee Danny moved well and was good at in-fighting. Although he was not the easiest guy to get along with, Dave McCabe was an extremely talented fighter and a man with great ability. Somehow or other, he seemed to fall at the final hurdle but, at his best, he could take complete control of a contest. All this talk takes me back to Chic Calderwood. I knew him well though I did not train or manage him. I loved him in action – his left jab was the finest I have ever seen. What a tragedy that his career ended up in that horror car smash on the banks of the Clyde.

The game is changing fast and I don't like some of things I see. These are not criticisms from an old traditionalist. They come from a man who loves boxing, who thinks it will always exist, who is of the opinion that is now as well run on the medical side as it can be and who does not want the clock turned back. One of the trends I dislike most is 'celebrity fights' – even if the money raised goes to charity and the contestants enjoy it. I just think the risks are too great. Put it this way, for people to plan something like this makes a mockery of the sport. I work with serious youngsters who I book in for a yearly medical. They get an MRI scan and all manner of precautions are taken. They train for months or years and, before we put fighters into the ring, they are checked out to ensure their skulls are not a millimetre too thin in a vulnerable area or whatever. Boxing is a very dangerous sport and contestants need to be properly prepared for it. It should not be the case of a few Hooray Henries going against each other after only a handful of sessions in training. It is worth considering that the vast majority of the lads who join gyms never actually fight. This kind of celebrity fighting, featuring such as Tommy Sheridan and ex-Celt Frank McAvennie (even if they are not of the Hooray-Henry cut) and others, is wrong.

Even less defendable is the growth of cage fighting. Boxing has moved on a long way from bare-knuckle fighting but this so-called sport is something of a harking back to the bad old days. Some commentators have called it 'human cock fighting'. Others have said that it goes back to the gladiatorial ethos of Rome but that gives it a certain historical dignity that it does not deserve. Two men in a cage knocking the s*** out of each other? Biting and eye gouging are barred and the contestants wear gloves but that is about it in the way of rules. Successful fighters can use techniques like 'ground and pound' in which an opponent's face is smashed into the canvas time after time. In America, it is branded as Mixed Martial Arts or MMA. It generates big money and some even think it might damage boxing as a spectator sport. It is not for me. And I do worry that, even here, it could damage legitimate, highly controlled boxing where, over the years, a safety-first attitude has developed. It is sad that cage fighting has already come to Scotland.

In contrast, boxing has had the Marquis of Queensberry Rules since 1867 though there have been revisions and changes over the years since Gentleman Jim Corbett beat John L. Sullivan to become the first world champion under the rules. Despite not knowing what they really mean, every schoolboy can talk about the Queensberry Rules though fights behind the bike shed are seldom conducted under the code. Now that women's boxing and cage fighting are around, it is interesting to look at the old original rules and ponder how sensible the legislators of the fight game were around 150 years ago. Are we really going to allow combat sport to go backwards with undercover bare-knuckle fight clubs and the rest of it? Not if I can do anything about it. The original Queensberry Rules are interesting and I suspect few who talk about them have ever read them:

1   To be a fair stand-up boxing match in a 24-foot ring or as near that size as practical.
2   No wrestling or hugging allowed.
3   The rounds to be of three minutes duration with one minute's time between round.
4   If either man falls through weakness or otherwise, he must get up unassisted, 10 seconds to be allowed for him to do so, the other man meanwhile to return to his corner and when the fallen man is on his legs the round is to be resumed and continued till the three minutes has expired.
5   A man hanging on the ropes in a helpless state, with his toes off the ground, shall be considered down.
6   No seconds or any other person to be allowed in the ring during the rounds.
7   Should the contest be stopped by any unavoidable interference, the referee to name the time and the place as soon as possible for finishing the contest: so that the match must be won or lost, unless the backers of both men agree to withdraw their stakes.
8   The boxing gloves to be fair full-sized boxing gloves of the best quality and new.
9   Should a glove burst or come off it must be replaced to the referee's satisfaction.
10 A man on one knee is considered down and if struck is entitled to the stakes.
11 No shoes or boots with springs allowed.

12   The contest in all other respects to be governed by
      the revised rules of the London Prize Ring.

So there you have it though I don't know what that stuff about
boots with springs is all about!

There is another modern development that I just don't take
to – women's boxing. Jane Couch, the best-known Brit in this
game, was recently awarded the MBE. I know her well and I
admire her tenacity in building a career despite opposition
from people like myself. I know that Jane credits boxing for
turning her life around. As a youngster she was a self-confessed
slob, a boozer and a rough-houser on the streets. When she
first saw professional women's boxing in the States, she decided
this was the road out of her way of life and turned to the gym.
She also has a sense of humour. After hearing that one opponent was a police officer out of the ring, Jane told the press it
was nice to beat up a cop without being arrested. Jane's first
pro fight in Britain was in Caesar's in London's Streatham Hill
in 1998. This was years after she had established herself fighting
in America and Europe where there was less hostility to women
in the ring. Jane, known on the posters as the 'Fleetwood
Assassin', got backing from the Equal Opportunities
Commission to take on the British Boxing Board of Control.
She claimed she was being discriminated against and the subse-
quent tribunal turned out to be highly embarrassing for the
Board. They were ridiculed for their contention that pre-
menstrual tension made women too unstable to box. The Board
was KO'd by the tribunal and Jane's fight in London – against
an eighteen-year-old from Yugoslavia – was the first women's
professional boxing match sanctioned by the Board. But I tend
to go along with Frank Maloney who was managing Lennox

Lewis at the time. He described the contest as a freak show. I agree. And Jane might not like me for pointing out that, although women's boxing dates back to the 1880s, in America it was, for many years, purely a fairground attraction.

I have a more serious reason for believing women should not be allowed to box. I am anti-abortion and the thought of an unborn child being damaged in a ring horrifies me. I know that there are stringent medical tests to stop a pregnant woman getting into a boxing ring but tests can fail, once in a while, to spot a condition. History has shown this. And, less than a year after Jane's first pro fight under Board rules, a woman died in the ring in Denver, Colorado. Thirty-four-year-old Becky Zerlentes died in what was to be her last appearance before retiring. She was wearing protective headgear at the time of the accident and spectators did not think the blow that floored her was a particularly hard one. Many remarked that this tragedy seemed to be real life mirroring fiction and remarked on the similarities to the plot of the Oscar-winning film *Million Dollar Baby*. In that movie, a contestant is left a quadriplegic as a result of a spinal cord injury suffered in her last fight. No, women in the ring is not part of the future I see for boxing.

My old-fashioned view that boxing is essentially a male sport is shared by Veronica. She told one interviewer, 'I support Tommy's opinion.' She added an extra, shrewd female comment: 'It is OK for female boxing promoters to say they don't mind seeing boxers naked at weigh-ins – but a fighter's wife or girl-friend might take exception.'

OK, that's the gripes out of the way. Let's look to the future. I don't ever see the game dying out. Scrapping and admiration for those good at it is in human nature. Boxers will box, racing drivers will race, skydivers will dive and mountaineers will take on the tallest, most dangerous peaks. We need adventure, we need an adrenaline rush. TV is now king at the top level and bouts for world titles attract huge global audiences. Thanks to that, you can walk into a remote village almost anywhere in the world and hold a conversation with the locals on the merits of the current crop, the champions and the contenders. And sporting clubs like my own St Andrew's will continue to thrive, giving punters a great night out, albeit there is more to the evening than the boxing. Local gyms and local fight nights are also making something of a comeback. Having young guys training in a gym for a licensed, well-controlled fight is a whole lot better than having them hanging out in pubs and looking for a rumble on the streets. Keep-fit clubs and gyms generally are booming. And a boxing gym can be an especially attractive place to keep in shape and garner the wisdom of the older guy. A lifetime around gyms tends to be a lifetime lived with an eye on good health and keeping in shape, even if your days inside the ropes are long gone. And a local gym can be a real community asset.

In recent years, I have been promoting in places like Kirkcaldy, Irvine and Clydebank as well as in the Glasgow venues. Not so long ago, I had the then Scottish sports minister Patricia Ferguson MSP ringside at the Fife Ice Rink to watch Kevin Anderson defend his Commonwealth welterweight title against Ali Nuumbembe. The politician was responding to criticism from me as Anderson's promoter and manager that our championship boxers were not getting the recognition their achievements merited. I had accused Alex Salmond's predecessor as First Minister, Jack McConnell, of failing to promote adequately champion boxers such as Anderson, Alex

Arthur and, before his fall from grace, Scott Harrison. With boxing a core event in Glasgow's quest to host the Commonwealth Games in 2014, Ms Ferguson accepted the invitation to go to Fife. I told *The Herald*'s Darryl Broadfoot that I was delighted to say that Ms Ferguson would see first-hand for herself that any money invested by the government in boxing is well worth it. I also told young Darryl that I was pleased that, at last, the government had sat up and taken notice of what was happening in the sport because it had long been my belief that our successful fighters had not been given due recognition.

This political breakthrough came after a meeting with Patricia Ferguson at which I aired my view that boxing in Scotland had been ignored in favour of traditionally more popular sports. I pointed out that, in England, boxing is to be rein-troduced at some schools to promote fitness, well-being and discipline and I urged Scotland to do the same. I was on my hobbyhorse that day in Edinburgh and I went on to tell the sports minister that, while boxing was not as popular as foot-ball, as a nation we were better at it. I underlined how it can help build community spirit and pointed out that it is a sport that gives discipline and confidence. I told her that I had seen many a timid young boy come into a gym and leave with real self-respect and belief in himself. I reminded her that the majority of people who come into a gym never fight in a ring – their target is fitness.

It is also true that boxing generally has raised millions over the years at charity nights and celebrity sports events. I have long been part of that and maybe that, as well as my contri-bution to the actual sport, led to the award of my MBE in 2007. I am immensely proud of the honour. And I was greatly moved by the literally hundreds of phone calls, e-mails, faxes, cards and old-fashioned snail-mail letters that poured through our letterbox when the award was announced. And I was also conscious it was an accolade to the sport and everyone in it as well as to myself.

My theory that boxing can bring discipline to youngsters and generally help communities got a boost when I was given a Services to Sport award from Glasgow City Council. I was honoured to get it and Christopher picked it up on my behalf as I was in Puerto Rico receiving a co-promoter of the year award, with Barry Hearn, from the World Boxing Organisation. Later I was awarded the Lord Provost's silver medal, the first time it had gone to boxing. On the same day I received that award, Midge Ure of Ultravox got a silver medal for services to music so I was in good company. No wonder I listen to the odd CD by his band on my Jag's stereo.

I always like to get involved in charities and boxing is a great game for fundraising. Even folk who might never attend another fight night in their lives seem to enjoy the atmosphere and tend to open their wallets more than they might normally do. The list of organisations the St Andrew's Sporting Club has been involved in is a long one. It includes: The Prince and Princess of Wales Hospice, Barnardo's, Help the Aged, the Variety Club, the Newspaper Press Fund, the Lord Provost's Charity, Erskine Hospice, the Anthony Nolan Bone Marrow Trust, the Beatson Oncology Centre and many more.

One piece of personal charity work Veronica and I look on with real pleasure came about through my friendship with Alistair Naismith who then managed the Holiday Inn at Glasgow Airport. Alistair was a boxing fan and his son Ross boxed as an amateur out of the Blantyre Miners' Welfare under the tutelage of John McDermott MBE. Alistair was also on the Parents' Association for Craighead School, near Blantyre, an establishment for children with learning difficulties. Alistair got me involved in events like prize-givings and I got to know the headmaster John McEnhaney. John mentioned one day that the school was looking for money to help create a sensory room for children with autism. He mentioned the cost, which he knew accurately as the children and parents were fundraising to pay for it. It seemed the local council would only pay for educational needs, not therapeutic needs. Veronica and I took this on board and set about to help. It was a great day when it was all completed. Veronica and one of the young children in the school did the honours with a ribbon-cutting ceremony followed by tea and cakes and sandwiches which the pupils had all helped to make. It was one of the happiest days of our lives – an achievement to rank with anything we have done in boxing.

You wander through life taking it day by day. Sometimes you get a shock when you scan the paper over breakfast. It startled me the other day to read that I was a 'veteran' promoter. Who would have thought that would happen to wee Thomas Gilmour from Oatlands? But there you are. Veteran or not, I have no plans to retire. Boxing still excites me. And I still have that fire in my belly that helped make me a shop steward and which, in my boxing career, got me into a few scrapes with the Board of Control and politicians and the so-called 'authorities' of all kinds. I am not slow to state my opinion and, when I think something is wrong, I go as hard as I can to sort it out. But, who knows, I might just mellow a little bit. Maybe when I am seventy and we are celebrating the fiftieth anniversary of the St Andrew's club, Christopher – a man with an honours degree in law as well as having boxing in his genes – will be in charge and getting the sort of support from his wife Tracey that I got from Veronica, getting the buzz from running the show but also taking the strain. And, at times, there is a lot of that! Then I will sit at the top table relaxing with the sporting elite who take it as an honour to be at our events. And I must admit I have a hankering to be the first President of the St Andrew's Sporting Club, something my father would have loved to be but sadly he died before it was possible. With Christopher promoting, the dynasty lives on. A 'veteran', too, is allowed time to enjoy his grandson's company. And I love nothing more than to dangle young Max Gilmour on my knee. I smile a lot most of the time but with the wee fellow on my knee I allow myself a secret grin or two. You just can't help thinking that Max Gilmour is a wonderful name for a boxing promoter.

APPENDIX

The following boxers have been managed or co-managed by Tommy Gilmour:

A
Paul Abercromby
Davie Adams
Tanveer Ahmed
Mike Allen
Kevin Anderson
Shaun Anderson
David Appleby
Paul Appleby
Henry Armstrong
Ray Atherton
Louie Atuna

B
George Baigrie
Sandy Bartlett
Steve Bendall
Willie Bilan
Drew Black
Steve Black
Robert Boardman
John Bothwell

Stevie Boyle
Peter Bradley
Ryan Brawley
Gordon Brennan
Mark Breslin
Billy Brough
Nathan Brough
Colin Brown
Albert Buchanan
Alston Buchanan
Billy Buchanan
Paul Burns (Liverpool)
Paul Burns
Gary Burrell
Pinky Burton
Paul Buttery

C
Alex Cairney
Glen Campbell*
Ronnie Carroll
Robert Carson

James Clamp
Pat Clinton
Billy Collins
Hugh Collins
Brian Connell
Jamie Coyle
Jan Cree
Peter Culshaw

D
John Davison*
Kenny Davidson
Chris Davies
Graham Delehedy
Gerry Devine
Harry Dhami
Craig Dickson
Alex Docherty
Craig Docherty
Drew Docherty
John Docherty
Willie Docherty
Wilson Docherty
John Donnelly
James Drummond

E
Keith Ellwood

F
Biagio Falcone

Andrew Ferrans
John Fewkes*
Bobby Finlay
Danny Flynn
Allan Foster

G
Michael Gale*
Al Garritt
Mark Geraghty
Andy Gibson
Jimmy Gilhaney
Joe Gillon
Allan Grainger
Stuart Green

H
Allan Hall
Duncan Hamilton
Billy Hardy
James Hare*
Robert Harkin
Colin Harrison
Peter Harrison
Mark Hastie
Barry Hawthorne
Robert Hay
Sean Heron
Mark Hobson*
Lee Hodgson*
Francis Hogg*

Brian Holmes
Jamil Hussein*

I
Alan Ingle

J
Mohammed Jamil
Darren Johnstone
Alan Jones
Gary Jones

K
Charlie Kane
Stevie Kane
David Keir
Damaen Kelly
Jim Kelly
George Kerr
Jawaid Khaliq*
Charlie King
Keith Knox

L
Russell Laing
Billy Lauder
Tommy Leverage
Adey Lewis
Walker Logue
Jamie Lowther*

M
Mally MacIver*
Kris McAdam
Gary McArthur
Jamie McBride
Dave McCabe
Tommy McCallum
Billy McClung
Joe McCluskey
Brian McConnell
Ian McGirr
Stevie McGuire
Davy McHale
George McIlroy
Jamie McIlroy
Jim McIntosh
Kevin McIntyre
David McKenna
Mike McKenzie
Jim McKeown
Terry McKeown
John McKinley
Herbie McLean
Ian McLeod
Joe McNamee
Tony McPake
Pat Mallon
Emmanuel Marcos
John Marshall*
Tommy Marshall
Scott Millar

Ian Millarvie
Joe Miller
Tommy Milligan
Darryl Mitchell
Lee Molloy
Jim Montgomery
Alex Moon
Jamie Moore*
Thomas Moran
Tony Moran
Barry Morrison
Adam Muir
John Mullen Jr
John Mullen Sr
Steven Mullin
Joe Murphy
Brian Murphy Jr
Brian Murphy Sr
Ritchie Murray

N
Gary Neville
Eddie Nevins*
Stuart Nichol

O
Alan Oag
Leo O'Reilly*
Damian Owen

P
Alan Peacock
Wayne Pinder*
Mitch Prince

Q
Tommy Quinn
Willie Quinn

R
Furhan Rafiq
Calum Rattray
Gary Reid
Mike Reid
John Ritchie
Derek Roche*
Sandy Robb
Dale Robinson*
Manny Romain
Gary Ryder

S
Archie Salmon
David Savage
John Sharkey
Lee Sharp
Charlie Shepherd*
John Simpson
Hughie Smith
John Smith

APPENDIX

Johnny Smith
Darren Spencer
Warren Stone*

T
Daniel Teasdale*
Jackie Townsley
Joe Townsley
John Townsley
Kevin Townsley
Glenn Tweedie

V
Bobby Vanzie*
Richard Vowles*

W
Gwyn Wale

Johnny Walker
Darren Walton*
Paul Watson
Paul Weir
Bradley Welsh
Dazzo Williams
Stephen Williams
Steve Williams
Craig Winter*
Stevie Woods
Derek Wormald*

Y
Andrew Young
Dougie Young

*as joint manager

Apologies to anyone left out in error! TG

INDEX

269

INDEX

INDEX

Turpin, Randy 235, 236
Tyson, Mike 57, 183

V
Vasquez, Robert 168, 178, 179

W
Warren, Frank 180, 222, 226, 236
Watson, Michael 226, 228

Watt, Jim 13, 19, 23, 57, 127, 140, 156, 157, 166, 167, 170, 173, 208, 210, 211, 215, 225, 252
Weir, Paul 174, 215, 245
Williamson, Roy 23, 31,
Wilson, Howard 43, 44
Wilson, Sammy 47, 141
Woolard, Gerry 190–219

Y
Young, Linda 14